BIRTH PASSAGES

BIRTH PASSAGES

Maternity and Nostalgia,
Antiquity to Shakespeare

THERESA M. KRIER

CORNELL UNIVERSITY PRESS
Ithaca and London

Wallace Stevens is cited from *Collected Poems* by Wallace Stevens, copyright © 1954 by Wallace Stevens. Reprinted by permission of Alfred A. Knopf, a division of Random House Inc., and permission of Faber and Faber Ltd.

Parts of chapters 3 and 4 originally appeared as "Generations of Blazons: Psychoanalysis and the Song of Songs in the *Amoretti*," from *Texas Studies in Literature and Language* 40 (3): 293–327. Copyright © 1998 by the University of Texas Press. All rights reserved.

First published 2001 by Cornell University Press

Printed in the United States of America

Library of Congress Cataloging-in-Publication Data

Krier, Theresa M., 1953-
   Birth passages : maternity and nostalgia, antiquity to
Shakespeare / Theresa M. Krier.
        p. cm.
   Includes bibliographical references and index.
   ISBN 0-8014-3893-4
   1. Mothers in literature. 2. Motherhood in literature.
   I. Title.

PN56.5.M67 K75 2001
809'.933520431—dc21

                                                         2001001968

To my mother and her sister,
to the memory of my grandmothers,
and in honor of their mothers

[Birth] is indeed a perilous adventure, this serious act of venturing into mortality, swimming in a sea strewn with wrecks, where none indeed go undamaged.

—Ralph Waldo Emerson, *Journals*, July–October 1851

Contents

Preface

OF GENERATION: So many works in so many art forms could take this as their titles, and so many more works engage discourses and verbal traditions dealing with generation. Yet we hardly know what to do these days with works unabashedly about fecundity, Dame Nature, or procreation once we have exposed the benighted ideologies that could give rise to their intertwined appropriations, idealizings, and defenses against the maternal. This critique has been carried out brilliantly and at length in feminist theory and ethics—not least by Luce Irigaray, who has everywhere enkindled my thinking—and poetry needs to engage the critique. I take on part of this task by arguing that certain writers of antiquity, the English Middle Ages, and the English Renaissance propose vigorous alternatives to the insistent nostalgia for the maternal pervading their cultures. Since nostalgia for the lost archaic mother dominates so much recent literary-historical work through the influences of psychoanalysis and philosophy, the old poems may have something to say to us as well as to their contemporary audiences.[1]

The strongest accounts abroad today concerning maternity and ambivalence toward mothers rely upon the premise of a moment when the infant undergoes alienation from an archaic mother, or of the subject's post-oedipal fantasizing of such a moment. No matter how and when this event occurs, the loss of merger with a provident, nurturing mother is thought to haunt us, to shape our desire, to fuel our actions. From the necessary loss of mother, so this account goes, we live permanently with desire for her and dread of her mighty, procreative, and engulfing powers. The passage itself is inevitable yet always precarious, imperfectly achieved, fraught with ambivalence, subject to all kinds of fantasy elaboration. It is the sacrifice that creates culture. As psychoanalytic theorists frequently point out, the notion of merger with the mother

---

1. See the bibliographical essay at the end of this book for pointers to these domains.

arrives as a deferred action, or *Nachträglichkeit*, a retroactive construction that makes possible object relations with a fantasized mother-*object*. But this fact does not make her figure less powerful in affect or in any cultural imaginary; rather the opposite—she thus *gains* power, unless, as in Irigaray's repeated sallies, she enters the Symbolic and finds release from her children's constructions. Such an account is especially powerful in analyzing masculine identity in patriarchies; it can articulate how the masculine imagination might idealize women, demonize them, split, dominate, confine, demean, abject, reify, disavow, murder . . . an endless array of mechanisms for negotiating the hazards of the first relationship with a woman. Readings of ancient, medieval, and Renaissance poetic texts in the last twenty years have emphasized the separation from the mother as a trauma, and critiqued literary works' displacement of maternity into tropes and figures, an imaginative work understood to be performed at the expense of literal and historical mothers.[2]

As an instrument for exposing the structure of gender relations in many discourses and verbal forms, this broad account remains unsurpassed. It makes possible brilliant readings and explanatory accounts, and it can be historicized to meet many moments in Western history. The notion of nostalgia for the maternal—and its precedent assumption of a merger (or fantasy of merger) with an archaic mother from which we are exiled—has begun to have the status of a truism. I think it *is* true, or true enough.

Yet it is worth joining with those voices which challenge this assumption of a primal union with a mother to be lost, and the assumption that sundering from this union is imperative just to the degree that it is so naturally resisted, as if mothers and infants were under a spell and needed awakening. Separation is not identical to loss; the impossible quest for a lost archaic mother is not the only possible relation to the maternal; there is more than mourning work to launch the nascent subject into action and invention, history and ethics, though we might not always guess this from surveying the landscape of literary scholarship.[3] Masculine desire for and dread of the maternal body is only one of the

2. See the bibliographical essay.

3. As Valerie Traub suggests in "Prince Hal's Falstaff: Positioning Psychoanalysis and the Female Reproductive Body," *Shakespeare Quarterly* 40 (1989): 456–74, "in its emphasis on the excessive, overwhelming, engulfing mother, psychoanalysis exposes its own paranoia that, were it not for the decisive entrance of the father, the contiguity of the pre-oedipal period would seductively go on and on" (471). She expands this remark in *Desire and Anxiety: Circulations of Sexuality in Shakespearean Drama* (London: Routledge, 1992), 65–68.

responses to the maternal that bears scrutiny. Even works populated with monstrous or idealized mothers may register other forms of maternal relations. There are more forms and tones of aggressive energy between mother and child, for instance, than the child's renunciation and abjection of the mother. Aggression, as I understand it here, is a means of sustaining the open space between mother and child, holding open the intersubjective field within which mother and child are each *present, at some distance.* For this argument I look to the Song of Songs, Lucretius's *De rerum natura,* Chaucer's *Parlement of Foules,* Spenser's *Amoretti* and *Faerie Queene,* book 4, and Shakespeare's *Love's Labor's Lost* and *The Winter's Tale.* In the process, I offer counterreadings to now widespread assumptions about currently disgraced forms like erotic blazon (the Song and the *Amoretti*), about unfashionable traditions like hexaemeral accounts of the biblical Creation and their kin in medieval encyclopedia and hymn (the *Parlement* and *Love's Labor's Lost*), and about cosmology and philosophical poem (*De rerum natura*). Other works suggested themselves as germane to my argument—Virgil's *Georgics,* Statius's *Thebaid,* Bernardus Silvestris's *Cosmographia,* Marie de France's *Lai le Fresne,* Chaucer's Man of Law's Tale and Clerk's Tale, Spenser's *Mutabilitie Cantos,* Shakespeare's *Pericles*—but fleeting time, not to mention the patience of readers, advised excluding these. Moreover, I remain committed to extended readings of individual works, the amplitude of which seems to require individual chapters.

To articulate my points about distance and aggression between mother and child, I engage Melanie Klein with D. W. Winnicott, and Winnicott with Luce Irigaray. This may seem such an unlikely grouping for psychoanalytic study of early poetry that here I want to say a few words about them generally—and especially about Irigaray, whom we rarely consider in relation to the British psychoanalytic movement.

Klein has received attention from feminist psychoanalytic critics, and her place within the battles of the early psychoanalytic movement has been documented, but both her work and Winnicott's have often remained peripheral to the great tide of literary criticism emergent from the different emphases of Jacques Lacan and Julia Kristeva. Fortunately, as Irigaray says, the maternal-feminine "cannot be collected into *one* volume."[4] This book is meant in part as a good word spoken on behalf of Klein's and Winnicott's British psychoanalysis and its uses in literary

4. Luce Irigaray, "Volume-Fluidity" (1974), in *Speculum of the Other Woman,* trans. Gillian Gill (Ithaca, N.Y.: Cornell University Press, 1985), 227–40, at 240.

thinking. Klein and Winnicott are little indebted to European philosophy in any direct way (although the effects of Romanticism are marked
in them, as in Freud). Formed by the great wars and the Freud of the
1910s and 1920s, their work has considerable explanatory power and is
often underestimated. Klein's papers are dense with responses to Freud
and to Winnicott (and Abraham and Ferenczi, although I do not pursue
these), Winnicott's with responsiveness to Freud and Klein. It seems
likely to me, furthermore, that Irigaray owes something to both Klein
and Winnicott. In any event, her work can carry the Kleinian and Winnicottian concerns of early to midcentury into our own time, and link
them with more recent gender analysis.

I think we find it easy enough to take Klein seriously, partly because
her papers explicitly acknowledge colleagues and predecessors: plenty
of footnotes, plenty of rigorous interchange with others. But we underread Winnicott, not to say misread him. (I have found that only one of the
many passing statements about him in exegeses of Lacan, for instance,
happened to be true or accurate.) His papers are reticent, not to say mad-
deningly oblique, in their acknowledgments and citations, even more
than is generally true of much psychoanalytic writing from both Britain
and France. Written within the highly charged setting of the British Psycho-Analytical Society, often in response to papers delivered by others
only weeks before, they tend to assume not just specialized knowledge
but the intimacy of Society gatherings; they tend to make only the most
casual nods to their precursor texts. Moreover, Winnicott intentionally
deployed the offhand to devious purposes, including (to borrow a notion
from Robert Frost) that of seeming altogether obvious. To do justice to
Winnicott's laconic, apparently transparent prose, we need alertness to
its rhetorical gestures and patience with its white spaces until they fill up
with the traces of other voices with whom he is in constant conversation.
These empty spaces are not restful for Winnicott; the feeling of emptiness
is one of the things that he would class among "unthinkable agonies"
always near at hand to the individual subject. Learning to tolerate emptiness is one of the difficult achievements of the Winnicottian subject—and
a challenge for his readers. There are abysses in this simple description of
his: "emptiness is a prerequisite for eagerness to gather in. Primary
emptiness simply means: before starting to fill up."[5]

5. D. W. Winnicott, "Fear of Breakdown" (1963), in *Psycho-Analytic Explorations*, ed. Clare
Winnicott, Ray Shepherd, and Madeleine Davis (Cambridge: Harvard University Press,
1989), 87–95, at 94.

Among the conversants who fill his white spaces are the mothers with whom he worked in clinical practice. Their specific circumstances—their financial strains and labor and class expectations and family ties and makeshifts in wartime—constantly incited his own thinking, though his intellectual tradition and his genres afforded him little space to give voice and form to maternal experience. Some such detail occurs in his case histories, but more often we can look to Winnicott for *implicit* opportunities to historicize psychoanalysis. Similarly with gender: his focus on the mother involves gender implicitly, but he had little interest in gender difference per se and was uninterested in social critique. But he did leave open spaces in his work, in which analysis of culture and gender could be done.

To hear such resonances in his work, and such developments of his key concepts, I turn to Irigaray, whose resources in and contributions to late-century feminisms allow us to tease out the potentialities of Winnicottian concepts. We can do this not only with her vigorous critical readings of philosophical texts, chiefly written in the 1970s, but also with her surprising turn in the 1980s to terms and thinkers familiar to premodern poets and philosophers: the four elements of earth, air, fire, and water, the pre-Socratics, the physics of motion and space; medieval mystics, wonder, the divine; biblical figures of angels and nuptials and annunciation and *parousia*.[6] All of these figures aim to draw into the symbolic the textures, processes, and possible experiences of the female body, and I hope to demonstrate how such gestures can be used more widely than they have been by literary critics. Irigaray's frequent recourse to processes of birth in concepts like passage, interval, threshold, contiguity, the placental economy, and "the between"—a phrase also used by Shakespeare in *The Winter's Tale*—draws out much that Winnicott left implicit in his papers and clinical work, and suggests new ways of reading for the maternal in early poetic traditions. It is Irigaray who, because of her concern with enunciating subjects' debt to mothers, makes possible the widening of Winnicott's range to encompass language and

6. Irigaray herself surveys this trajectory of her work in "The Question of the Other," trans. Noah Guynn, *Yale French Studies* 87 (1995): 7–19; Carolyn Burke discusses the turn and Irigaray's reasons for it in "Romancing the Philosophers: Luce Irigaray," in *Seduction and Theory: Readings of Gender, Representation, and Rhetoric*, ed. Dianne Hunter (Urbana: University of Illinois Press, 1990), 226–40. Two works situating Irigaray within continental theory are Rosi Braidotti, *Patterns of Dissonance: A Study of Women in Contemporary Philosophy*, trans. Elizabeth Guild (New York: Routledge, 1991), and Tina Chanter, *Ethics of Eros: Irigaray's Rewriting of the Philosophers* (New York: Routledge, 1995).

texts: "Language, however formal it may be, feeds on blood, on flesh, on material elements. Who and what has nourished language? How is this debt to be repaid?" She speaks of the desirability of bringing "the maternal-feminine into language: at the level of theme, motif, subject, articulation, syntax, and so on."[7] Furthermore, Irigaray thinks passionately about how to verbalize praise—a central concern of mine in these pages. Her catalogue of speech acts that humans direct toward God in *An Ethics of Sexual Difference* is striking for its outpouring of positive affect and energy, for its hosannas as well as laments: the modalities of enunciation in dialogue include "commands, prayers, appeals, graces, cries, dirges, glorias, anger, and questions."[8] Irigaray's work of the 1970s, sometimes criticized as essentialist, and that of the 1980s, sometimes criticized as utopian, may be seen as a gathering of resources that make possible such enunciations by and about women, in terms that pay our debt to the mother.

If Freud, Lacan, and Kristeva create a powerful discourse with which to speak of lack, loss, mourning, melancholy, and the past in the constitution of the subject, Irigaray, Klein, and Winnicott create a field in which literary critics may speak also of praise, celebration, exultation, exaltation, gratitude, and transformation as what comes *after* mourning. This book attends to the poetic utterance of thanks, benedictions, glorias, and questions, and asks what these enunciations have to do with maternity. Winnicott, in turn, provides some ballast for the utopian inclinations of Irigaray, with his models for the movement, freedom, and intersubjectivity for which she calls. He clarifies how Irigaray's nuptial hopes for encounters between men and women may extend to other encounters, regardless of gender or erotic valence. Irigaray is usually, and appropriately, read in the context of continental philosophy. But the reciprocal value of her work and that of British psychoanalysts needs emphasizing. It is not accidental that one of the best accounts of the Irigarayan imaginary in English, that by Margaret Whitford, acknowledges a general debt to Marion Milner, a colleague of Winnicott's.[9]

7. Irigaray, "An Ethics of Sexual Difference" (1984), in *An Ethics of Sexual Difference*, trans. Carolyn Burke and Gillian Gill (Ithaca, N.Y.: Cornell University Press, 1993), 116–29, at 127; "The Invisible of the Flesh: A Reading of Merleau-Ponty, *The Visible and the Invisible*, 'The Intertwining—the Chiasm' " (1984), ibid., 151–84, at 152.

8. Irigaray, "Love of the Other" (1984), in *Ethics*, 130–50, at 139. Irigaray means this as gender-specific, applying to "the relations between man and his God," but if there is any written Western discourse in which women speak so, it is surely in religious writing.

9. Whitford, *Luce Irigaray: Philosophy in the Feminine* (London: Routledge, 1991), headnote to chap. 3: "I should like to acknowledge my debt in this chapter to the work of Marion Milner."

The poetic texts studied in this book belong to the prehistory of psychoanalytic thought and make possible the kinds of thoughts that psychoanalysts have. Moreover, it is in large part psychoanalytic discourse that permits us to perceive this prehistory, and so to read poems of the distant past in a new way. Irigaray's furious and exalted readings of the philosophers demonstrate how such reading can open up new futures for them as well as for us.

Lacan suggests the reciprocal actions of temporality in the process of psychoanalysis in a beautiful and well-known passage: "What is realized in my history is not the past definite of what was, since it is no more, or even the present perfect of what has been in what I am, but the future anterior of what I shall have been for what I am in the process of becoming."[10] Irigaray too has hopes for new visions of old texts and their openings into our futures. In an essay written after the suicide of a friend who had failed the *passe* which would have qualified her as analyst in Lacan's school, Irigaray passionately calls on psychoanalysis to recognize the prophetic functions of the unconscious: "And if the unconscious were *both* the result of the acts of censorship, of repression forced on us in and by a certain history, *and also* a yet-to-come-into-being, the *reservoir of a yet-to-come*, your repudiations, acts of censorship and misrecognitions would seem to fold the future back into the past."[11] Her charge that Lacanian psychoanalysis thwarts the future by locking the unconscious into retroactive struggle with the past paradoxically emerges in her extension of Freud and Lacan on the temporality of psychoanalysis. She wants psychoanalysis to offer transformative possibilities: to the individual, to our culture, to past texts.

My hope is that this book conveys some of Irigaray's, Winnicott's, and Klein's aggressive energies for transformative movements into incalculable futures. The suppleness and errancy with which figuration eludes the cultural constraints so powerfully represented by our dominant accounts of maternity, and the varied, unpredictable relationships that readers form with poems, urge us to dwell ever more intently on the mobile gestures of works committed to figuration of

10. Jacques Lacan, "The Function and Field of Speech and Language in Psychoanalysis," in *Écrits: A Selection*, trans. Alan Sheridan (New York: Norton, 1977), 30–113, at 86.

11. Irigaray, "The Poverty of Psychoanalysis" (1977), trans. David Macey with Margaret Whitford, in *The Irigaray Reader*, ed. Whitford (Oxford: Blackwell, 1991), 79–104, at 82.

maternity and birth.[12] Winnicott, engaged with Klein and Irigaray, change what we can make of the literary past.

Authors these days often celebrate the collaborative, social nature of their thinking and writing processes. My sense is rather that, within the vast solitudes of writing, I am grateful for those who held up beacons: so shines a good deed. Among them at various moments in the past decade—they may not even remember—have been Janet Adelman, Judith Anderson, Harry Berger, Jr., Craig Berry, Carolyn Bitzenhofer, Joan Blythe, Barbara Bono, Gordon Braden, Jacqueline Brogan, Gerald Bruns, Helen Cooper, Heather Dubrow, Andrew Elfenbein, Elizabeth Fowler, Marshall Grossman, Graham Hammill, Bernhard Kendler, Clare Kinney, Joseph Loewenstein, Ellen Martin, Katharine Maus, David Miller, James Nohrnberg, Alexandra Olsen, Kathy Psomiades, Jon Quitslund, Amy Reese, John Rumrich, A. C. Spearing, Sheila Teahan, Jennifer Vaught, John Watkins, Susanne Wofford, my students at Notre Dame and Virginia, the anonymous readers for Cornell University Press, Ange Romeo-Hall and John LeRoy at the Press, and occasional patient auditors at conferences and lectures. None of these advisors is accountable for errors in which, in my folly, I have persisted. Special thanks to Bonnie Hanks, Karen Macdonald, and Catherine Sutton (and Tupelo, Foxy, and Benji). At the end of my work, the University of Virginia and the University of Notre Dame cooperated to provide me a year as visiting professor at Virginia. Although I might never have conceived this project without the rough weathers of a Great Lakes region, I surely would never have finished it without a year in the serene weathers and luminous skies of the Blue Ridge. The Charlottesville Friends' Meeting, though I was there for so short a time, remains for me a source of strength and clarity.

I am grateful for permissions to reprint generously granted by the presses cited on the copyright page and by those listed here. Earlier portions of chapters 5 and 6 appeared as "The Aim Was Song: Narrative and Lyric in Chaucer's *Parlement of Foules* and Shakespeare's *Love's Labour's Lost*," in Theresa Krier, ed., *Refiguring Chaucer in the Renaissance*

---

12. Lacan is celebrated for giving us the power to account for the errancy of figuration, of course, but it is striking how single-mindedly literary critics, anyway those working in the periods I read about, use this power to dwell with dolorous phenomena and affect. It need not be so, as Ellen Martin demonstrates to witty effect in her weave of Winnicott and Lacan in "*Sir Orfeo*'s Representation as Returns to the Repressed," *Assays: Critical Approaches to Medieval and Renaissance Texts* 8 (1995): 29–46, and "Raiding Jonah: Reading through Object Relations Theory," *Essays in Literature* 20 (1993): 70–83.

(Gainesville: University Press of Florida, 1998), 165–88; reprinted with the permission of the University Press of Florida.

"Ana Halach Dodeach" is cited from Vicki Hearne, *In the Absence of Horses*, copyright © 1983 by Princeton University Press; reprinted by permission of Princeton University Press.

Spenser's *Epithalamion* and *Amoretti* are cited from William Oram et al., *The Yale Edition of the Shorter Poems of Edmund Spenser*, Yale University Press, copyright © 1989; used with permission.

The Parlement of Foules is cited from Larry D. Benson, ed., *The Riverside Chaucer*, 3d ed., copyright © 1987 by Houghton Mifflin Company; reprinted with permission.

Love's Labor's Lost and *The Winter's Tale* are cited from Evans, G. Blakemore, ed., *The Riverside Shakespeare*, 2d ed., copyright © 1997 by Houghton Mifflin Company; used with permission.

Passages from Lucretius are copyright © Oxford University Press 1947. Reprinted from Lucretius: *De Rerum Natura*, vols. 1–3, edited with Prolegomena, Text and Critical Apparatus, translation and commentary by Cyril Bailey (1947, reissued 1986) by permission of Oxford University Press.

The English translation of Lucretius is reprinted by permission of the publishers and the Trustees of the Loeb Classical Library from *Lucretius*, translated by W. H. D. Rouse, rev. by Martin F. Smith, Loeb Classical Library (Cambridge: Harvard University Press, 1992). The Loeb Classical Library ® is a registered trademark of the President and Fellows of Harvard College.

Angela Carter is reprinted from "Overture and Incidental Music from *A Midsummer Night's Dream*," copyright © Angela Carter 1985; reproduced by permission of the Estate of Angela Carter c/o Rogers, Coleridge & White Ltd., 20 Powis Mews, London W11 1JN.

This book is made possible in part by support from the Institute for Scholarship in the Liberal Arts, College of Arts and Letters, University of Notre Dame.

PART ONE

Hazards of Birth

1
Cradle and All

———————

In the dewy wood tinselled with bewildering moonlight, the bumbling, tumbling babies of the fairy crèche trip over the hem of her dress, which is no more nor less than the margin of the wood itself; they stumble in the tangled grass as they play with the coneys, the quick brown fox-cubs, the russet fieldmice and the wee scraps of grey voles, blind velvet Mole and striped Brock with his questing snout—all the denizens of the woodland are her embroiderings, and the birds flutter round her head, settle on her shoulders and make their nests in her great abundance of disordered hair, in which are plaited poppies and the ears of wheat.

The arrival of the Queen is announced by no fanfare of trumpets but the ash-soft lullaby of wood doves and the liquid coloratura blackbird. Moonlight falls like milk upon her naked breasts.

She is like a double bed; or, a table laid for a wedding breakfast; or, a fertility clinic.

—Angela Carter

Mythopoeic Mothers and Tropes of Generation

Angela Carter's description of Titania, comic and magnificent, at once celebrates and guys the literary traditions that she draws together so as to mark both their original magnitude and their latter-day relegation to the nursery: those of romance and mythopoeia, of the goddess Natura and the fairy queen, of a voluptuous, animate, and animal-filled natural world, of a verdant wood; rhetorical strategies like the leisurely, uninhibited envisioning of the naked female body; literary figures like similitude, catalogue, personification.[1] The bathos of the phrase "or, a fertility clinic", with its wonderful fall from the stately parallel similes, nonetheless elevates even the belated forms of fertility worship that we manage through a disquieting technology. Carter's passage identifies the literary kinds and figures I address in this book. What are we, at the outset of the twenty-first century, to make of works that brazenly revel in such literary conventions, which seem to invite every imaginable objection to hegemonic ideologies of gender and the normative coercions of representation? How are we to take a sentence like "Moonlight falls like milk upon her naked breasts"—if we choose to receive it at all?

This book is about a surprising literary tradition; indeed it has not even been considered a tradition. Works in this vein, drawn to topics and tropes of generation, scrutinize and critique their own cultures' forms of nostalgia for a lost merger with the mother, a nostalgia that they recognize within their literary cultures as a temptation to a glamorous but false, even disabling, fantasy. Lucretius, the composer of the Song of Songs, Chaucer, Spenser, Shakespeare lodge maternity and its possible representations in their works, as part of their linked attraction to worlds of created objects and to the tropes and forms of praise. All of them elaborate on the linked conditions of maternity and infancy, and, like Angela Carter in the epigraph to this chapter, they recognize as well as challenge a powerful nostalgia for a nurturant maternal presence, ample and benign. They clearly do not comprise a genre, but they do constitute a loose family—kith if not kin—with interests in acknowledging and hailing their precursors as part of their meditation on maternity. The works to which I listen in this book—the Song of Songs, *De rerum natura*, the *Parlement of Foules*, the *Amoretti*, *The Faerie Queene*, *Love's Labor's Lost*, *The Winter's Tale*—acknowledge the lure of nostalgia for an

---

1. Angela Carter, "Overture and Incidental Music for *A Midsummer Night's Dream*," in *Black Venus* (London: Chatto and Windus, 1985), 72–73.

archaic mother, indeed evoke it, but urge alternatives to both longing for and dread of her. They work out new ways of making room for the paradoxes and variousness of mother-child relationships and new ways of understanding the actions of literary forms and tropes as they turn from nostalgia. They offer representations of birth less as an irreparable wound of separation from the mother than as *a claiming of distance from or proximity to her within a charged, articulated, and volatile space.*

Like Angela Carter, these writers deploy exorbitant tropes of maternity, birth, and infancy. Like Carter, they embrace the conventions they adopt even as they fight against them. Like Carter, they do so to figure and to claim places in literary history for fluent systems of unpredictable identifications, desires, and aggressions. Each has strong intertextual ambitions and invents a poetic tradition for itself. They share a concern with the relationships of their vernacular to prior poetic and narrative traditions, moving to popularize in their own culture whatever counts for them as classic. Their different cultures, ideologies, and historical contexts notwithstanding, they participate in a branching project of vernacularization. To this end they each oppose what they construe as the constrictions of powerful and loved textual traditions—neoplatonism, Petrarchism, biblical prophecy, heroic codes, Graeco-Roman myth—then open up alternatives to these traditions' thinking in matters of gender, sexuality, and generation. Each develops relationships among biological and poetic conception, creation, and reproduction. Each opens itself to the allure and risks of a mythopoeic ontology of maternal, terrestrial fecundity. Each attends to the creation of the world, sometimes as in cosmological and scientific traditions, sometimes as in a biblical array of creatures. In each, this network of concepts is urgent to the writer or the speaker, a matter not just of preservation and transformation of the past in their art, but of a philosophic, ethical challenge: —You must change your life. This means a quest for social forms, feeling states and linguistic resources which transform and supersede that structure of the maternal-feminine which Emmanuel Levinas critically calls "ontology of nature, impersonal fecundity, faceless generous mother, matrix of particular beings, inexhaustible matter for things."[2]

Maternity, birth, and generation circulate through these works so pervasively that the fact of male authorship has significance. The writers whom I address are major, canonical, erudite, densely figurative, influ-

---

2. Emmanuel Levinas, *Totality and Infinity: An Essay on Exteriority*, trans. Alphonso Lingis (Pittsburgh: Duquesne University Press, 1979), 46.

ential, male writers, treating of creation and procreation in patriarchal cultures whose failures in regard to women writers, mothers, and the feminine generally have been massively documented. We will be more frustrated than satisfied if we look to them for extensive representations and narratives of maternal characters-as-subjects. Their works argue that before such stories can flourish, readers and cultures must undertake a prior labor of invention and figuration. This labor is my subject. It is the labor of transforming that mesmerizing cultural conviction of an originary fusion with maternal plenitude, and the consequences of such a fantasy: idealization of maternity, fear of the hostile or angry mother, the desire for union with and dread of engulfment by maternal power, mythopoeic elaborations of a chthonic mother earth with which men imagine they might be reunited and so made whole.[3] The ethical challenge, vigorously mounted, forms a crisis that initiates the reader into new linguistic forms figured as new births, fresh conditions of exposure. Thus each offers a meta-narrative about poetic language—say, about catalogues and naming, or about similitude, or about the emergence of the vernacular.

Above all, I study works that engage with the problems of praise and the affective partner of praise, gratitude—rhetorical and psychic issues that Angela Carter exposes in her "Overture," where the impulse to praise (to praise Titania, the maternal body, romance, Shakespeare all at once) is both sustained and ironized. Praise and gratitude are at the heart of these early poets' enterprises in *translatio*, carrying the poetic achievements of their pasts into their vernacular present. But the works I discuss do not assume any easy access to praise; indeed they raise the very question of the grounds of praise in any instance. Their writers concern themselves not with the praise of grandees, nor exclusively with adored ladies, but with a more general exultation in conditions of creatural existence. Robert Pogue Harrison discusses this kind of praise, and the nature of the object, in his Heideggerian turn away from what seem to him the confinement and narcissism of discourses about the subject:

> Praise is without doubt the inner, nostalgic vocation of poetry in general. Poetic praise allows that which is praised—the hero, the athlete, the statesman, the lady, the homeland, the mountains, the "lake effects," the seasons of nature—to reveal itself in its own essential light, which is not the light of poetry but which, without poetry, lacks the space in which to shine forth. . . .

3. Cf. Louis Althusser, *Lenin and Philosophy*, trans. Ben Brewster (New York: Monthly Review Press, 1971), 222: a text may evince an "internal distantiation" from ideologies to which "it alludes and with which it is constantly fed."

The onto-dependence that obtains between the praiser and the praised cannot . . . be traced back to mechanisms of poetic subjectivity.[4]

It will be clear from the following pages that I think it *is* possible to address such ontological praise poetry by talking about the subject, if not about "all that the concept of poetic subjectivity has come to imply in recent literary criticism" (34). In this study, the link between poetic praise of objects and subjectivity is the Winnicottian notion of *use of an object*—in his peculiar twist on the idiomatic senses of "use" and "object," which I discuss in the next chapter. The praised objects in this book include the world's phenomena and flux found in classical cosmological thinking, the living things of the biblical Creation, the temporality of seasons, as well as more specific sets of circumstances, like the familiar Chaucerian narrators' gratitude for access to old books.

The Chaucerian example of gratitude, widespread among early writers—if not always as genial and radiant as Chaucer makes it seem—is not fortuitous. Gratitude for the materials from which to fashion a poetic history infuses the big poetic works in the traditions I consider here. Poetic gratitude and its frequent manifestation in praise comprise a theme, a topos, a subject matter, an homage to admired precursors, and a reservoir of imagery neighboring on the lexical fields of maternity, birth, and infancy. These instances of praise have an immediate object— the summer, for example, or the beloved—but they are also meant to exult in the aesthetic risk of aspiring to praise, and in the material, linguistic, formal, and psychic resources for doing so. Early writers regularly join themes of creation to the rhetorical challenge of praise and to the ethical challenge of representing the maternal. Furthermore, they pose unexpectedly vigorous analyses and interrogations to the literary traditions that they work so hard. What are legitimate grounds for praise and the condition of gratitude? When would praise be unearned or cheapened? How can the orthodoxies and restrictions of received language, as well as that language's resourcefulness, be refreshed? Individual poets' meditations on these issues proceed via figurations of maternity and birth, or more accurately through a poet's entertaining for some interim the impulse to nostalgia for and idealization of the mother, then blocking it and turning from it, toward previously unimaginable ways of greeting a demystified maternal. It is as if these writers ask,

4. Robert Pogue Harrison, *The Body of Beatrice* (Baltimore: Johns Hopkins University Press, 1988), 34. This book I have found useful to read side by side with Joel Fineman's work on epideictic rhetoric in *Shakespeare's Perjur'd Eye: The Invention of Poetic Subjectivity in the Sonnets* (Berkeley: University of California Press, 1986).

with Luce Irigaray, how to repay the debt to the mother, how to conquer the cultural inclination to sentimentalize and so refuse acknowledgment of maternal subjectivities.

I join with currents of gender analysis in pressing beyond generalized indictments of tropes of the maternal, on the grounds that they repress the maternal only to construct upon it masculine identity and masculine cultures. Recent feminist theory and literary commentary have developed more flexibly theorized interpretation of figures in poetic works, understanding figuration as a crucial path to the transformation of cultural impulses to abject and idealize the maternal.[5] It is possible, for instance, for writers to internalize a notion of the mother as a structure or ground for language and action (mother as object) and yet to acknowledge, or work their way toward, mothers' subjectivities, via the capacity for gratitude in their writings. Irigaray herself fuses the most powerful critiques of troping maternity with refreshed figures for the maternal.

The poems that speak in this book register their discovery that gratitude unexpectedly requires owning and marshaling forms of *aggression* involved in birth and early relations to the mother. I will be describing various psychic economies of gratitude specific to individual works, but here I say a few general things about it, not least because the relation of gratitude to aggression that I pursue in this book through Melanie Klein, D. W. Winnicott, and Irigaray is underdiscussed in treatments of all of them, and because all of them demonstrate a passionate use of textual objects in their engagements with precursors.

The grounds for poetic praise of general conditions, figured synecdochically via maternity, birth, and infancy, are neither evident nor simple. Though speakers may come to celebrate the givenness of such conditions, this givenness is an invention as well as a discovery, and very often a triumph, as if over felt conditions of bareness and exposure, or conversely, over the *trauma* of excess—what Emerson calls "the fearful extent and multitude of objects."[6] Sequences of poetic events within each work make it clear that gratitude arises not when the singer simply

5. For a survey and discussion of theoretical objections to metaphor see Domna Stanton, "Difference on Trial: A Critique of the Maternal Metaphor in Cixous, Irigaray, and Kristeva," in *The Poetics of Gender*, ed. Nancy Miller (New York: Columbia University Press, 1986), 157–82; see Drucilla Cornell, *Beyond Accommodation: Ethical Feminism, Deconstruction, and the Law* (London: Routledge, 1991) for the positive potentialities of metaphor to feminist theory.

6. Ralph Waldo Emerson, "Nature," in *Works*, 6 vols. (Philadelphia: John D. Morris, 1906), 3:5–75, at 33.

picks up the manifold conditions of mortal life as if they lay scattered about for the taking, but when he or she discovers, through others' poems, "the great and crescive self";[7] it marks the strength and movements of the singer as well as the discovery of the givenness of the world. This praise arises through a certain kind of aggression in the speaker. It may coexist with tenderness, as in the Song of Songs, or with genial bemusement, as in Chaucer. It is not precisely the emulative aggression and domination that govern much social gift-giving, nor always the oedipal strife of poets as in Harold Bloom's account, but a specific form of aggression that I understand by means of the proposals of Klein, Winnicott, and Irigaray about the roots of aggression in infancy's complex relationship to the mother.

Klein places this aggression before theory—an innate fact, not to be interrogated. As we shall see at more length in the next chapter, this aggression takes as its early form an insatiable greed fueling a fantasy of destroying the mother's body because she is the mysterious source (both container and provident agent) of nourishment. The aggression aroused by the infant's grievance against the breast and by its fear of retaliation from the mother manifests itself in elaborate fantasies of biting, devouring, cutting, degrading, and destroying the mother-object. It is certainly easy, almost irresistible, to slide from this envy to the postulate of a prior mother/infant fusion or plenitude at the breast, for which we pine ever after.[8] And the pathos of nostalgia for an imagined merger with the mother may be intensified by cultural circumstances, for instance ancient Roman property law or the late Elizabethan successes in higher education, both of which formed cohorts of ambitious young men whose exercise of power and autonomy was checked by generations of fathers who persisted in living on and controlling the material resources of such exercise.

For Winnicott, Kleinian fantasies of destroying the mother and then atoning by reparative action are less useful for thinking out aggression's

7. Emerson, "Experience," in *Works*, 5:292–322, at 316.

8. See, for example, Freud, "Female Sexuality" (1931), in *Standard Edition of the Complete Psychological Works of Sigmund Freud*, ed. James Strachey et al., 24 vols. (London: Hogarth Press and Institute of Psycho-Analysis, 1953–73 [henceforth *SE*]), 16:231, and this from "Femininity" (1932), in *SE*, 22:122: "The reproach against the mother which goes back furthest is that she gave the child too little milk—which is construed against her as lack of love. . . . But . . . it is impossible that the child's reproach can be justified as often as it is met with. It seems, rather, that the child's avidity for its earliest nourishment is altogether insatiable, that it never gets over the pain of losing its mother's breast." All of Melanie Klein's work brings out vividly the infant's greed and insatiability, but she understands these chiefly as responses to the *internal* threat of the death instinct.

relation to gratitude than what he describes as the infant's fantasied destruction of objects and the subsequent, happy discovery that objects (including the mother but not only her) survive this destruction, thus becoming independent beings as well as sources of materials for use in signifying. Winnicott works out this scheme as an alternative to the Kleinian infant's chief motivation of guilt. Because the surviving object is discovered to exist externally, independent of the infant, this mother remains more complicated and unpredictable than infant fantasies can envision. For Winnicott, Kleinian infantile fantasy locks the subject into an orientation to the past; it works through a rich but fixed repertoire of fantasy objects and dynamics: the organs and parts of the maternal body, the mesmerizing movement of the unconscious inward and downward to the dark interior of the body. Winnicott's clinical work stresses by contrast movements into air and openness. His exchanges with clients, like Irigaray's evocations of a new female imaginary, put the unconscious at the service of creating the future. Winnicott might say that Klein remains thrall to mourning, unable to create a space between mother's body and infant that is neither destructive nor merely reparative. Winnicott, opposing a Kleinian notion of creative action that can be only reparative and guilt-ridden, aims to venture beyond grief for the loss of an archaic mother and to create clinical practices to free his clients and himself from paralysis into movement, gesture, and inventive exchange. But without feminist theory Winnicott reaches a limit in his own transformative terms. Irigaray, reworking both modern philosophy's notion of the interval and the notion of the unconscious, can return us to Winnicott's potential space, its temporality and its capacities for positive affect, even for what she calls the divine.

The manifold figures of space in Klein, Winnicott, and Irigaray can tell us much about the treatment of maternity, birth, and birthing in poetic fictions that turn away from nostalgia toward the paradoxes of mother-child relationships. The fluctuant, variously passionate space between mother and child, repeatedly figured in Klein, Winnicott, and Irigaray, provides a resource, a field upon which language, gesture, and creative action might be possible. It is also a formal relationship: fluid in shape, sometimes including others, but always coordinating, creating longitude and latitude between mother and child. "The sky isn't up there: it's between us," says Irigaray.[9] Such distance becomes formative literally in

---

9. Luce Irigaray, "When Our Lips Speak Together" (1977), in *This Sex Which Is Not One*, trans. Catherine Porter (Ithaca, N.Y.: Cornell University Press, 1985), 205–18, at 213.

the birth process, then in the handling of the baby in space and time. Feeding, holding, carrying, wrapping, warming, clothing, cleaning; age of the child at the various junctures when total care recedes; degree of bodily contact and face-to-face exchange; degree of responsiveness and hardiness expected from baby: all these vary widely from culture to culture. But the space between mother and child is also figurative and formative because it structures the becoming of the emergent subject. Because of our enrollment in this formal temporal and spatial relationship, formal process is part of our lives with relationships and objects, and we cannot do justice to a text, a fellow creature, or the social imaginary of maternity without some kind of formal analysis.

I use the term *parturition* for the long-term maintaining of space between mother and child, of whatever ages, whether between living characters or within the psyche, and I think of it as springing from certain forms of aggression. Parturition figures the ways in which both infant and mother may enfranchise each other after the confinement of labor and birth, may be *at large*—have elbow room, an openness of space between them, a passionate, shifting interplay of proximity and distance. This space may exist between mother and child, or within either of them. Moreover, since parturition in this extended sense pervades each culture relevant to this book, its entire symbolic range may be available even to mothers and children who have been lost to one another. Psychoanalytic theory often collapses the distinction between this space and loss more generally. Thus Kaja Silverman, in a passage to which I will return, describes a moment in Lacan's mirror stage: "Subjectivity is thus from the very outset dependent upon the recognition of a distance separating self from other—on an object whose loss is simultaneous with its apprehension."[10] But there is no evident reason that recognition of a distance is prima facie *loss* of an object, nor for the frequent slippage in psychoanalytic discourse from loss to lack, thence to castration and nostalgia. Mother and child, relieved of the burdens of lack, might well shape and sustain a space between them for fluencies of

---

10. Kaja Silverman, *The Acoustic Mirror: The Female Voice in Psychoanalysis and Cinema* (Bloomington: Indiana University Press, 1988), 7. Cf. Victoria Hamilton, *Narcissus and Oedipus: The Children of Psychoanalysis* (London: Routledge and Kegan Paul, 1982), 259: "the newborn does not only wish to be *fused*; therefore, he does not need to be prised away. He may seek out near-continual proximity, togetherness, mutuality and synchrony, but these goals are very different to the wish for total womb-like fusion, as described in the primary narcissism thesis." The range of desire for degrees of contact rather than for merger characterizes many mothers' published accounts of their relations with their children.

language, affect, thinking, and formal creation. Not a Lacanian mirror, but a Winnicottian space-between, is what Irigaray argues for in "Divine Women," in another passage to which I will return: "Though it may at times help us to emerge, to move out of the water, the mirror blocks our energies, freezes us in our tracks, clips our wings. What protects me from the other and allows me to move toward him or her is more often the settling of a space, an enclave of air rather than the interposition of mirrors and glasses whose cutting edge all too often threatens to turn against me."[11]

In this enclave of air we might take as a model for the mother/child space the words of Vicki Hearne's speaker in her poem on the Song of Songs: "From my mountain of words I can see / You on your mountain."[12] So might mother and child speak to each other, as if glad of the spacious ground between mountains. Or we might take as corporeal metaphor of our complex interface with a separate mother the placenta. Irigaray, putting forward work by Hélène Rouch, refers to "the placental economy" of exchange between mother and fetus, two discrete organisms in one; the placenta is "neither one nor the other."[13] As Rouch says, the placenta is a tissue formed by the embryo, not "a mixed formation, half-maternal, half-fetal." It is

> the mediating space between mother and fetus, which means that there's never a fusion of maternal and embryonic tissues. . . . This relative autonomy of the placenta . . . cannot be reduced either to a mechanism of fusion (an ineffable mixture of the bodies or blood of mother and fetus), or, conversely, to one of aggression (the fetus as foreign body devouring from the inside . . .). These descriptions are of imaginary reality and appear quite poor indeed—and obviously extremely culturally determined—in comparison to the complexity of the biological reality. (38–39)

Part of the blame for this impoverished imaginary, for Irigaray and Rouch, lies with psychoanalysis. For psychoanalysis "justifies the imaginary fusion between a child and its mother by the undeveloped state of the child at birth and by its absolute need of the other, its mother. It's

11. Luce Irigaray, "Divine Women" (1984), in *Sexes and Genealogies*, trans. Gillian Gill (New York: Columbia University Press, 1993), 55–72, at 66.

12. Vicki Hearne, "Ana Halach Dodeach," in *In the Absence of Horses* (Princeton: Princeton University Press, 1983), 13.

13. Luce Irigaray, interview of Hélène Rouch, "On the Maternal Order" (1987), in *Je, Te, Nous: Toward a Culture of Difference*, trans. Alison Martin (London: Routledge, 1993), 37–44, at 41.

this fusion, implicitly presented as an extension of the organic fusion during pregnancy, which, it would seem, simply has to be broken [by a third term, by the father] in order for the child to be constituted as a subject" (42). Imagining a placental economy allows us to imagine a bodily intimacy of mother and child that is always already not a fusion or merger; distinctness exists from the start. Biological birth is a transformation of this interface, an extension of distinctness. But this version of birth needs to be brought into the symbolic, figured, and interpreted in order to be acknowledged.

It is in *not* acknowledging parturition that fantasies of fusion with an archaic mother arise; not to acknowledge the dynamic distances between mother and infant in birth is itself the loss. Rouch says, "The differentiation between the mother's self and the other of the child, and vice versa, is in place before it's given meaning in and by language, and the forms it takes don't necessarily accord with those our cultural imaginary relays: loss of paradise, traumatizing expulsion or exclusion, etc. I'm not accusing these forms of the imaginary of being wrong, but of being the only ways of theorizing what exists before language."[14]

Trapped in the melancholia of unperformed mourning for a fusion that we do not allow ourselves to know we have never exactly had, we consign ourselves to the pathos of nostalgia for an idealized first home. This work of mourning, which relies on naming birth adequately, would make possible the unalienated jubilation for which Irigaray's recurrent topos is free movement in the air: "Once we have left the *waters* of the womb, we have to construct a space for ourselves in the *air* for the rest of our time on earth—air in which we can breathe and sing freely, in which we can perform and move at will. . . . To construct and inhabit our airy space is essential. It is the space of bodily autonomy, of free breath, free speech and song, of performing on the stage of life."[15]

14. Quoted in Irigaray, "On the Maternal Order," 42. See also Irigaray, "Body against Body: In Relation to the Mother" (1980), in *Sexes and Genealogies*, 7–21, at 16: "The insatiable character of what we . . . call orality, the unquenchable thirst, the desire for the mother to fill us to the brim, is the subject of much discussion in analysis. . . . [Yet] there is no real reason to believe that an infant's thirst . . . is insatiable. . . . that mouth cavity of the child, like any desire, becomes a bottomless pit if the time spent in utero is a taboo issue."

15. Irigaray, "Divine Women," 66. This mourning of birth so as to get on with the jubilation of living in air is a crucial step that I leave largely unexamined in this book, not least because it would require an interweaving of Irigaray and Kristeva that would exceed my present scope. Many medieval Christian Nativity and Holy Family narratives would work well in marking the steps of such mourning work; so would Spenser's Garden of Adonis. On the former, see, for example, Theresa Coletti, "Purity and Danger: The Paradox of

Our poems articulate the release into positive affect that follows acknowledgment, placing, and interpretation of parturition. To achieve freedom of movement in the air, the prerogative of Irigaray's angels, is ideally a prerogative of birth, as Winnicott suggests in his papers on transitional space. But to achieve it, the poets of this study suggest, requires resistance to the pathos of nostalgia and a commitment to articulating the endlessly varied, charged spaces between mother and child. Klein, Winnicott, and Irigaray aid my argument that the impulse to poetic praise gathers when the individual speaker or poet owns his or her own aggression as a means of claiming a ground of relationship without the coercions of compliance from the other. This stance Irigaray builds into the preposition *à* in her nonidiomatic title *J'aime à toi*. Of this phrase she says: "*I love to you* means I maintain a relation of indirection to you. I do not subjugate or consume you. I respect you (as irreducible). I hail you: in you I hail. I praise you: in you I praise. I give you thanks: to you I give thanks for . . . I bless you for . . . I speak to you, not just about something; rather I speak *to* you. I tell you, not so much this or that, but rather I tell *to* you."[16]

It is not accidental that Irigaray's paradigmatic catalogue lodges hailing, praising, thanking, and blessing in close proximity; together they suggest that what Irigaray calls "indirection" might be that space between mountains, between two speakers, between mother and child, between lovers, that would allow for the rising up of praise poetry.

Weathering Birth

Symbolizing, interpreting, and then making something of such parturition entails an initial acknowledgment of the roughness of birth for both mother and infant, something we find in topoi throughout early periods. "We came crying hither, / Thou know'st the first time that we smell the air / We wawl and cry." Lear's cold comfort to Gloucester is the most haunting articulation of a topos widely developed in early writing, on the infant's experience of birth. Lucretius: "And then the

Mary's Body and the En-gendering of the Infancy Narrative in the English Mystery Cycles," in *Feminist Approaches to the Body in Medieval Literature*, ed. Linda Lomperis and Sarah Stanbury (Philadelphia: University of Pennsylvania Press, 1993), 65–95; and Kathleen Ashley and Pamela Sheingorn, *Interpreting Cultural Symbols: Saint Anne in Late Medieval Society* (Athens: University of Georgia Press, 1990).

16. Luce Irigaray, "I Love to You," in *I Love to You: Sketch of a Possible Felicity in History*, trans. Alison Martin (London: Routledge, 1996), 109–13, at 109; ellipses in original.

infant, / like some sailor tossed / from savage seas, lies naked, speech-less, helpless / to keep alive, when nature first has heaved and spilled him into the light from mother's womb; / he fills the world with wails—and well he might, / such pain awaits his passage through this life!" The prophet Jeremiah: "Cursed be the day on which I was born! / The day when my mother bore me, let it not be blessed! / Cursed be the man who brought the news to my father . . . / because he did not kill me in the womb; / so my mother would have been my grave, / and her womb forever great." The book of Wisdom: "And I too, when born, inhaled the common air, and fell upon the kindred earth; wailing, I uttered that first sound common to all. . . . For no king has any different origin or birth, but one is the entry into life for all; and in one same way they leave it." The Old English *Solomon and Saturn* II observes, "When a mother bears a son, then she has no control / over how long his journey through the world may last. / She will often nourish her child to woe, / to her own sorrow." The Spirit who visits Boccaccio's dreamer in the *Corbaccio* laments: "How many babies, entering life against their [mothers'] will, are tossed into the arms of fortune! Look at the hospitals! How many more die before they have tasted mother's milk? How many are abandoned to the woods, how many to the beasts and the birds?" Tristram in all the versions of his story is named for the sorrow of his birth; Malory's plainness brings out with particular pathos the exposures of both mother and child:

> And whan she was farre in the forreste she myght no farther, but ryght there she gan to travayle faste of hir chylde, and she had many grymly throwys. . . .
>
> And so by myracle of oure Lady of Hevyn she was delyverde with grete paynes, but she had takyn suche colde for the defaute of helpe that the depe draughtys of deth toke hir, that nedys she must dye and departe oute of thys worlde; there was none othir boote. . . .
>
> And whan she sye hym [the baby] she seyde thus: "A, my lytyll son, thou haste murtherd thy modir! And therefore I suppose thou that arte a murtherer so yonge, thow arte full lykly to be a manly man in thyne ayge; and bycause I shall dye of the byrth of the, I charge my jantyllwoman that she pray my lorde, the kynge Melyodas, that whan he is crystened let call hym Trystram, that is as muche to say as a sorowfull byrth."

"When I was born," says Shakespeare's Marina, "Never was waves nor wind more violent." Jonson, apostrophizing Pliny's "infant of Saguntum," grimly approves his second thoughts about being born at all: "Ere thou wert half got out, / Wise child, didst hastily return, / And mad'st thy mother's womb thine urn."[17]

One reads the lines of Jeremiah or of Jonson with alarm for the glancingly acknowledged mothers; childbirth is a rough experience for the mother too, and its topoi begin with the earliest written records of our traditions. The Lord says to Eve, "in pain you shall bring forth children." The Lord who speaks through Isaiah obsessively compares himself to a mother, both in his tender love and in his suffering: "I have kept still and restrained myself; / now I will cry out like a woman in labor, I will gasp and pant." When Chaucer's Custance, torn away from her young children, makes bold to utter the closest she comes to a complaint: "I have noght had no part of children tweyne / But first siknesse, and after, wo and peyne." The composer of *Cleanness* contrasts the Nativity story, and the purity in which Mary and her infant separated, with other mortal births: "For þer watz seknesse al sounde þat sarrest is halden, / And þer watz rose reflayr where rote hatz ben euer, / And þer watz solace and songe wher sorz hatz ay cryed." Margery Kempe, in the account of her madness after the birth of a child, speaks of the ills that all pregnant women are heir to: "aftyr þat sche had conceyued, sche was labowrd wyth grett accessys tyl þe chyld was born, & þan, what for þe labowr sche had in chyldyng & for sekenesse goyng beforn, sche dyspyred of hyr lyfe, wenyng sche mygth not leuyn." Erasmus's Fabulla, a new mother engaged in spirited conversation with the family friend Eutrapelus, asserts, "Now, though you [men] make a special point of boasting of your martial valor—there's not a single one of you who, if he once experienced childbirth, would not prefer standing in a battle line

17. Sources of these birth passages: Shakespeare, *King Lear* 4.6.178–80 (all references to Shakespeare come from *The Riverside Shakespeare*, ed. G. Blakemore Evans et al. [Boston: Houghton Mifflin, 1974]); Lucretius, *De rerum natura* 5.222–27 (*The Nature of Things*, trans. Frank Copley [New York: Norton, 1977], 118); Jeremiah 20:15–17 and Wisdom 7:3–6, from the New Revised Standard Version (Grand Rapids, Mich.: Zondervan, 1993); *Solomon and Saturn* II, in *Anglo-Saxon Didactic Verse*, ed. and trans. Louis Rodrigues (Felinfach: Llanerch, 1995), p. 179, lines 193–96 ["Modor ne rædeð, ðonne heo magan cenneð, / hu him weorðe geond worold widsið sceapen. / Oft heo to bealwe bearn afedeð, nu / seolfre to surge"]; Boccaccio, *The Corbaccio*, trans. Anthony Cassell, 2d ed. (Binghamton, N.Y.: MRTS, 1993), 28 (but I follow John Boswell's translation here; see his note on the verb "se n'uccidono," in *The Kindness of Strangers: The Abandonment of Children in Western Europe from Late Antiquity to the Renaissance* [New York: Pantheon, 1988], 414); Malory, *Works (Morte Darthur)*, ed. Eugene Vinaver (London: Oxford University Press, 1954), 275; Shakespeare, *Pericles* 4.1.59; Ben Jonson, "To the Immortal Memory and Friendship of that Noble Pair, Sir Lucius Cary and Sir H. Morison," 1–8, in *Complete Poems*, ed. George Parfitt (New Haven: Yale University Press, 1975).

ten times over to going through what we must endure so often."
Spenser's Amavia says of the birth of her child, "Lucina came; a man-
child forth I brought: / The woods, the Nymphes, my bowres, my mid-
wiues weare, / Hard helpe at need. So deare thee babe I boughte, /
Yet nought too deare I deemd." Titania wistfully remembers the
friend who died in childbirth, whose son she now rears: "But she,
being mortal, of that boy did die." Shakespeare's Posthumus dreams of
a mother who says of his birth, "Lucina lent not me her aid, / But took
me in my throes, / That from me was Posthumus ripped, / Came crying 'mongst his foes, / A thing of pity!" Donne's Niobe, perhaps
speaking for the now-mute Anne Donne, says simply and epigrammat-
ically, "By childrens births, and death, I am become / So dry, that I am
now mine owne sad tombe."[18] Nor have the material, social, and medical conditions that make possible such topoi of birth changed much in
most of the world; even in the most industrialized cultures birth and
child rearing were risky and burdensome until well into this century.[19]
The people likely to read or write a book like this one are fortunate in

18. These examples are from Genesis 3:16; Isaiah 42:14; Chaucer, the Clerk's Tale, *Canterbury Tales* fragment IV(E), lines 650–51 (Chaucer citations come from *The Riverside Chaucer*,
3d ed., ed. Larry Benson et al. [New York: Houghton Mifflin, 1987]); *Clannesse*, in *The Poems
of the Pearl Manuscript*, ed. Malcolm Andrew and Ronald Waldron (Berkeley: University of
California Press, 1978), lines 1078–80; Kempe, *The Book of Margery Kempe*, ed. Sanford
Brown Meech, notes by Hope Emily Allen (London: Oxford University Press, 1940), 6;
Erasmus, *Puerpera* (1526), in *The Colloquies of Erasmus*, trans. Craig Thompson (Chicago:
University of Chicago Press, 1965), 271; Spenser, *The Faerie Queene*, ed. A. C. Hamilton
(New York: Longman, 1975), 2.1.53; Shakespeare, *A Midsummer Night's Dream* 2.1.135 and
Cymbeline 5.4.43–46; John Donne's epigram "Niobe," in *Poetical Works*, ed. J. C. Grierson
(Oxford: Oxford University Press, 1971), 67.

19. Studies of the perils of birth in premodern Western eras now comprise a vast field;
see the bibliographical essay. Roger Schofield argues for tempered estimates of the number
of women who died in childbirth or through complications of pregnancy and birth in early
modern Europe; see "Did the Mothers Really Die? Three Centuries of Maternal Mortality
in 'the World We Have Lost,' " in *The World We Have Gained: Histories of Population and
Social Structure*, ed. Lloyd Bonfield, Richard Smith, and Keith Wrightson (Oxford: Oxford
University Press, 1986), 231–60. Demographic data are hard to come by and intractable to
interpretation, but it may be, as Boswell points out repeatedly, that maternal and infant
mortality, and risks to these populations generally, worsen in periods of instability, for
example, after the fall of Rome or during and after the decimations of population and
social structure caused by the Black Death. In any case, for this book what matters are the
perceptions, anxieties, and linguistic responses to the charged proximity of birth and
death, and both as exposures to the onslaughts of the world. Furthermore, if we take such
anxieties as intrinsic to the extended immaturity of the human infant, then relatively good
times for the survival and rearing of children would still give rise to such topoi in many
cultural forms.

the degree of buffering that our costly civilization permits, but we remain radically vulnerable to the mortal ills that flesh is heir to, and I take the exposures of birth for mother and child alike as synecdochic for such vulnerability. It has always been true that in most places in most times, resources are scarce, survival not guaranteed, thriving a distant hope. Psychoanalysis is one discourse within a tradition that acknowledges such difficulties. Freud and Klein, among the early pioneers, fashion moving testimonials to birth's vulnerability and the human need for protection.

Winnicott and Irigaray also bring into psychoanalysis models of birth that acknowledge its vulnerability and exposures, and make space for its work of mourning. But their models, drawing on many different historical versions of vitalism, further entertain hopes for an endless becoming, a capacity in the subject to pay the debt to that which gives it life, in an exultation that surges past the bittersweet melancholy of nostalgia. We ought to bear in mind that none of the written acknowledgments of birth I have cited expresses any experience of, much less fondness for, a mother/baby fusion; this remains a separate fantasy embedded in different topoi. When they do represent the paradoxes of gestation and birth events, it is more in terms like those of Christine Battersby: "the 'other' emerges out of the embodied self, but in ways that mean that two selves emerge and one self does not simply dissolve into the other. . . . This 'self' does not emerge out of the exclusion or abjection of the 'other.' . . . Instead, it is from intersecting force-fields that a 'self' and 'other' emerge."[20] These intersecting force-fields, in which the edges of objects meet, overlap, blur, and reform, constitute Winnicott's notion of potential space, as we shall see in the next chapter.

At one time during its writing I wanted to name this book *Weathering Birth*. The phrase has been demoted to the title of a section only, but it has its uses. I want to retain the phrase's connotation of exposure to the elements, the wildness and rigors of birth, the long-term vulnerability of human infancy, the physical endurance and dangers for the mother. But on the whole I do not want the sense of erosion, of diminishment that may come with "weathering" anything—as it clearly diminished Anne Donne. If I take as paradigmatic for human life generally the neonate's primordial exposure, all the risks of birth to both mother and child, and the passionate currents of love and hate that can flow in the spaces

---

20. Christine Battersby, *The Phenomenal Woman: Feminist Metaphysics and the Patterns of Identity* (London: Routledge, 1998), 8.

between them in my texts, I also demonstrate their commitment to the amplifications and exhilarations of sturdily weathering birth. In these works that treat of maternal and infant vulnerability, to acknowledge and represent birth is to discover sources of imaginative strength and exultation. Parturition may occasion praise of the condition of perceptible distinctness, and this on the part of the mother also. The space created by mother and child in varied, historically specific ways, the tangle of presence, absence, love, resentment, hate, friendship, need, protection, exposure, mourning of the dead, mourning of the living—these are inadequately addressed through a priori or careless equating of loss, lack, and absence—topics needing the complementary notions of presence, gratitude, and intervals between speaking, listening subjects. What Freud unforgettably called "the impressive caesura of the act of birth" has a wide array of functions and feeling tones.[21] Freud probably thought of this caesura in terms of the cut which figures the infant's sundering from the mother and castration. But readers of poetry may also want to retain and bring to psychoanalytic texts the sense of caesura as a breathing space, an expansion of line.[22]

Though Klein and Winnicott share (like this book) the attachment of psychoanalysis to the child's point of view, they are manifestly concerned with mothers and maternity, as well as with possible relationships between birth and creative action, largely through their elaborations of objects: what things count as objects, what life objects have in the psyche, how objects are structured as formal fields of complex forces and processes, how mental objects bear on objects in the world, including persons. The work of Klein and especially Winnicott on aggression is central to the tracing of alternatives to a melancholic or fatal nostalgia for the maternal. Winnicott, moreover, is far less cozy and ahistorical about family structure and affect than is often thought. He makes room for maternal subjectivity, for mothers' historical circumstances, and for a feminine symbolic grounded not in biological essentialism but in mutable historical processes and forms—issues at the center of Irigaray's thinking. All three of these pioneers, furthermore, make it possible to

21. Freud, *Inhibitions, Symptoms and Anxiety* (1925), in *SE*, 20:138. Dubrow argues at length that "poststructuralist paradigms that direct our attention to the subject [of loss] . . . often oversimplif[y] loss" (*Shakespeare and Domestic Loss* [Cambridge: Cambridge University Press, 1999], 2 and passim).

22. On the etymological tradition behind the phrase "Caesarean birth" see Renate Blumenfeld-Kosinski, *Not of Woman Born: Representations of Caesarean Birth in Medieval and Renaissance Culture* (Ithaca, N.Y.: Cornell University Press, 1990), 143–53.

see how, as Jonathan Dollimore among others argues, premodern ideas about sexuality, desire, death, and origins "remain obscurely active inside modern psychoanalysis."[23]

For these reasons the next chapter begins with Klein's and Winnicott's work on aggression. The chapters that follow, not strictly chronological, build an argument about nostalgia for an archaic mother, poetic language, psychoanalysis, and aggression as the gift unexpectedly attending adequate symbolizations of birth. As each chapter builds on the argument in previous chapters, two salient psychoanalytic notions gradually emerge. First, the book moves from aggression in its peculiar Winnicottian inflection as nearly synonymous with motility to aggression more commonly understood, freighted with hostility and violence, as in *The Winter's Tale*. Second, the sequence of chapters traces increasingly intricate mechanisms of nostalgia, from the radiant tenderness acknowledged in the Song of Songs, through confused longings and defenses (for example, the *Amoretti*), toward ambivalent hostility (*Love's Labor's Lost*), concurrence of longing for and aversion to female sexuality and reproductive power (*De rerum natura*), finally to hatred and fear mingled with idealization (*The Winter's Tale*).

Because of the value of their challenges in stirring our own thinking, I have chosen works which are formally sophisticated and complex, yet can seem to us worst possible cases of objectionable ideologies about the maternal, the feminine, the body: the Song of Songs and the *Amoretti*, with their flamboyant blazons of the beloved's body; Lucretius, with his abstracting, perhaps abjecting, of the maternal as a necessary condition for his philosophical cosmology; a romance sequence from Spenser's *Faerie Queene*, book 4, notable for its assemblage of mindlessly combative knights and damsels-made-trophies; Chaucer's *Parlement of Foules* with its unabashed celebration of the heterosexual and the procreative, concentrated in the figure of Dame Nature; Shakespeare's *Love's Labor's Lost* with its male aristocrats' posturings and infatuations. *The Winter's Tale* concludes the book because it presents to recent criticism a powerful and most difficult instance of nostalgia for the maternal. All these works might invite from twentieth-century readers challenges and

23. Jonathan Dollimore, "Desire Is Death," in *Subject and Object in Renaissance Culture*, ed. Margreta de Grazia, Maureen Quilligan, and Peter Stallybrass (Cambridge: Cambridge University Press, 1996), 369–86, at 385. See also Carla Mazzio and Douglas Trevor, "Dreams of History," in their collection *Historicism, Psychoanalysis, and Early Modern Culture* (New York: Routledge, 2000), 1–19, for further comments on the usefulness of psychoanalysis to historical inquiry, and recent rapprochements between historicism and psychoanalysis.

questions like those that Luce Irigaray fires at the major philosophical texts with which she wrestles in both love and aggression; I hope to demonstrate that the poetic works contain within themselves such questions, such wrestling with the dangerous angels of major traditions.

Since I also hope to demonstrate that ethical meditations on issues of maternity and birth have always been present in the poetic histories that poets make for themselves—if not in commentary traditions—I discuss these large poetic works in pairs so as to make arguments for intertextual relationships. Thus the Song of Songs and the *Amoretti* make possible extended discussion of figures of similitude, the movements of trope within a Winnicottian potential space, and the function of blazons at the present time. The chapters on Chaucer's *Parlement of Foules* and Shakespeare's *Love's Labor's Lost* link rhetorico-poetical matters of narrative and temporality, catalogue, hexaemeral writing, and the aspiration to song, with the functions of maternity and aggression that make song possible. The chapters on Lucretius's *De rerum natura* and Spenser's *Faerie Queene*, book 4, engage cultural fantasies of longing for reabsorption into a chthonic maternal matrix that would relieve the ethical burdens of our inevitable boundedness. Here my argument entails the uses of ancient myth and the ways that inheritance of myth is a resource as well as an obstructive challenge to the strong poet. Finally I turn to *The Winter's Tale*, the work that started the whole question for me, in order to consider one last time that most Winnicottian, idiomatic, cagey, and maddening notion of "enough"—as in "good-enough mothering." What is enough of anything?

2

Aggressive Movements in Psychoanalysis: Klein, Winnicott, and Irigaray

The philosophy we want is one of fluxions and mobility.
—Ralph Waldo Emerson

In this chapter I make constellations of Klein's, Winnicott's, and Irigaray's thinking on relations between infant and mother. Their array of figures for space and aggression (appearing now as mobility, now as hate) will prove resources for the literary-historical arguments of subsequent chapters. Aggression will prove a resource *against* nostalgia—much as mobility and aggression are resources for Emerson, who presides over this chapter and represents an antecedent American inflection of the British and French thinkers.[1] My thoughts in this chapter are partial in both senses of the word: they comprise a specific argument and they are not meant as a comprehensive overview. It will seem odd at first to read Irigaray along with Klein and Winnicott. Aside from the fact of their inhabiting different historical and intellectual universes, Klein remained committed to specific fantasies of the body's organs, corporeal containers, and alimentary systems in ways that Irigaray rejects; and Winnicott, who had little interest in theorizing language, would proba-

1. The epigraph comes from Ralph Waldo Emerson, "Montaigne," in *Works*, 6 vols. (Philadelphia: John D. Morris, 1906), 1:136–72, at 147.

bly have deflected Irigaray's pursuits of "male" and "female" as categories within discourse. But Klein and Winnicott open up unexpected, oblique, and fruitful ways to use Irigaray's powerful critiques of gender and figurative writing. And Irigaray's poetic elaborations of movement, passage, fluids, air, interval, and paying the debt to the mother are elegantly anticipated in the gestures of Winnicott's papers and clinical practice. I turn the absence of linguistic theorizing in Klein and Winnicott to positive tactical advantage for the duration of this book: this absence frees us to think about phenomena of poetic language outside the structuralist paradigms undergirding Lacanian and Kristevan analyses of language, paradigms which may *block* efforts to imagine maternity beyond loss and lack. Lynne Huffer speaks of the "Western, deconstructive tradition of thought that looks at language as the differential play of presence and absence" and argues that deconstruction *requires* nostalgia for an absent mother:

> Within that tradition, the logic of replacement can be described as a system whereby a term—the word or the sign—can come to the fore only by effacing another term—the thing or the referent—that it ostensibly sets out to name. If we further contextualize that logic of replacement within a psychoanalytic tradition of thought, the play of presence and absence can be articulated in the vocabulary of gendered subjects. . . . Significantly, this logic of appearance and disappearance, of moving toward something only to erase it, describes [a] nostalgic structure. . . . A nostalgic structure both creates and obliterates a lost object. . . . nostalgia requires an absent mother.[2]

Making no structuralist assumptions about language, Winnicott and Klein give us instruments with which to think about maternity in language outside dominant linguistic models; Irigaray turns structuralist implications against themselves and looks to nonstructuralist symbolic traditions (from pre-Enlightenment Europe, from the Far East) for new ways to bring mothers and birth into the symbolic. For instance, Winnicott's and Irigaray's splendid insistence on breath and mobility—effec-

---

2. Lynne Huffer, *Maternal Pasts, Feminist Futures: Nostalgia, Ethics, and the Question of Difference* (Stanford: Stanford University Press, 1998), 3. For other analyses of maternity and deconstruction, see two essays in *Derrida and Feminism: Recasting the Question of Woman*, ed. Ellen K. Feder, Mary C. Rawlinson, and Emily Zakin (New York: Routledge, 1997): Kelly Oliver, "The Maternal Operation: Circumscribing the Alliance," 53–68; and Ewa Plonowska Ziarek, "From Euthanasia to the Other of Reason: Performativity and the Deconstruction of Sexual Difference," 115–41.

tively a secular pneumatology—activates us to consider how old poems figure animation, inspiration, personification, apostrophe, and voice.[3]

While Melanie Klein made aggression, especially that of the very young infant, her special province, Winnicott is not often linked with this concept. It is widely assumed that Winnicott's picture of preoedipal life is about a reassuring mama, playing, and merger—and this in distinction to the Kleinian preoedipal during which the infant suffers the tortures of its own fears, violence, and hatred. Winnicott has been chastised for sentimentality about mother-and-baby, for influencing Benjamin Spock and Bruno Bettelheim, for idealizing mothers in theory but mistrusting the capacities of actual mothers, for deflecting attention from the mother's subjectivity, for managing and preaching to mothers, for neglecting the functions of the father, and for evading questions of the unconscious, gender formation, the oedipal complex, and the entry into language. Winnicott accrues objections possible to raise against normative uses of his work by others, among them social workers with their impulse to manage mothers, and literary critics with overly safe notions of play.[4] With such notions of Winnicott abroad, it is no wonder that Melanie Klein, Winnicott's teacher, predecessor, coworker, and antagonist, has undergone a wave of popularity: her tough-mindedness, her development of Freud's proposals about a death instinct, her grim vision of human aggression are all extremely useful to feminist and

3. See extensive treatments of ancient and Renaissance texts using these figures in Elizabeth Harvey, *Ventriloquized Voices: Feminist Theory and English Renaissance Texts* (London: Routledge, 1992), and Lynn Enterline, *The Rhetoric of the Body from Ovid to Shakespeare* (Cambridge: Cambridge University Press, 2000).

4. Exceptions tend to occur in drama studies, because drama critics are interested precisely in conflict and aggression, and because theatrical space, fictional space, and Winnicottian "transitional space" share many features. Among critics who take Winnicott on aggression seriously, see, for example, Meredith Skura, *Shakespeare the Actor and the Purposes of Playing* (Chicago: University of Chicago Press, 1993); C. L. Barber, *Creating Elizabethan Tragedy: The Theater of Marlowe and Kyd* (Chicago: University of Chicago Press, 1988); C. L. Barber and Richard Wheeler, *The Whole Journey: Shakespeare's Power of Development* (Berkeley: University of California Press, 1986). For an exception in the study of poetry and prose, see Anna Nardo, *The Ludic Self in Seventeenth-Century Literature* (Binghamton: State University of New York Press, 1991). Psychoanalytic and feminist work taking Winnicott seriously on the matter of aggression include Elsa First, "Mothering, Hate, and Winnicott," in *Representations of Motherhood*, ed. Donna Bassin, Margaret Honey, and Meryle Kaplan (New Haven: Yale University Press, 1994), 147–61; see also the appendix to this book.

social theorists. Using her work is a way to have object relations theory without Winnicott's assumed softness. All too often Winnicott figures, in primers of psychoanalysis, as a simplified carrier of twentieth-century nostalgia for an idealized maternal.

Conserving Winnicott

As we can see easily enough in retrospect, Winnicott's formative professional years led inevitably to his role in the postwar expansion of the medical and psychiatric professions, and postwar pressures to have mothers managed by experts.[5] But as Elsa First points out, Winnicott was in fact disturbed by "the resentimentalizing of housework and motherhood attending the postwar shift of women from the industrial work force back to the home," and he addresses this trend with characteristic frankness in a 1947 paper: "Sentimentality is useless for parents, as it contains a denial of hate, and sentimentality in a mother is no good at all from the infant's point of view."[6] Yet critiques of his work continue to rely on remarkably little reading and less historical situating. Here I mention just two points to illustrate the case and to clear a way in which we can use Winnicott more vigorously.

First, the notion that Winnicott idealizes merger with a nurturant mother can be sustained only by a certain vigilant refusal to grant enough of his writing a serious reading. Winnicott most often refuses the notion of merger with which he is too often identified, and insists rather on the earliest state as a more alarming "unintegration." As he says in a talk late in his life,

> I'm not sold on just taking over the concept of "symbiosis" because this word for me is too easy. It's as if, as in biology, it just happens that two things are living together. I believe it leaves out the extremely variable thing which is the ability of the mother to identify with the infant. . . . Her ability varies with different children not [only?] with her temperament but with

5. There are good discussions in Denise Riley, *War in the Nursery: Theories of the Child and Mother* (London: Virago, 1983), and Rozsika Parker, *Mother Love/Mother Hate: The Power of Maternal Ambivalence* (New York: Basic Books, 1995). A sustained polemic appears in Janice Doane and Devon Hodges, *From Klein to Kristeva: Psychoanalytic Feminism and the Search for the "Good Enough" Mother* (Ann Arbor: University of Michigan Press, 1992).

6. First, "Mothering," 152; D. W. Winnicott, "Hate in the Counter-transference" (1947), in *Through Paediatrics to Psycho-Analysis: Collected Papers* (New York: Brunner/Mazel, 1992), 194–203, at 202.

her experiences, and with the way that she is at the time, and this seems to me to be a more fruitful line of inquiry.[7]

Maternal nurture, far from being guaranteed, is a labor and an achievement, and there are assertions throughout the writing that this labor takes a good deal out of the mother—for example, this passage from 1945: "The normal child enjoys a ruthless relation to his mother, mostly showing in play, and he needs his mother because only she can be expected to tolerate his ruthless relation to her even in play, because this really hurts her and wears her out. Without this play with her he can only hide a ruthless self and give it life in a state of dissociation."[8] Even more strongly, "The mother . . . hates her infant from the word go."[9] Winnicott fights steadily *against* the idealized mother, which comes to him as a Kleinian notion trapped in its own jargon (and for that matter against non-psychoanalytic idealizations of infant): "a good breast introjection [which Kleinians take to be a good] is sometimes highly pathological, a defence organisation. The breast is then an idealized breast (mother) and this idealization indicates a hopelessness [within the infant] about inner chaos and ruthlessness of instinct."[10] Winnicott sees his clinical task as drawing his clients nearer to their own chaos and ruthlessness, so that they can hold these as resources *against* the sentimental idealization of the mother—an idealization that alienates them from their own powers as well as from mothers as subjects.

Second, Winnicott never ignores forces and vicissitudes of the world outside the nursery. On the contrary, his insistence on the importance of the historical mother, and his conviction that everything depends upon precisely how the early infant is managed over time, are lifelong oppositions to Kleinians' absorption in the phantasmatic world within the infant. Winnicott was pleased to learn that researchers of child rearing in Russia confirmed some of his ideas, but he would be unsurprised by, say, harsh practices in impoverished regions of Brazil, where mothers guard themselves against too quick an attachment to neonates, who may after all wish to die very young, or by the frequency and manifold

7. D. W. Winnicott, "D. W. W. on D. W. W.," in *Psycho-Analytic Explorations*, ed. Clare Winnicott, Ray Shepherd, and Madeleine Davis (Cambridge: Harvard University Press, 1989), 569–82, at 579.

8. D. W. Winnicott, "Primitive Emotional Development" (1945), in *Through Paediatrics*, 145–56, at 154.

9. Winnicott, "Hate in the Counter-transference," 201.

10. D. W. Winnicott, "The Depressive Position in Normal Emotional Development" (1954), in *Through Paediatrics*, 262–77, at 276.

forms of parents' divestment of their children in premodern cultures.[11] The subject's emergence, Winnicott allows, depends upon the formally complicated, culturally encoded relationship; maternal handling unfolds within social realities, but neither of these is reducible to the other. Within the context of British psychoanalysis, Winnicott could represent in our minds not chiefly a resistance to historicizing but an invitation to bring into theory the experience of culturally specific families.

To the degree that we rest with notions based on weak readings of Winnicott's work, we not only serve him badly but also thin out the possible relationships among psychoanalysis, poetry, and history. The Winnicottian infant's potential vitality is nearly Emersonian in strength and idiosyncrasy, as I have said. For Winnicott, "feeling real" and living creatively are close to what Emerson in his journals and essays calls originality, power, sturdiness, poise, receptivity to the present, a willingness to await surprise. They require not only a good-enough start through protection of infant vulnerability, but an adult capacity for fluent movement between an internalized structure of vulnerability protected and nurtured, on the one hand, and the exhilaration of risk, the resiliency to weather experience, on the other. Thus in a discussion of the cruelty entailed in clinical practice Winnicott says, "If we [analysts] are successful we enable the patient *to abandon invulnerability and to become a sufferer. If we succeed life becomes precarious* to one who was beginning to know a kind of stability and a freedom from pain, even if this meant non-participation in life and perhaps mental defect."[12] His attunement to vulnerability places Winnicott, with psychoanalysis generally, in a philosophical tradition extending from antiquity that reflects on our

11. Nancy Scheper-Hughes, *Death without Weeping: The Violence of Everyday Life in Brazil* (Berkeley: University of California Press, 1992), demonstrates how the Brazilian urban slum might be a world that could pulverize the infant before it can ever manage a "life force": Brazilian babies may be like the abandoned child she adopted and reared in 1965, who was so sickly that "my strong North American belief . . . in the natural resilience and hardiness of babies was forever shaken" (361). "And so a good part of learning how to mother on the Alto includes knowing when to let go of a child who shows that he wants to die. The other part is knowing just when it is safe to let oneself go enough to love a child, to trust him or her to be willing to enter . . . this life on earth" (364). I am indebted to David Wallace for putting me on to this harrowing book when it first appeared. See also the range of materials from antiquity through the fourteenth century discussed in John Boswell, *The Kindness of Strangers: The Abandonment of Children in Western Europe from Late Antiquity to the Renaissance* (New York: Pantheon Books, 1988).

12. D. W. Winnicott, "The Concept of Clinical Regression Compared with That of Defence Organisation," in *Psycho-Analytic Explorations*, 193–99, at 199.

radical vulnerability in a world of overwhelming stimuli. For Winnicott, the ability to register experience as real is not a given condition of human life but a psychic achievement, and the capacity for reception of experience manifests itself in the ability to use objects in the elaboration of a unique idiom. The vigor of this relationship between person and objects resembles the one that, Emerson suggests, holds between the poet and nature: "he loves the earnest of the northwind, of rain, of stone, and wood, and iron"; he loves them for the ways they require him to weather experience, for the ways one may pitch into them, or make something of their marks on him.[13] What the infant may learn, says Winnicott, is "Not, 'Ask and it shall be given,' so much as 'Reach out and it shall be there for you to have, to use, to waste.' "[14] I shall return to this sense of the word "use," and to Winnicott's use of apparently bland rhetoric for shock value (in this he is much like Emerson). But first I turn to Winnicott's sense of aggression, because without it nothing he says about baby's use of mother makes sense.

Theoretical Responses to Catastrophe

Some of the same historical materials that have brought renewed attention to Melanie Klein—for example, the Controversial Discussions of the British Psycho-Analytic Society during World War II, or Winnicott's letters—require literary thinkers to situate him more precisely and to attend to his prose more intently than we have done.[15] As a start, I place Klein and Winnicott between the two world wars in order to focus on the role of aggression in Winnicott's thinking. Like the poetic works I discuss in the following chapters, Winnicott's work is revisionary in a strong sense. That is, it searches within the discipline of psychoanalysis

---

13. Emerson, "The Poet," in *Works*, 5:271.

14. D. W. Winnicott, "Living Creatively" (1970), in *Home Is Where We Start From: Essays by a Psycho-Analyst* (New York: Norton, 1986), 35–54, at 50.

15. These have been available for some time, but have yet to affect most literary critics' close reading of Winnicott. One exception is Peter Rudnytsky, *The Psychoanalytic Vocation: Rank, Winnicott, and the Legacy of Freud* (New Haven: Yale University Press, 1991). See Winnicott's letters in *The Spontaneous Gesture: Selected Letters of D. W. Winnicott*, ed. F. Robert Rodman (Cambridge: Harvard University Press, 1989). Documents from the Controversial Discussions are gathered in *The Freud-Klein Controversies, 1941–45*, ed. Pearl King and Ricardo Steiner (London: Tavistock/Routledge, 1991). For accounts of the early history of psychoanalysis in Britain, see also Eric Rayner, *The Independent Mind in British Psychoanalysis* (New York: Jason Aronson, 1991); John Padel, "The Psychoanalytic Theories of Melanie Klein and Donald Winnicott and Their Interaction in the British Society of Psychoanalysis," *Psychoanalytic Review* 78 (1991): 325–45.

models for relationship to precursors other than those available from the painful examples of the first psychoanalytic thinkers. He discovers for himself an English vocation to vernacularize a discourse, and this vocation intersects with the psychoanalytic *translatio studii* westward that had intensified with continental psychoanalysts' flight from war. British psychoanalytic theory and professional organization were shaped by the world wars. This is not to underestimate earlier events on the continent that brought psychoanalysis to Britain.[16] But Freud's own work during and just after World War I, and throughout the 1920s, brings war into psychoanalysis as a trope pertinent to the formation of the subject; the European experience of war came to pervade many British theoretical formulations on the level of lexical choice, models of parental behavior, models of infantile vulnerability, and a large-scale sense of human vulnerability before the harshness of the world. These themes are intensified by Freud's personal catastrophes during the war and postwar years. "Mourning and Melancholia" and *Instincts and Their Vicissitudes* appeared in 1915 (the former in English in 1917); *Beyond the Pleasure Principle* was published in 1920, the same year as the death of Freud's daughter Sophie; *The Ego and the Id* appeared in 1923, the year in which Sophie's son died and Freud was diagnosed with cancer; 1924–26 saw Freud's protracted and unhappy break with Otto Rank, his late hope for a filial successor; *Inhibitions, Symptoms and Anxiety* appeared in 1926, in part as a response to Rank's *The Trauma of Birth*; *Civilization and Its Discontents* was published in 1930. These works were central to psychoanalysis in Britain, where thinking about infancy before the oedipal crisis had already begun, and where there was awareness of the difficult filial relationships within the psychoanalytic movement between the wars.

Part 2 of *Beyond the Pleasure Principle* opens with the well-known discussion of traumatic neurosis of the type brought on by experience of

16. Ernest Jones had pursued work with psychoanalytical thinkers on the continent in his twenties (during the first decade of the twentieth century), was a force in founding the American Psychoanalytical Association in 1910, founded the London Psycho-Analytic Society in 1913, broke it up in 1919 when he wanted to distance it from Jungians, then formed (without Jungians) the British Psycho-Analytical Society. The next year brought into existence the *International Journal of Psycho-Analysis*; in 1924 both the Institute of Psycho-Analysis and the International Library of Psycho-Analysis were formed, and in 1926 the London Clinic of Psycho-Analysis. Melanie Klein came from Berlin to lecture in 1925, bringing news of her analysis of children and her treatment of their play as equivalent to adult free association in its openness to interpretation; she moved to England the next year, where she was a formidable presence in the Society until her death in 1960.

war, and war neurosis continues both literally and figuratively throughout the book. Part 4 concerns itself extensively with the human organism's defenses against stimuli from the world, and famously creates a
little fiction in which the "living vesicle" of the brain, "with its receptive
cortical layer,"

> is suspended in the middle of an external world charged with the most
> powerful energies; and it would be killed by the stimulation emanating
> from these if it were not provided with a protective shield against stimuli. It
> acquires the shield in this way: its outermost surface ceases to have the
> structure proper to living matter, becomes to some degree inorganic and
> thenceforward functions as a special envelope or membrane resistant to
> stimuli. In consequence, the energies of the external world are able to pass
> into the next underlying layers, which have remained living, with only a
> fragment of their original intensity. . . . By its death, the outer layer has
> saved all the deeper ones from a similar fate. . . . The protective shield must
> above all endeavour to preserve the special modes of transformation of
> energy operating in it against the effects threatened by the enormous ener-
> gies at work in the external world—effects which tend towards a levelling
> out of them and hence towards destruction.[17]

This is an extraordinarily urgent representation of the vulnerability of
the organism/psyche, and of subjectivity as a defensive reaction formation. Freud's fiction of the traumatized brain, deadening itself so that the
tender innermost layers of life might flourish, would be a major force in
Melanie Klein's powerful development of the idea of mother and psyche as containers, and in her concern with boundaries of self. It would
also be a force subtending two Winnicottian models of the emergent
subject: the subject as an integrated, bounded body making pugnacious
contact with other firmly bounded objects in space, but also as something more like a sheer energy pattern, capable of suspending a defensive sense of boundedness. These models make much of the world's
enormous energies, as Freud does with particular force in *Beyond the
Pleasure Principle*, *Instincts and Their Vicissitudes*, and *Inhibitions, Symptoms and Anxiety*. For Freud, war and trauma argue against the easily
granted "instincts of self-preservation, of self-assertion and of mastery";
these are not the great powers that we have thought but part of a larger
drive toward death, "instincts whose function it is to assure that the

17. Freud, *Beyond the Pleasure Principle* (1920), in *Standard Edition of the Complete Psychological Works of Sigmund Freud*, ed. James Strachey et al., 24 vols. (London: Hogarth Press
and Institute of Psycho-Analysis, 1953–73), 18:27.

organism shall follow its own path to death, and to ward off any possible ways of returning to inorganic existence other than those which are
immanent in the organism itself. . . . the organism wishes to die only in
its own fashion. Thus these guardians of life, too, were originally the
myrmidons of death."[18]

Beyond the Pleasure Principle is internally contradictory and frankly
perplexing in many useful ways, as readers have always recognized.[19]
One of its rich confusions, and one of Freud's examples of the way
pleasure and unpleasure continually turn into each other, is a condensation of cataclysmic war events—say, bombs—with orgasmic satisfaction.
Orgasm in *Beyond the Pleasure Principle* is paradoxical enough in itself,
since what constitutes its pleasure is both the climax of excitation and
the surcease of excitation. Moreover these are what also constitute its
unpleasure. Such linked problems posed a generative challenge to Winnicott, who throughout his career refused to the polarity of excitation vs.
stasis any part in his models of health in pleasure, affect, attachment,
object seeking, and action. He resists both the trauma of bombs going off
and the trauma or shattering of orgasmic release as intrinsic to subjectivity; he resists ruptures in preference to continuities. The world's
assaults do not make what Winnicott calls "going-on-being" easy to
achieve. Winnicott seeks to name conditions that could make possible
the achievement of going-on-being, by swerving from Freud's stark
alternatives of excitation and stasis or eros and thanatos; the drama of
the Winnicottian infant's life is the quest for something like a steady-
state process, open to transformation but not obliterated by energies and
objects from the world. At the start, the vulnerable Winnicottian infant
needs as a shield not external layers of brain but a mother who can
measure and filter the phenomenal influx of the world, which would
otherwise be experienced as an assault creating the "unthinkable anxieties" of going to pieces, falling forever, having no orientation: "All failures (that could produce unthinkable anxiety) bring about a reaction of

18. Ibid., 39.
19. For discussions germane to the present argument, see Jean Laplanche, *Life and Death
in Psychoanalysis* (1970), trans. Jeffrey Mehlman (Baltimore: Johns Hopkins University
Press, 1976); Richard Boothby, *Death and Desire: Psychoanalytic Theory in Lacan's Return to
Freud* (London: Routledge, 1991); Luce Irigaray, "Belief Itself" (1980), in *Sexes and Genealo-
gies*, trans. Gillian Gill (New York: Columbia University Press, 1993), 23–53; Margaret
Whitford, "Irigaray, Utopia, and the Death Drive," in *Engaging with Irigaray: Feminist Phi-
losophy and Modern European Thought*, ed. Carolyn Burke, Naomi Schor, and Whitford (New
York: Columbia University Press, 1994), 379–88; Michael Eigen, *Psychic Deadness* (London:
Jason Aronson, 1996), 5–23.

the infant, and this reaction cuts across the going-on-being. If reacting that is disruptive of going-on-being recurs persistently it sets going a pattern of fragmentation of being . . . loaded in the direction of psychopathology."[20] Or again: "It is especially at the start that mothers are vitally important, and indeed it is a mother's job to protect her infant from complications that cannot yet be understood by the infant, and to go on steadily providing the simplified bit of the world which the infant, through her, comes to know. . . . Only on a basis of monotony can a mother profitably add richness."[21]

The value of a mother at the start is vividly realized if we grasp Winnicott's prior sense that mother and baby may never find each other. Thus he describes the nursling's and mother's finding of each other in terms of lines of direction and force, which may just as well go in different directions:

> The baby has instinctual urges and predatory ideas. The mother has a breast and the power to produce milk, and the idea that she would like to be attacked by a hungry baby. These two phenomena do not come into relation with each other till the mother and child *live an experience together.*
>
> I think of the process as if two lines came from opposite directions, liable to come near each other. If they overlap there is a moment of *illusion*—a bit of experience which the infant can take as *either* his hallucination *or* a thing belonging to external reality.[22]

The bearing of these vectors, with mother and child as two lines of force launched on all but arbitrary, solitary paths that *may* take them near each other, form unsettlingly random paths. Winnicott deploys a certain whimsicality of expression ("mother has . . . the idea that she would like to be attacked by a hungry baby") to carry the appalling exposures and risks of birth relations. In this moment potential space seems remarkably chancy, an achievement pulled out of circumstances of radical poverty.

It was through the interaction of his pediatric work, his analysis, and his absorption of Freud's work of the 1920s that Winnicott developed a vivid sense of the infant as absolutely vulnerable, risking the onslaught of the "enormous energies" of the world, requiring the protective shield

20. D. W. Winnicott, "Ego Integration in Child Development"(1962), in *The Maturational Processes and the Facilitating Environment: Studies in the Theory of Emotional Development* (Madison, Conn.: International Universities Press, 1965), 56–63, at 60–61.

21. Winnicott, "Primitive Emotional Development," 153.

22. Ibid., 152.

that mother could provide, in danger of psychosis if the environment could not be filtered and moderated. The risk of psychosis forms a universal human birthright for Winnicott; it is a consequence of being born unintegrated and dependent. The Winnicottian ideal is not to conquer internal chaos nor even to relieve it through interpretation, as in Klein, but to find means of dwelling equably with it, of surviving immaturity.

> All along, according to the age and the maturational stage of the infant, the parent is engaged in preventing clinical breakdown from which recovery occurs only through organisation and reorganisation of defences. It is by minute-to-minute care that the parent is laying down the basis of the future mental health of the infant. . . . And on the whole, parents have always tended to succeed in this, their essential, tremendous task, the reason being that for this purpose what they need to be is themselves, and to be and do exactly what they like being and doing; and by doing just this they save their children from jerky reorganisations of defences, and from the clinical distress that lies behind each of these reorganisations.[23]

This passage shows the characteristic Winnicottian paradox (sometimes it can be an incoherence or evasion) of making high demands on the parents, who nonetheless mostly succeed just by being themselves. As in *Beyond the Pleasure Principle*, the world for the Winnicottian baby is initially that which brings intense pressures upon emergent impulses of activity and growth, threatening to disfigure or deform them.

But the Winnicottian neonate, infinitely fragile, dependent utterly on the environmental protection managed by mother, is simultaneously possessed of strong impulses: toward growth, respiration, movement, survival, relationship, self-assertion, becoming. These all count as aggression for Winnicott. "At the start the baby's ego is both feeble and powerful."[24] To describe the most primitive forms of aggression "it would be necessary to go back to the impulses of the foetus, to that which makes for movement rather than for stillness, to the aliveness of tissues and to the first evidence of muscular erotism. We need a term here such as life force."[25] He means a Bergsonian life force and motility

---

23. D. W. Winnicott, "Further Remarks on the Theory of the Parent-Infant Relationship" (1961), in *Psycho-Analytic Explorations*, 73–75, at 74–75.

24. D. W. Winnicott, "The Importance of the Setting in Meeting Regression in Psycho-Analysis" (1964), in *Psycho-Analytic Explorations*, 96–102, at 101.

25. D. W. Winnicott, "Aggression in Relation to Emotional Development" (1950), in *Through Paediatrics*, 204–18, at 216.

Laplanche has shown how the anaclitic drive for Freud is a matter of the "*leaning originally* of infantile sexuality on . . . that which orients the 'bodily function essential to life' . . .

as opposed to Freud's death instinct and stasis; he also means life force as opposed to Klein's conception of the death instinct as anxiety, greed, envy, and murderousness. He would have been happier with Emerson's formulation of aggression as the excess of life force: "To every creature nature added a little violence of direction in its proper path, a shove to put it on its way; in every instance, a slight generosity, a drop too much."[26]

Birth, aggression, war, and psychoanalysis form powerful constellations throughout Klein's life as well. The year 1914, for instance, saw the outbreak of war, the death of Klein's mother, the birth of her third son, her first reading of Freud (*On Dreams*), and perhaps the start of her analysis with Ferenczi.[27] The end of the war in Hungary—she was living in Budapest—led to a Bolshevik uprising, followed hard by an antisemitic counterrevolution and by corresponding crises in the professional status of Ferenczi; by 1919 she had separated from her husband and gone to live with his parents. During the Second World War she left London temporarily for Scotland, where one of her patients was the child Richard, whose many anxieties had been compounded by the bombing of his home and then, in 1940, of Klein's own house in London; the material of his sessions included much about invasion, bombing, catastrophic destruction. War, aggression, and murderous violence pervade her work; strikingly, though, they appear chiefly as manifestations of the internal forces of the death drive. As she argued in a 1948 paper:

---

the [Freudian] terms *function, need*, and *instinct* characterize generally the vital register of self-preservation in opposition to the sexual register" (*Life and Death*, 16). For his whole career, Winnicott's concern would be to elaborate this "vital register," which is one aspect of Freud's inheritance of thinking on human vulnerability, rather than the sexual register. We have become accustomed to granting how the subject's entry into the sexual register and into signification, through the dynamics of the Oedipal process, makes for the figures of metaphor and metonymy. The remarkable thing is how much room Winnicott's emphasis on the vital register makes for proposals about figuration. This is so partly because the vital register is never entirely separate from the sexual. Laplanche describes the sexual register in terms to which Klein, Winnicott, and Irigaray would devote their life's work: the sexual zone "is a kind of breaking or turning point within the bodily envelope, since what is in question is above all sphincteral orifices: mouth, anus, etc. It is also a zone of exchange, since the principal biological exchanges are borne by it. . . . This zone of exchange is also a zone for care . . . by the mother" (*Life and Death*, 23–24).

26. Emerson, "Nature," in *Works*, 5:390.

27. Evidence is inconclusive about this latter date; it may have been 1912, when she began working with Ferenczi, although in old age she remembered it as belonging to the eventful year 1914.

The interaction between external and internal danger-situations persists throughout life.

This was cleverly shown in the analysis carried out in war-time. It appeared that even with normal adults anxiety stirred up by air-raids, bombs, fire, etc.—i.e. by an "objective" danger-situation—could only be reduced by analysing, over and above the impact of the actual situation, the various early anxieties which were aroused by it.[28]

The Kleinian death drive is violent in itself, but it also awakens the anxiety of that sleeping giant, the life instinct and its wish not to die. Insofar as the death drive takes the form of animosity toward the mother, the infant who rages against the mother also recoils from its own hatred and from the hatred it imagines radiating toward itself from the mother. The world of the Kleinian infant is made up of objects like Mama's breast, Papa's penis (which is sometimes inside of the breast, sometimes inside of Mama where it mysteriously turns into babies), milk, feces; but also of forces which are persecutory weapons. We call these forces by names like projection, introjection, and projective identification, but the child experiences them as a raging oral desire to devour, rob, tear, and rend the mother and also fear of her imagined talion desire to devour, engulf, rob the baby.

Klein's earliest formulations about children emerged from analyzing her own children, chiefly Erich, who figures largely in her papers of the early 1920s, but it is the troubled children of her practice who populate her moving 1932 book, *The Psycho-Analysis of Children*. Because this book articulates the strong positions from which she never wavered, and because it had a powerful effect on Winnicott, who first discovered Klein's work through reading the book in manuscript, it is worth reviewing some of its lines of thought.

The Kleinian infant inhabits an economy of scarcity created by the death instinct, and therefore is constantly susceptible to envy, impulses to rob, tendencies to guard itself and to view others as thieves, and aggressive anal/urethral desires to expel, burn, smash, and defile. Everything in the circumstances of the neonate conspires to intensify the death instinct with which it comes equipped:

I hold that anxiety arises from the operation of the death instinct within the organism, is felt as fear of annihilation (death) and takes the form of fear of

28. Melanie Klein, "On the Theory of Anxiety and Guilt" (1948), in *Writings*, ed. Roger Money-Kyrle, 4 vols. (New York: Free Press, 1975), 3:25–42, at 39.

persecution. The fear of the destructive impulse seems to attach itself at once to an object—or rather it is experienced as the fear of an uncontrollable over-powering object. Other important sources of primary anxiety are the trauma of birth (separation anxiety) and frustration of bodily needs; and these experiences too are from the beginning felt as being caused by objects. Even if these objects are felt to be external, they become through introjection internal persecutors and thus reinforce the fear of the destructive impulse within.[29]

Lest the controversial workings of the death instinct remain too abstract or too easily denied, Klein insists on the incredible violence of fantasy:

The idea of an infant of from six to twelve months trying to destroy its mother by every method of its sadistic trends—with its teeth, nails and excreta and with the whole of its body, transformed in phantasy into all kinds of dangerous weapons—presents a horrifying, not to say an unbelievable picture to our minds. . . . But the abundance, force and multiplicity of the cruel phantasies which accompany these cravings are displayed before our eyes in early analyses so clearly and forcibly that they leave no room for doubt.[30]

Furthermore, once oral frustration awakens the child's unconscious knowledge of its parents' sexual pleasures, which it imagines to be "of an oral sort," the buildup of its frustration increases its hatred and envy of the parents: "Its cravings to scoop and suck out now lead it to want to suck out and devour all the fluids and other substances which its parents (or rather their organs) contain, including what they have received from one another in oral copulation" (130–31). Klein's contemplation of the ways that the infant covets the organs, substances, and fluids within Mother and tries to destroy their possessor creates a rhetoric of abundance in an economy of scarcity: "All these elements taken together give rise to sadistic phantasies whose number, variety and richness are all but inexhaustible" (132). Her economy of scarcity is linked to her own

29. Melanie Klein, "Notes on Some Schizoid Mechanisms" (1946), in *Writings*, 3:1–24, at 4–5.

30. Melanie Klein, *The Psycho-Analysis of Children* (1932), in *Writings*, 2:128–30. In "Notes on Some Schizoid Mechanisms" and other papers written after World War II, Klein would develop the powerful notion of projective identification to name the process of splitting off hated aspects of the self and driving them into another, where they can be harmed and controlled. See Michael Eigen's case for the centrality of Klein's 1946 "Notes on Some Schizoid Mechanisms" and especially of the 1961 *Narrative of a Child Analysis*, which "shocks one into awareness of Mother's body as a war zone" (Eigen, *Psychic Deadness*, 26).

compliance with Freud's anal economy and its symbolic equations between penis, feces, baby, and gift, an economy in which, as Margaret Whitford says, "each of these . . . can be detached from the giver (or in the case of the penis, be imagined to be detachable) and thereby circulated from one person to another."[31]

In Klein's cases the child confronting the hostile, grudging world feels itself excluded from the primal scene, or from the locus of gestation (if the mother is pregnant) or from the mother's breast, which is the great original and model of what the child takes to be the full contents of the mother's body. Thus Klein tells four-year-old Ruth "how she [Ruth] envied and hated her mother because the latter had incorporated her father's penis during coitus, and how she wanted to steal his penis and the children out of her mother's inside and kill her mother. . . . [and] that this was why she was frightened and believed that she had killed her mother or would be deserted by her."[32] Or again there is six-year-old Erna, whose lavishly violent games position her now as sadistic, now as masochistic because of her sense of exclusion and scarcity in relation to her parents:

> [Erna's] sense of guilt [about sucking] can be explained by the fact that sucking also represented biting off and devouring her mother's breasts and her father's penis. I may refer here to my thesis that it is the process of weaning which, together with the child's wish to incorporate its father's penis, and its feelings of envy and hatred towards its mother, sets the Oedipus conflict in motion. This envy is founded on the child's early sexual theory that in copulating with the father the mother incorporates and retains his penis. (55)

The parents' copulation throws into disarray the child's emergent sense of coherently bounded bodies, its sense of the proper: What body parts, contents, or shapes belong to Erna herself? What belongs to her mother? Does the penis belong to the father or the mother? Are babies the same kind of creation, and the same kind of gift, as feces?

Later Klein would link these torments to the earliest nursing experiences of the neonate. The earliest stage or position, the paranoid-schizoid, is characterized by anxieties over such issues of bodily integrity, greed, theft, danger of invasion, the nature of corporeal property. But "anxiety" is perhaps too static a word for the infant's sufferance

---

31. Margaret Whitford, *Luce Irigaray: Philosophy in the Feminine* (London: Routledge, 1991), 187.
32. Klein, *Psycho-Analysis of Children*, 28.

of the life instinct and the death drive as they are galvanized by issues of bodily cohesion and ego integrity; in its first few months the infant undergoes something like the trauma of warring, besieging tribes whose aggressions devastate themselves as well as their enemies:

> The primary danger-situation arising from the activity of the death instinct within is felt . . . as an overwhelming attack, as persecution. . . . We may assume that the struggle between life and death instincts already operates during birth and accentuates the persecutory anxiety aroused by this painful experience. It would seem that this experience has the effect of making the external world, including the first external object, the mother's breast, appear hostile.[33]

The only defense for the primitive ego is actively to split off and expel painful, bad experiences or introjected objects, and project them into the mother. Yet "as far as the ego is concerned the excessive splitting off and expelling into the outer world of parts of itself considerably weaken it. For the aggressive component of feelings and of the personality is intimately bound up in the mind with power, potency, strength, knowledge and many other desired qualities."[34]

Klein is familiar for her vivid fantasy scenarios of bodily organs and parts, but it is the additional element of the vectors of force and momentum in splitting, projection, introjection, and so on that make those scenarios so traumatic. Splitting alone is no inconsiderable management problem to the infant. From birth the nursling incorporates split images of the hated breast (which causes frustration, fails to feed on demand, etc.) and of the loved, idealized breast. The early ego's active splitting is a defense against its own death-instinct and anxieties that it arouses, but in turn causes other difficulties; its experience of fragmentation in this splitting arouses a primitive anxiety about falling to pieces, a threat that the baby imagines coming from the mother: "The result of splitting is a dispersal of the destructive impulse which is felt as the source of danger. . . . the primary anxiety of being annihilated by a destructive force within, with the ego's specific response of falling to pieces or splitting itself, may be extremely important in all schizophrenic processes."[35] To thwart this feeling, the infant then splits off the feeling and projects it out of itself, onto the mother. We might say that splitting proceeds from

---

33. Klein, "Theory of Anxiety and Guilt," 31.
34. Klein, "Notes on Some Schizoid Mechanisms," 8.
35. Ibid., 5.

splitting-as-dichotomizing to splitting-as-fragmenting to splitting as disavowal of chaos within the primitive ego.[36]

Range of Motion

"We wawl and cry," as Lear said, but we do so with a necessary assertiveness, in order to fill our lungs with those first vital and precious draughts of air, more, to discover breath as a primordial way of feeling real and alive, a theme that recurs throughout Winnicott's writing. Thus in 1949: "During the birth process, in reaction to the construction [construction?] of the maternal tissues, the infant has to make what would be (if there were any air available) an inspiratory movement. After birth, if all goes well, the cry establishes the expression of liveliness by expiration. This is an example in terms of physical function of the difference between reacting and simply going on 'being.' " And in late 1968:

> In the individual's early development it is not a case of fusion [with mother], because what is there in the activity that characterises the baby's aliveness starts [baby] off as a unit or unity. To get quickly to the idea that I have in mind one could profitably use the idea of the fire from the dragon's mouth. I quote from Pliny who (in paying tribute to fire) writes, "Who can say whether in essence fire is constructive or destructive?" Indeed the physiological basis for what I am referring to is the first and subsequent breaths, out-breathing.[37]

Winnicott's insistence on breathing, especially on the forcefulness with which the neonate takes in breath (the dragon breathes fire), swerves strategically from Kleinian conditions of scarcity. Irigaray will later develop topoi of air independently. For both Winnicott and Irigaray, it is true to say: of breath and air, and a concomitant sense of aliveness, there is always enough. For Winnicott, to suppress breath is to lack a sense of aliveness or a sense that one has a right to be alive—to be unable to know and claim the fact that one has been born. For Irigaray, to forget to breathe is to have disavowed the vital process of celebrating parturition; it is to deny the debt to the mother, to court nostalgia:

36. On splitting, see Melanie Klein, "Personification in the Play of Children" (1929), in *Writings*, 1:199–209; "Notes on Some Schizoid Mechanisms"; "Theory of Anxiety and Guilt."

37. The first passage comes from D. W. Winnicott, "Birth Memories, Birth Trauma, and Anxiety" (1949), in *Through Paediatrics*, 174–93, at 188; the second from Winnicott, "Comments on My Paper 'The Use of an Object' " (1968), in *Psycho-Analytic Explorations*, 238–40, at 239.

This air that we never think of has been borrowed from a birth, a growth, a *phusis* and a *phuein* that the philosopher forgets.

To forget being is to forget the air, this first fluid given us gratis and free of interest in the mother's blood, given us again when we are born, like a natural profusion that raises a cry of pain: the pain of a being who comes into the world and is abandoned, forced henceforth to live with the immediate assistance of another body.[38]

Winnicott would have welcomed this poetico-philosophical use of the element of air. To suppress respiration is to deny the debt of which Irigaray speaks, by complying with impingements from the world. In Winnicott's work, the world not only pulverizes archaic impulsiveness like a bomb, sometimes doing so in bad circumstances, but—being populated with adults who wish to manage the infant and who are implicated in complex power relations—it may require the infant to organize defenses, one of which is to comply by fashioning a false self to placate the world.

Compliance is among the catastrophes that all humans risk, just by virtue of being born into a culture. But it is not inevitable, nor need the world remain a potential bomb waiting to interrupt continuity of being. For if the mother's earliest obligation is to protect the newborn from impingements and exposures in order that nascent "aliveness" can unfold into aggressive and erotic drives, she very soon needs and wants to initiate a graduated failure to meet baby's needs. This long, intricate weaning process Winnicott came to call disillusionment. It will cause discomfort and pain but need not form only dolorous emotional structures in the infant; it may but need not be corrosive. "Disillusionment" is a usefully general term for a very wide range of possible relationships, attitudes, and consequences of an equally wide range of infant care: thinking of disillusionment not only as something that befalls the infant but as something created by the mother reminds us of mother's need for the space between herself and the infant. Disillusionment elicits infantile aggression in specific ways, aside from any later-developing resentment, dread, desire, hatred of mother. First, the mother's gradual and necessary refusal to sustain the infant's omnipotence by perfectly matching its needs summons the infant's aggression, understood sim-

38. Luce Irigaray, "An Ethics of Sexual Difference" (1984), in *An Ethics of Sexual Difference*, trans. Carolyn Burke and Gillian Gill (Ithaca, N.Y.: Cornell University Press, 1984), 116–29, at 127; see also "A Breath That Touches in Words," in *I Love to You: Sketch of a Possible Felicity in History*, trans. Alison Martin (London: Routledge, 1996), 121–28.

ply as impulses-toward. Gradual disillusionment could be traumatic—
but it could be generative as well.[39] The infant starts to take her part in
traversing the space that mother gradually enlarges and sustains. Second, the mother's measured withholdings of provision give baby an
obstacle to push against, and so the baby is launched on the unending
process of discovering external reality. The world becomes not (or not
always) a looming danger or a tempest, not a surfeit of arousing stimuli,
not a reality principle requiring submission or resignation, but a field for
active exercise of capacities.

The first experience of this field occurs in what Winnicott calls a transitional or potential space. In this alternative to the Kleinian infant's
defensive spinning of intrapsychic fantasy, "the person is reaching out
in some way so that if an object is in the way there can be a relationship."[40] The traversing of the field becomes, among other things, an
adult capacity to use, or enter into complex relationship with, a person
or an artifact. Winnicott thus develops this sense of world as a place of
endeavor and objects to be used, or contacted as truly external, most
immediately in relation to Melanie Klein, who never saw the external
world as a resource in the active way that Winnicott does.

Winnicott's conviction that the fragile vulnerability of the neonate
paradoxically allows for the eventual discovery of the world's wealth
emerged in opposition to Klein's vivid evocations of the terrors that
beset the youngest infant from within. "Object use" is also Winnicott's
turn away from Klein's corporeal substantives—breast, feces, babies
and other things within the mother's body—and a marker of his inclination to discuss instead the complex behavior, attitudes, feelings, bearing,
and temporality of the mother. In his elaborations of potential or transitional space where boundaries of identity are put into question, Winnicott creates an alternative to the reification of bodies and others as containers, on the grounds that there is something unwieldy or crude in
conceiving of persons as containers if they are not simultaneously conceived as processes of becoming, or if we fail to see the interaction

39. See Masud Khan, "The Concept of Cumulative Trauma," in *The British School of Psychoanalysis: The Independent Tradition*, ed. Gregorio Kohon (New Haven: Yale University
Press, 1986), 117–35. Khan notes that "the infant has also a great inherent resilience and
potentiality (strength). It not only can and does recover from breaches in the protective
shield, but it can use such impingements and strains . . . toward further growth and struc-
turation" (132–33).

40. D. W. Winnicott, "Living Creatively," 35–54, at 41.

between two subjects like mother and infant as blurring, overlapping events. Had he encountered the feminist theory of the 1970s and 1980s, he might have endorsed one of Irigaray's criticisms of the "phallic economy" as a legitimate charge against Klein. In *Elemental Passions*, Irigaray's female speaker addresses a male discourse that has appropriated and defined her jouissance: "I was the source and resource of all your objects. . . . I had become all kinds of things at stake, all kinds of sound. Which you would take, hold or reject. Through all your orifices. Full of things, a container for your things, reduced to things: to eating, voiding, seeing, hearing, possessing . . ."[41] Winnicott would also have objected to Klein's account of the baby's fantasy of the replete breast, in that it fails to name the different kind of organ, the skin (which we might expand, in the spirit of an Irigarayan labial economy, to include all the folds, surfaces, and textures of the body). The skin, a Winnicottian might add, is an organ that allows perceptual delineation of objects, hence of orientation in space to other spatial objects, at the same time that it allows contact with others' flesh and surfaces. The skin, as Irigaray suggests, is porous, secretes fluids, links discrete beings.[42] Winnicott aims for something like this positive envisioning of contact with others in his notion of a transitional space where the categories of inside and outside are confounded; this is a notion that Irigaray will develop from other discourses, in her sense of the fluxions of identity.

Nonetheless, we also need to keep Klein in view for her salutary reminder that contacts between surfaces like skin, bodily folds and orifices, or Irigaray's mucous, are exposures and risks, experienced as emanations of passion from objects into the self. For Klein such contacts are charged with danger, while Winnicott and Irigaray hold out the utopian possibility of contacts that are like a touch of breath or air. Klein laid out the dynamics of envy with unparalleled richness and force; it would be Winnicott who would find ways to develop a notion of gratitude as envy's opposite, in large part because he opposed the Kleinian psychic economy of scarcity with an economy of hard-won abundance, and the

41. Luce Irigaray, *Elemental Passions*, trans. Joanna Collie and Judith Still (London: Routledge, 1992), 61–62.

42. See, for example, Luce Irigaray, "On the Maternal Order" (1987), in *Je, Te, Nous: Toward a Culture of Difference*, trans. Alison Martin (London: Routledge, 1993), 37–44; "Volume-Fluidity" (1974), in *Speculum of the Other Woman*, trans. Gillian Gill (Ithaca, N.Y.: Cornell University Press, 1985), 227–40; "The 'Mechanics' of Fluids" (1977), in *This Sex Which Is Not One*, trans. Catherine Porter with Carolyn Burke (Ithaca, N.Y.: Cornell University Press, 1985), 106–18.

classical urethral/anal economy with reciprocally transformative exchange across an interval—a placental economy, to adopt Rouch's and Irigaray's model. In her 1957 publications on envy and gratitude, Klein links envy with the perception of dearth within and abundance elsewhere:

> If we consider that deprivation increases greed and persecutory anxiety, and that there is in the infant's mind a phantasy of an inexhaustible breast which is his greatest desire, it becomes understandable how envy arises. . . . The infant's feelings seem to be that when the breast deprives him, it becomes bad because it keeps the milk, love, and care associated with the good breast all to itself. He hates and envies what he feels to be the mean and grudging breast.[43]

All Klein's concepts can be traced back to a presumed nostalgia for that from which one is always already excluded: a plenitude contained within the breast and then the mother's body generally, making it seem a self-sufficient container of all desirable things. All Kleinian infants know envy. Just to the degree that we discover or enter a discrete, bounded identity separate from the mother, we envy and desire that which the other is, and the other is always apprehended as an object-container replete in itself, not subject to the vicissitudes of need or desire.

To envy and idealize the other's identity in this nostalgic fantasy of a paradisal repleteness is to constrict its mobility, and Winnicott would develop an almost Blakean allergic reaction to the death drive as this kind of binding. He hews instead to a notion of boundary formation as a process of movements that take form, often stable or delineated but also transformable, permeable, fluent, overlapping with others' forms and identities. He would have saluted Irigaray's theorizing about fluids as a useful model to oppose to Klein's emphasis on the solid organs populating the Kleinian phantasmatic. For encounters within Winnicott's "potential space" function, as Irigaray says of the physics of fluids, according to a "dynamics of the near and not of the proper."[44] Having swerved from the alimentary intensities of Klein and developed other senses of what might count as a gift from child to parent, he might have relished the fierce wit in her objection to the solid mechanics of Lacan's

43. Melanie Klein, *Envy and Gratitude: A Study of Unconscious Sources* (1957), in *Writings*, 3:183.

44. Irigaray, " 'Mechanics' of Fluids," 111.

objet a: "will feces—variously disguised—have the privilege of serving as the paradigm for the *objet a*? Must we then understand this modeling function . . . of the object of desire as resulting from the passage . . . from the fluid to the solid state? The object of desire itself, and for psychoanalysts, would be the transformation of fluid to solid?"[45]

In his own work, however, Winnicott develops movement and fluency not according to a physics of fluids, like Irigaray, but in terms of the traversal of space and line. These traversals constitute a potential space; in the present context, the best model for it arises in Winnicott's consultation practice of the squiggle game. Winnicott's game, in which the child patient and the analyst take turns drawing squiggles and improvisatory developments of the other's lines, *makes something* of dynamic lines incipient with future shapes. Here lines do not bind but open out; squiggles "are incontinent."[46] Furthermore they elicit not only a clinical transference from child to analyst, but also a response in the analyst toward the child. It is conversation in its old, large sense of reciprocally transforming exchange. Winnicott thus acknowledges the centrality of the countertransference to the therapeutic relationship, and opens access to "surprise"—the analyst's unconscious, say, and its interaction with the child's unconscious. Winnicott's "surprise" is akin to the Irigarayan unconscious, "*the reservoir of a yet-to-come*," and Winnicott intends it as a repudiation of the determinisms of Kleinian theory.[47] For Winnicott in the squiggle game and in other clinical settings, it is as Irigaray says in her challenge to psychoanalysis: "any living body, any unconscious, any psychical economy brings its order to analysis."[48] In contradistinction to Klein, the Winnicottian clinician gives to the child an immediate and eliciting responsiveness, not an axiomatic, dominating, unilateral interpretation: "These phenomena of the play area have infinite variability, contrasting with the relative stereotypy of phenomena that relate either to personal body functioning or to environmental actuality."[49] Klein's authoritative and inflexible interpretations are objectionable to Winnicott in the same way that Lacanian interpretations become objectionable

45. Ibid., 113.

46. D. W. Winnicott, "The Squiggle Game" (1964–68), in *Psycho-Analytic Explorations*, 299–317, at 302.

47. Luce Irigaray, "The Poverty of Psychoanalysis" (1977), trans. David Macey with Margaret Whitford, in *The Irigaray Reader*, ed. Whitford (Oxford: Blackwell, 1991), 79–104, at 82.

48. Ibid., 83–84.

49. D. W. Winnicott, "The Location of Cultural Experience" (1967), in *Playing and Reality* (London: Routledge, 1991), 95–103, at 98.

to Irigaray: their unforgiving theoretical stringency tells the same story over and over again, refuses "surprise" (Winnicott) or "ceaseless becoming" (Irigaray); such clinical operations foreclose the very workings of the unconscious that they claim to interpret.[50] For Winnicott, this amounts to a claim that Klein fails to acknowledge the child; Klein is the tormenting analyst/mother in whom one cannot make a dent—as she often was to Winnicott himself.[51] It is less the absent past than the incipient future that Winnicott invites into the generative here and now of the consulting room. The adult variously attends, passes by, engages, lets be, leaves traces and structures, improvises, reciprocates, makes and holds a space whose boundaries either party can reshape. As Jessica Benjamin says, transitional space is "something that forms a boundary and opens up into endless possibility."[52]

Moreover, his experiences with Klein, as well as his internalization of her ideas, would have made useless to him some of the most powerful

50. See, for example, Irigaray, " 'Mechanics' of Fluids," 115, where she charges that the analyst's "repeating the same story . . . is . . . in part the *death instinct*"; Irigaray, "Poverty of Psychoanalysis." See also Elizabeth Hirsh, "Back in Analysis: How to Do Things with Irigaray," in *Engaging with Irigaray*, 285–315, at 292: "Lacan's dialectic remains for Irigaray a theoretically closed system, fully 'axiomized' and constitutionally incapable of producing anything new. . . . Lacan and Freud alike stand charged with failing to listen to their analysands in part . . . because analytic listening entails putting oneself into play, and at risk, in the scene of analysis." Rigidity of axiom and a failure to listen are among the charges that Lacan levels at Melanie Klein; see Jacques Lacan, "Discourse Analysis and Ego Analysis" and "The Topic of the Imaginary," in *The Seminars of Jacques Lacan*, bk. 1, *Freud's Papers on Technique, 1953–54*, ed. Jacques-Alain Miller, trans. John Forrester (New York: Norton, 1991), 62–70, 73–88, which respond to Klein's case history in "The Importance of Symbol Formation in the Development of the Ego," in *Writings*, 1:219–32. Mary Jacobus discusses these papers by Klein and Lacan in *First Things: The Maternal Imaginary in Literature, Art, and Psychoanalysis* (New York: Routledge, 1995), 129–52. As the work of Freud, Lacan, Klein, Winnicott, and Irigaray themselves show, psychoanalytic discourse allows for more flexibility of explanatory account than they often feel. Nonetheless, I think literary critics need to do more stretching toward such variegation in analysis of the literary.

51. In his work this personal difficulty with Klein leads to a belief in the necessity for the analyst to restrain the impulse to interpret prematurely, and to wait while the patient finds his or her way. In 1968 he said, "It appals me to think how much deep change I have prevented or delayed in patients . . . by my personal need to interpret. If only we can wait, the patient arrives at understanding creatively and with immense joy, and I now enjoy this joy more than I used to enjoy the sense of having been clever. I think I interpret mainly to let the patient know the limits of my understanding." D. W. Winnicott, "The Use of an Object and Relating through Identifications" (1968), in *Playing and Reality* (London: Routledge, 1991), 86–94, at 86–87.

52. Jessica Benjamin, "A Desire of One's Own: Psychoanalytic Feminism and Intersubjective Space," in *Feminist Studies/Critical Studies*, ed. Teresa de Lauretis (Bloomington: Indiana University Press, 1986), 78–101, at 94.

psychoanalytic notions articulating nostalgia for the mother: mother as origin of a semiotic, preverbal realm of the chora, or outside the Symbolic, or in need of repression or casting out so that her child might enter the realm of fathers and culture. On the contrary, he labors all his life to understand the process of birth and the experiences of mothers and infants—mothers' experiences of trying to sustain babies within families, infants' experiences of the great world—and to bring them into the Symbolic, where they can bear interpretation and find a place within discourse. For Winnicott, the honesty of this potential discourse opposes Kleinian idealization and Kleinian bondage to the pathos of envy, guilt, and nostalgia for the maternal. There is more to be built in a Winnicottian life than recurrent substitutions for or monuments to the mother.

Winnicott first articulated his position on aggression only in the late 1940s and early 1950s, after working in pediatrics and psychoanalysis for nearly a quarter of a century. It took this long both because his ideas on aggression evolved from his experience in both world wars and because his theorizing about aggression was a function of his relationship to Melanie Klein and his internal requirement to find a way of opposing the obstacle she presented, as when in 1950 he claims the earliest motility of the organism under the aegis of aggression: "Prior to integration of the personality there is aggression. A baby kicks in the womb; it cannot be assumed that he is trying to kick his way out. A baby of a few weeks thrashes away with his arms; it cannot be assumed that he means to hit. A baby chews the nipple with his gums; it cannot be assumed that he is meaning to destroy or to hurt. At origin aggressiveness is almost synonymous with activity."[53] This little anaphoric catalogue, so concrete, challenges Klein only obliquely. By 1955 he is willing to go further:

> Unfused motility potential *needs to find opposition*. Crudely, it needs something to push against, unless it is to remain unexperienced and a threat to well-being. In health, however, by definition, the individual can enjoy going around looking for appropriate opposition. . . . the individual *must* be opposed, and only if opposed does the individual tap the important motility source. . . . The sense of real comes especially from the motility (and corresponding sensory) roots.[54]

53. Winnicott, "Aggression in Relation to Emotional Development," 204.
54. Ibid., 212–13.

"Crudely," he says, but we may also think that Winnicott speaks metaphorically, or rather that he articulates a means by which the infant discovers a capacity for metaphoricity simultaneous with a discovery of an external reality: the baby discovers external reality because it manifests itself as an obstacle. Indeed, in 1954 Winnicott had, in reaching for adequate representation of aggression's thrust, discovered the comic shouldering of the baby into birth (just the opposite to Jonson's infant of Saguntum):

> In normal birth the opposition encountered provides a type of experience which gives effort a head-first quality. . . . there seems to be a general validity in the association between pure effort and a head-first relationship to opposition. . . . . The impulsive gesture reaches out and becomes aggressive when opposition is reached. There is reality in this experience, and it very easily fuses into the erotic experiences that await the new-born infant. I am suggesting: *it is this impulsiveness, and the aggression that develops out of it, that makes the infant need an external object*, and not merely a satisfying object.[55]

Finding promise rather than peril in the birth trauma is typical of Winnicott's thinking. The protective arc of the mother's shelter does more than safeguard the vulnerable neonate from the tempestuous world; the baby also needs things against which to make contact, and she needs for things to get out of her way ("if an object is in the way there can be a relationship"). Together these constitute important aspects of her thriving. The mother's initiatives in playing need to become increasingly expansive spatially and to present just-safe-enough risks for the child, and also to allow the child more truly dangerous sallies.

The articulation of aggression first as an archaic impulse, then as the need to push against an obstacle, both ruthless or pre-ruth, makes sense of Winnicott's best-known description of aggression, the fantasized destruction of the object. In a very late paper widely cited by literary critics, he constructs the famous comic dialogue: "The subject says to the object: 'I destroyed you,' and the object is there to receive the communication. From now on the subject says: 'Hullo object!' 'I destroyed you.' 'I love you.' 'You have value for me because of your survival of my destruction of you.' 'While I am loving you I am all the time destroying you in (unconscious) *fantasy*.' "[56]

What could this "all the time" destruction be? It may be a Kleinian

---

55. Ibid., 215, 217.
56. Winnicott, "Use of an Object," 90.

rage and hatred, but Winnicott's emphasis transforms the struggles for scarce resources into a kind of marvel that the object world survives and, for a fortunate enough infant, has enough to go around. Elsa First glosses: "Something like: 'I imagine that if I use you I am using you up, exhausting you, obliterating you.' Also: 'If I assert myself there will be no room for you.' Perhaps also: 'I wish to have all of you, all to myself'; or, 'I might have destroyed you in my exuberance. You were blotted out for me, but I see you remain.' "[57]

"Survival" of the object ("you have value for me because of your survival of my destruction of you") means that the mother, in her own self-interest, refuses to be made simply absent, either in the world or in the infant's psyche, by the infant's aggression; her refusal makes possible for the infant the first steps toward differentiation and accommodation of mother's complex otherness. Furthermore, in order to have a structuring force in the emergence of the subject, the negating gesture of destruction recurs. We must *always* be destroying objects psychically, says Winnicott; if we are not, we are alienated from our own inner chaos. This destruction is unlike other forms of negation—say, abjection, repression, disavowal—in that it may lead to surprise, curiosity, and release at finding that the object has survived. Destruction is an action that tests the reliability of the environment, a notion of which Winnicott became convinced in his work with children sent away from London in World War II: delinquent behavior, actually a testing of the environment, was in this context a sign of resilience and health, whereas the compliance of the quiet children was more likely a mark of their despair.

A later passage from Winnicott's "Use of an Object" is less often cited but is essential as a way of expanding the repertoire of feelings available through aggression. It is untrue, he says, that aggression implies hostility when it occurs at the early developmental stage that Winnicott describes here, in a passage directed against Klein's vivid representation of infantile rage and also against her intense focus on the object as intrapsychic: "*There is no anger* in the destruction of the object to which I am referring, though there could be said to be joy at the object's survival. From this moment, or arising out of this phase, the object is *in fantasy* always being destroyed. This quality of 'always being destroyed' makes the reality of the surviving object felt as such, strengthens the

---

57. First, "Mothering," 158. See also Benjamin, "Desire of One's Own," 93–95, for one of the best articulations of destruction and potential space.

feeling tone, and contributes to object-constancy. The object can now be used" (93). However the infant contacts what it recognizes as other, this contact includes negation or destruction. As Benjamin suggests, "the negativity that the other sets up for the self has its own possibilities, a productive irritation, heretofore insufficiently explored."[58] Benjamin might be thinking of Winnicott's reversal of Freud: "The assumption is always there, in orthodox theory, that aggression is reactive to the encounter with the reality principle, whereas here it is the destructive drive that creates the quality of externality."[59] The discovery of the world's objects, and their discreteness, is visceral and kinetic; it involves a physics of pressure, force, gravity, and defines the body not only as a discrete, dense object, but also as a locus of intersecting fields of force.

If Winnicott had gone no further than this notion of the infant's discovering obstacle-objects to push against, then we might fairly charge him with obscuring a phallic foundation to his birthing model; the infant's emergence from the birth canal would be little more than a moment in a penetrative economy of coming to knowledge of objects. Along with Irigaray, we might object that such a model of birth-as-aggression makes the (male) child the one with determinate form, while the female parent is merely the material condition of form, outside awareness and discourse, perceptible only in the ways that a masculine discursive order repetitively remakes uterine homes in the world: "Within this nourishing home screenplays, oral, anal, phallic are rerun. . . . This fiction exacts a high price from the one from whom this excess is borrowed, as the first house is used, used up without any debt, any payment, without any record made of it. And therefore without consciousness, without memory, except the terror of abandonment?"[60] This is the maternal-feminine as no more than a container or envelope, "the starting point from which man limits his things." And, as Irigaray argues repeatedly, "the *relationship between envelope and things* constitutes one of the aporias, or the aporia, of Aristotelianism and of the philosophical systems derived from it."[61] The maternal-feminine as imagined in this discourse is to be resisted because it is static.

But as we have already seen, for Winnicott there are also incalculable

58. Jessica Benjamin, *Shadow of the Other: Intersubjectivity and Gender in Psycho-Analysis* (London: Routledge, 1998), 85.

59. Winnicott, "Use of an Object," 93.

60. Luce Irigaray, "The Limits of the Transference" (1982), trans. David Macey with Margaret Whitford, in *Irigaray Reader*, 105–17, at 111–12.

61. Luce Irigaray, "Sexual Difference" (1982), in *Ethics*, 5–19, at 10.

movements within transitional space, movements that first arise as aggression. The space-between and its openness to motility anticipate a good deal that Irigaray would later put in many figures: that of contiguous lips, of metonymy, of fluids, of thresholds and intervals, of angels face to face over the ark of the covenant, of movement, flight, passage, crossing, the suppleness of motility.[62] In the space created by the vis-à-vis we can see that transitional space fosters meetings that blur, overlap, and refashion the contours of subjective identity.[63] Or, to delineate its transgressive movements more clearly, we might adduce Irigaray's own *practice* of engagements with philosophers—fierce, joyful, intimate, intricate, always in motion. The outcomes of such interaction are irreducible to any one theoretical model, and so invite the future. Parties in transitional space, like those in an Irigarayan interval or in the processes of birth, shape between themselves a space-time of passage, movement, and above all freedom from coercion. Of the mother/child space, for instance, Irigaray like Winnicott points out how the mother, by being a subject herself, puts herself and her child in a state of intimacy and transformation that survives long after temporal infancy and caretaking: "If after all this [use by man, by baby], she is still alive, she continuously undoes his work—distinguishing herself from both the envelope and the thing, ceaselessly creating there some interval, play, something in motion and unlimited which disturbs his perspective, his world, and his/its limits."[64] This would be to allow for the exhilarations, and not just the pain, of what Winnicott calls "disillusionment," which is tantamount to parturition in its extended sense. The interval or transitional

62. In these figures, Irigaray variously tropes many philosophers—Aristotle, Heidegger, Derrida, Levinas, Merleau-Ponty; an important instance is her development of place and interval through a reading of Aristotle's *Physics* IV (on space), mediated by Heidegger's reading of Aristotle on time (also in *Physics* IV). See Luce Irigaray, "Place, Interval: A Reading of Aristotle, *Physics* IV" (1984), in *Ethics*, 34–55. The phenomenologist Henri Bergson seems a likely influence on Irigaray's thinking about interval (as he was for Winnicott); see Dorothea E. Oklowski, "The End of Phenomenology: Bergson's Interval in Irigaray," *Hypatia* 15, 3 (summer 2000), 73–91.

63. Winnicott on the mother/child space, Irigaray on the mother/daughter relation, and Irigaray on the meeting of lovers share a certain vitalism and motility that extend to all encounters between subjects. For strong descriptions of the corporeal patterns that arise between mother and infant—breathing, movement, touching—see Judith Kestenberg and Joan Weinstein, "Transitional Objects and Body-Image Formation," in *Between Reality and Fantasy: Transitional Objects and Phenomena*, ed. Simon Grolnick and Leonard Barkin with Werner Muensterberger (New York: Jason Aronson, 1978), 83–88; and Kestenberg, "Transsensus-Outgoingness and Winnicott's Intermediate Zone," ibid., 63–73.

64. Irigaray, "Sexual Difference," 10.

space is a perpetual challenge, yet also a resource and resting place where the engaged parties can experience going-on-being in freedom: "for both, a possibility of unhindered movement, of peaceful immobility without the risk of imprisonment."[65]

One consequence of taking parturition as generative, aggressive, and mobile is that specular relations are not the only foundation of perception of things in the world as discrete entities; the discovery of things is also a matter of mass, volume, and kinesis, a result of having something to push against, then air in which to expand the boundaries of self. Perception of boundedness and discrete objects becomes an achievement in the fostering and gathering of energy and, insofar as the infant's first words tend to be nouns and namings, links that headfirst aggression to language and poetry. As Emerson says, "By virtue of this science [knowledge of things in the world] the poet is the Namer, or Language-maker, naming things sometimes after their appearance, sometimes after their essence, and giving to every one its own name and not another's, thereby rejoicing the intellect, which delights in detachment or boundary."[66] Such a sense of parturition or the space between constitutes Winnicott's transformation of what we often call *loss to the infant* into destruction *by* the infant. If there is mourning in the infant's discovery that it does not own or possess the breast—or before this, in parturition itself—and if the mother can acknowledge the infant's feelings of sorrow and rage, then she makes possible the infant's discovery of its own appetite. "For if it does not develop appetite," says Harold Boris, "it only has its grievances as things upon which to nurse and gnaw." Only with reciprocal acknowledgment of giving and receiving between mother and infant, and acknowledgment of the aggression this entails in both parties, "can gratitude become linked with what previously stimulated only envy. And only then can admiration grow up to become a reason for identification."[67]

Only then can the subject expand into figuration, Winnicott might have said. He sustains a lifelong antagonism to Klein's certainties of interpretation, what Lacan would call her brutality. For Lacan, Klein's forcefulness is as much conceptual coarseness as it is aggression toward the children she analyzed; these two things are linked as over-literal-ness, which is for Lacan an aspect of her failure to address the linguistic.

65. Ibid., 12.
66. Emerson, "The Poet," 275.
67. Harold Boris, *Envy* (Northvale, N.J.: Jason Aronson, 1994), 36.

For Winnicott the over-literalness contributes to Klein's deadening effect on the British Psycho-Analytical Society because it forecloses the transformative reservoir of the unconscious; the explicitness of Klein's intrapsychic mechanisms and fantasies prevents *surprise* and its creation of the future, both in clinical practice and in theory.[68] At the other end of their century, it seems to me that we need both Klein and Winnicott, with Irigaray, to augment psychoanalytic readings of poetic texts. For we have been telling ourselves the same story over and over again: that texts replicate the phallic order, repudiate the mother, abject the feminine, marginalize women. This is not an untrue story so much as just one story, mesmerizing to us because of the illusions generated by our own gender arrangements. No story can be told in just one volume, and with Klein, Winnicott, and Irigaray I hope to hear other stories in poetic texts. I begin with the Song of Songs, because it proffers the most hope for transformation of reading practices and gender relations alike.

68. On surprise, see, for example, Winnicott, "Living Creatively," 51, 53; "The Pill and the Moon" (1969), in *Home Is Where We Start From*, 196–97; "The Squiggle Game," 219–317.

PART TWO

Generations of Blazons

3
The Providence of Similitude in the Song of Songs

The mind is a baby giant who, more provident in the cradle
than he knows, has hurled his paths in life all round ahead
of him like playthings given—data so-called. They are
vocabulary, grammar, prosody, and diary.

—Robert Frost

In this chapter and the next I discuss lyric speakers in love, the
woman of the Song of Songs and the poetic amorist of Edmund
Spenser's *Amoretti*—a sonnet sequence happily in debt to the biblical
book, not least in its ambitious blazons, successors to the ancient
Hebrew praise song. Each of the two speakers is possessed of a mind
like the one Robert Frost describes as a baby giant, provident in the
cradle and prodigal in the abundance of verbal resources hurled outward like playthings.[1] The prodigality of the Song's blazons—the
scope of objects named in the similes, the catalogue form that implicitly threatens to overrun several kinds of decorum, the untrammeled
commitment to representation, the boldness of erotic desire, the
nakedness of exultation—these features of blazon which make them

---

1. Robert Frost, "The Constant Symbol," in *Collected Poems, Prose, and Plays*, ed. Richard
Poirier and Mark Richardson (New York: Library of America, 1995), 790.

vulnerable to attack in our time by some strains of feminist critique are the very features performed most beautifully in the utterances of the two speakers.

I begin simply by gathering the Song's references to mothers, offspring, shelter, and food provision in order to delineate the female speaker through the symbolic actions of the verses, chiefly her claiming of her position as daughter. Here I deploy perhaps the most familiar contributions of Winnicott: playing, potential space, the mechanisms by which a provident mother may rear a generous child. Then I turn to a form of aggression in the Song, and use Irigaray's suggestions about metonymy and poetic language in the book, especially the difficult similitudes that have come under attack and dismissal in recent years.

Mothering and the Song's Creatural Object World

It is a peculiar fact that both lovers in the Song, as well as many other human and animal creatures there, are insistently marked as the children of mothers, and as siblings. The woman refers to "my mother's sons" (1:6); the man calls her "the only one of her mother . . . the choice one of her that bore her" (6:9); reference is made to the mother who crowned the king "in the day of his espousals" (3:11), and to the mother who gave birth to the man (8:5); in repeated passages, the woman longs to make the man as a brother to herself, and to bring him into her mother's house (3:4, 8:1–2); the verses are filled with ewes, their lambs, and undomesticated animal offspring like fawns and young gazelles.[2] These references, used variously in figures of similitude, address, and deixis, comprise a coherent motif of mother/child relations. But commentary is not clear that such a motif even exists, much less what significance it could have; perplexity is a common response. Roland Murphy muses, "It is a strange fact that the mother is so frequently referred to in the work. . . . The mother is mentioned also in the Egyptian love poetry, but it is not clear why her role is so prominent"; again, speaking of Song 3:11, "Nothing is known about any practice in which the queen mother would have crowned her son, whether at his coronation or on his wedding day"; again, "no matter who speaks these lines [at 8:5], the allusions remain obscure. Why is the arousal to love now associated with

---

2. Biblical passages are cited from the Masoretic text (Philadelphia: Jewish Publication Society, 1955).

the place where the mother had once conceived or given birth?"[3] Michael Fox attends to biblical verse structures but underestimates the resourcefulness of parallelisms to signify. Thus of 3:4, the woman's assertion that she "had brought him into my mother's house, / And into the chamber of her that conceived me," Fox simply notes: " 'Room' here is a poetic automatism, in which a near-synonym is used for the sake of completing the parallelism without changing the denotative meaning of the sentence."[4]

But traditional commentary is challenged by an increasingly sophisticated feminist discourse. Phillis Trible, beginning with the simple desideratum to read for the feminine, has interpreted the dominant presence of the woman in the Song as a contrast with and healing of the human wounds borne in Genesis 2–3.[5] Of the Song's passages about maternal figures, Trible suggests that the "references to the mother, without a single mention of the father, underscore anew the prominence of the female in the lyrics of love"—and, I would add, the prominence of the mother and child pair.[6] Song of Songs 3, opening with the desolate woman's search for her beloved, resolves into relief and the safety of their union, with her declaration that she has taken him into her mother's house: "Scarce had I passed from them, / When I found him whom my soul loveth; / I held him, and would not let him go; / Until I had brought him into my mother's house, / And into the chamber of her that conceived me" (3:4). Chapter 8 reiterates: "Oh that thou wert as my brother, / That sucked the breasts of my mother! / When I should find thee without, I would kiss thee; / Yea, and none would despise me. / I would lead thee, and bring thee into my mother's house, / That thou mightest instruct me; / I would cause thee to drink of spiced wine, / Of

3. Roland Murphy, *The Song of Songs: A Commentary* (Minneapolis: Fortress, 1990), 146, 152, 191. For surveys of speculations about the mother's house, see Marvin Pope, *The Anchor Bible Song of Songs: A New Translation and Commentary* (New York: Doubleday, 1977), 421–22; on mothers elsewhere in the Song, 496–97; on the woman's wish that her beloved were as her brother, 655–57; on her evocation of the beloved's conception by his mother, 663–66.

4. Michael Fox, *The Song of Songs and the Ancient Egyptian Love Songs* (Madison: University of Wisconsin Press, 1985), 118–19.

5. Phillis Trible, *God and the Rhetoric of Sexuality* (Minneapolis: Fortress, 1978), 144–65; Pope, *Anchor Bible Song of Songs*, 205–10. Others who write on the relationship of the Song to Genesis 2–3 include Athalya Brenner, *Song of Songs*, Old Testament Guides (Sheffield: JSOT, 1989), and *A Feminist Companion to the Song of Songs* (Sheffield: Sheffield Academic, 1993), 83.

6. Trible, *God and the Rhetoric of Sexuality*, 158.

the juice of my pomegranate" (8:1–2). Carol Meyers argues for the importance of the mother's house as a sociological reality of ancient Israel, and cites instances from Ruth and from the story of Rebekah, as well as from the Song.[7] Michael Goulder proposes a reading of the mother's house which takes seriously both the literal and the figurative, or rather the corporeal meaning of the phrase, which equally needs recuperation: "The meaning is sexual. . . . 'I have brought him into the house of my mother' is a euphemism for her welcoming him into her womb. 'The chamber of her who conceived me' underlines this intention."[8] The structure of sexual intimacy here is grounded in a stability identified with the dwelling of her mother, a stability emergent from the mother's own erotic, reproductive, and social history.

We can begin to see what is at stake in this poetic link between mother and daughter if we first listen to Irigaray on the strains of the mother/daughter relationship.[9] The 1979 essay "And the One Doesn't Stir Without the Other" registered the strains and mutual suffocations of the mother/daughter bond in Western culture. But soon afterward Irigaray argued that women need to find paths around the mother's theoretical lack of identity: "How, as daughters, can we have a personal relationship with or construct a personal identity in relation to someone who is no more than a function? . . . we need to say good bye to maternal omnipotence (the last refuge) and establish a woman-to-woman relationship of reciprocity with our mothers, in which they might possibly also feel themselves to be our daughters."[10] The alternative to

7. Carol Meyers, " 'To Her Mother's House': Considering a Counterpart to the Israelite *Bêt 'ab*," in *The Bible and the Politics of Exegesis,* ed. David Jobling, Peggy Day, and Gerald Sheppard (Cleveland: Pilgrims, 1991), 39–51.

8. Michael Goulder, *The Song of Fourteen Songs* (Sheffield: JSOT, 1986), 27, 61–62.

9. Although this theme runs throughout Irigaray's work (for instance, in her constant prodding that we think out Antigone's relationship to her mother, Jocasta) relevant pieces in the present context include "And the One Doesn't Stir without the Other," trans. Hélène Vivienne Wenzel, *Signs* 7, 1 (1981): 60–67; "When Our Lips Speak Together" (1977), in *This Sex Which Is Not One,* trans. Catherine Porter with Carolyn Burke (Ithaca, N.Y.: Cornell University Press, 1985), 205–18; "The Limits of the Transference" (1982), trans. David Macey with Margaret Whitford, in *The Irigaray Reader,* ed. Whitford (Oxford: Blackwell, 1991), 105–17; "On the Maternal Order" (1987), in *Je, Te, Nous: Toward a Culture of Difference,* trans. Alison Martin (London: Routledge, 1993), 37–44; "The Bodily Encounter with the Mother" (1980), trans. David Macey, in *Irigaray Reader,* 34–46; "Love of Same, Love of Other" (1984), in *An Ethics of Sexual Difference,* trans. Carolyn Burke and Gillian Gill (Ithaca, N.Y.: Cornell University Press, 1984), 97–115; "The Forgotten Mystery of Female Ancestry" (1989), in *Thinking the Difference: For a Peaceful Revolution,* trans. Karin Montin (New York: Routledge, 1994).

10. Luce Irigaray, "Women-Mothers, the Silent Substratum of the Social Order," in *Irigaray Reader,* 47–52, at 50.

mother-blaming within psychoanalysis is to create alternative accounts of mothering, accounts that take the complaining child beyond "a relationship with need": "Complaints . . . that is what does remain to us of our relationship with our mothers. A little child complains, cries . . . But if mothers could be women, there would be a whole mode of a relationship of desiring speech between daughter and mother, son and mother, and it would, I think, completely rework the language that is now spoken."[11]

It is this hope of a new discourse, built upon remembering the mother, that the Song of Songs offers. Specifically, as Irigaray argues in 1982, the possible identification between daughter and mother needs to be transformed from a model of substitution (the daughter in the place of the mother) to a model of contiguity (the daughter alongside the mother):

> The love of self among women, in the feminine, is very hard to establish. Traditionally, it is left in the undifferentiation of the mother-daughter relationship. And this relationship has to be given up, Freud tells us, if the woman is to enter into desire for the man-father. A dimension that must be denied in word and act. . . . Does this mean that love of the mother among women can and may be practiced only through *substitution*? By a taking the place of? Which is unconsciously colored by hate?
>
> Since the mother has a unique place, to become a mother would supposedly be to occupy that place, without having any relationship to the mother in that place. The economy, here, would be either the one woman or the other, either her or I-me.[12]

This is an economy of sacrifice: if there can be only one mother, then women compete for that scarce resource which is the place of the mother. Rivalry leads to *"quantitative estimates* of love that ceaselessly interrupt love's attraction and development," and prevents our hailing the mother as subject or fellow creature. Identifications by substitution and sacrifice arise from a cultural refusal to claim parturition as a condition of knowing the mother as fellow woman. A sacrificial economy of identification will have relevance for an analysis of metaphor and metonymy in the Song of Songs, as we shall see. But first the contiguity between mother and daughter in the Song calls for more detail.

The creative acts of the woman speaker in the verses about the mother's house are made possible by her claiming of daughterhood as the very condition of her creatureliness. The intensification of precision

11. Ibid., 52; ellipses in original.
12. Irigaray, "Love of Same, Love of Other," 101–2.

in the tiny, final parallelisms as she moves first inward—"into my mother's house, / And into the chamber of her"—and then to a sidelong memory of the precise moment when she "conceived me"—situates amorous stability not only in the precious space of the mother's chamber but also in time, with the subordinate reference to the mother's conception of the daughter who now utters this song. The imaginative urgency with which the girl regards her own origins in an earlier amorous act of her mother, identifying with her mother-then, and the way that the grown daughter now draws her lover into the protective shelter of the mother's household, manifest what it means for the woman to be a daughter as well as a lover—or rather, an adult daughter and *so* a lover.

The benign detachment required to identify with the mother within her own history (as desiring subject rather than as mother) is no small achievement. Winnicott speaks of the infant's coming to learn that the mother is outside its control, but the discovery and cherishing of the mother's subjectivity is something that challenges every child growing up in Western cultures with a strong affective investment in motherhood, no matter what the normative family structure. The acknowledgment of the mother as a desiring subject is learned and relearned, in stages, through a constant choreography of nearness to and distance from the mother; it is difficult to sustain, as our nostalgic constructions of motherhood demonstrate, and may never be learned at all. The woman of the Song has this discovery and cherishing as a resource, and it accounts in large part for her poetic persona and point of view.

When the expression about drawing the beloved into the mother's house recurs in chapter 8:1–2, it begins with such a resonance from chapter 3. Now the creative act of the speaker takes the form of wish rather than recounted deed, a wish for something like an ideal siblinghood. "Oh that thou wert as my brother . . . then they should not despise thee" (8:1). Within the rudimentary narrative in the Song, the woman wishes for her family's acceptance of the man, and for an end to the apparent hostility of her brothers. More important for my purposes is her wish that he could be not just her lover in the future but also her intimate in the past, from her own earliest times, her fellow in origins— an origin represented as knowledge of and nourishment at the maternal breast. The charge of this yearning is very great. It condenses the adult's erotic desire with the infant's attachment, and it displaces attachment to the breast to cherishing of the desired milk-sib. This compressed yearning carries pathos, as well, in that the fantasy of the lover as fellow nursling adumbrates a potential wish of adult lovers to have had a shared knowledge of the same other and the same household in infancy. That this wish is generally impossible of fulfillment does not lessen the importance of the fantasy for adult lovers, nor the imperative to create a way of being offspring together, quasi-sibs. Song 3:4 and 8:1–2 often elicit commentators' anxious reassurances that no incest wish is involved, and that the verses can be entirely accounted for by the woman's longing for social approval. Ilana Pardes, though, moves in a more likely direction when she recognizes "a wish to return to a paradisiacal phase—infancy—in which nakedness and desire . . . can be exhibited without shame."[13]

The next verse reiterates and varies the motif of the mother's house, where the woman will cause the groom to "drink of spiced wine, / Of the juice of my pomegranate" (8:2). In this extension of Song 3:4, the mother still presides over the union of lovers in the daughter's wish; the maternal body now yields to the maternal house, an enclosure as welcoming and as erotic as the better-known enclosed garden. For the mother's house of 8:2 suffuses adult erotic desire with the infantine attachment to the mother evoked by the woman's fantasy-recollection of nursing. But now the intimate otherness of the maternal body, giving milk to the infant daughter, yields place to the beloved's body, given wine to drink by the woman, who has assumed the place of the nurturant mother. The woman takes on the function of the mother as food provisioner, but, through an imaginative displacement, not exactly that of the nurturant maternal body. Now it is the adult who feeds a fellow adult, and with wine rather than milk. This wine is both literal and figurative, as Goulder notes: " 'eššoq^{e}kā , I would kiss you, in v. 1 leads on by assonance to 'ašq^{e}kā, I would give you to drink. The sexual meaning is not in doubt."[14]

These verses mark a transfer of authorship of provision from mother to daughter/female lover; the valence of taking infantile milk at the breast carries over to the wish for giving wine to the beloved. In both verses the identification of the woman with her mother is crucial: she wishes to be the giver of nurture. But in 8:1 she wishes also that she and her beloved could be fellow receivers of mother's milk; milk and wine

---

13. Ilana Pardes, *Countertraditions in the Bible: A Feminist Approach* (Cambridge: Harvard University Press, 1992), 137. See also the surveys of commentary in Pope, *Anchor Bible Song of Songs*, 655–56; Fox, *Song of Songs*, 166; Murphy, *Song of Songs*, 156, 188.

14. Goulder, *Song of Fourteen Songs*, 62.

together carry a wish, simultaneously active and passive, to be given to as well as to bestow. The mother is temporally displaced, not to be obliterated or forgotten but to be lodged elsewhere, nearby. The frankness of the adult, erotic wish to surrender to dependence as radically as does the human infant amounts, in this context, to an acknowledgment and honoring of the mother. Giving to and receiving from the other becomes a joint project for the two lovers in the woman's wish, and it is a retrospective consequence of her imagining herself and the man as infants at the breast of the same mother, near each other through contact with the mother. These actions of the woman and of the two lovers in their imagined shelter are available only through an adult daughter capable of imaginatively displacing a remembered dependency into a now freely bestowed interdependency, and of welcoming her mother and that mother's desire into discourse.

Themes of orality and the maternal body link up with another important set of verses, those on the apple and the apple tree (2:3–5, 8:5), via a Canaanite religious association of trees with female divinity and fertility:[15]

> As an apple-tree among the trees of the wood,
> So is my beloved among the sons.
> Under its shadow I delighted to sit,
> And its fruit was sweet to my taste.
>
> (2:3)
>
> Under the apple-tree I awakened thee;
> There thy mother was in travail with thee,
> There was she in travail and brought thee forth.
>
> (8:5)

These are passages about which commentators often resist full explicitness. Of the latter passage Murphy says, "the significance of the apple tree in 8:5b is not immediately apparent, though it may reflect the motif of 'love under the trees' which is found in Egyptian love songs."[16] This suggestion is likely enough. Goulder, though, raises the requisite questions.

> Why is it thought necessary to give such a physical description of the conception? . . . Why is it mentioned twice? Why the emphatic double

15. Carol Meyers, *The Tabernacle Menorah: A Synthetic Study of a Symbol from the Biblical Cult* (Missoula, Mont.: Scholars, 1976), 95–164; on sacred groves, see Savina J. Teubal, *Sarah the Priestess: The First Matriarch of Genesis* (Athens, Ohio: Swallow, 1984), 91–93.

16. Murphy, *Song of Songs*, 191.

"there"? . . . it could be that the place where she aroused him is an anatomical place as well as a place in a glade; and that it is thought of as an apple-tree by virtue of the two fruits hanging down above the "trunk"; that there is a special force to "under," because it is at the under end of this tree that the nerves are concentrated that make for such arousal.[17]

Explicitness about the apple tree as a trope for the genitals of the loved man, and about the woman's exclamation "refresh me with apples; / For I am love-sick" (2:5), is in no way indelicate. Indeed the fruit tree carries more complex gender connotations than this. I have already noted the woman speaker's partial identification with her own mother and the repetition of the motif of the mother's house in conjunction with taking in nourishment (8:2); at 8:5 the cumulative force of these passages extends into a new identification of the adult daughter with the beloved's mother, and the birthing that gave rise to his life.[18] It is further to identify the maternal with place itself, but not to limit the maternal to place. If the experience of place, or of a space within which events and cognitive experience develop, is constituted through relation to the maternal, then that maternal-as-function (or as envelope, to follow Irigaray) must be included within our eventual acknowledgments of and repayments to the mother. Here the mother-as-place is both reconstituted and transcended, for and by the adult child, in imaginative memorialization of the beloved's earliest origins. Thus the site of origin in conception, imagined as if remembered, provides the very basis of identity claimed and celebrated by the daughter, along with the mother: the ground beneath the apple tree lodges both women's erotic experience in a resonant historical depth. The density of imagined acts of memory, and of remembering as if for another, makes this passage both an identification-with and an honoring of difference between the woman of the prior generation and the woman singer in the Song. The apple tree of the Song is surely, as Goulder suggests, a figure for the phallus of the

17. Goulder, *Song of Fourteen Songs*, 7–8. On apples in traditions relevant to biblical studies, see Pope, *Anchor Bible Song of Songs*, 371–72, 374, 381–83. Apples are unlikely to be the fruit of the Hebrew; see Pope, *Anchor Bible Song of Songs*, 371–72. I stay with apples here because of their importance in Christian literary traditions.

18. Ascription of voice at 8:5 is debated in the commentary; see Pope's survey, *Anchor Bible Song of Songs*, 661–62; Murphy, *Song of Songs*, 191. Arguing as I am for the lovers' honoring of mothers' historical, corporeal experience, I would like to think that, since 3:4 seems to suggest that the location of the mother's erotic experience was the bedchamber, then 8:5 and its reference to the mother conceiving the child under the apple tree is spoken by the woman, about the groom's mother. But the point need not be sustained for my argument to hold.

beloved. But it is also a maternal apple tree, by virtue of the literal, intimate events that once took place on the ground beneath it and by virtue of the complex symbolic actions of the woman who celebrates her identification with and difference from an earlier woman. The man is in turn cherished for being the son of a woman who experienced these events—for being a fellow creature.[19]

When the woman voices the wish that her lover could have been a milk-sib and praises the fruit tree, she evinces an apprehension of creatureliness pervading the Hebrew Bible, especially the recurrent, joyful acknowledgment of human dependence upon objects populating the world ("objects" in both the biblical and the Winnicottian senses). Many of these are sources of nourishment; hence the abundance of herbs, spices, fruits, nuts, wine, juice, milk, honey; hence too the frequency of acts of feeding, nursing, and grazing: they occur in about one-third of the book's verses, sometimes more than once.[20] The fauna of the Song, the doves, gazelles, goats, ewes, lambs, young roes, horses, foxes who animate its extraordinary landscapes bear scrutiny too. Of the nine verses in which animals are associated with the woman, five are about young animals, and two of these are repetends intensifying and refining the initial assertion. There is the man's apparently teasing response to her question about where he feeds and rests his flock: "If thou know not, O thou fairest among women, / Go thy way forth by the footsteps of the flock / And feed thy kids, beside the shepherds' tents" (1:8). Twice we read, "Thy teeth are like a flock of ewes all shaped alike, / Which are come up from the washing; / Whereof all are paired, / And none faileth among them" (4:2, 6:6); and twice "Thy two breasts are like two fawns / That are twins of a gazelle, Which feed among the lilies" (4:5 and 7:4; the latter drops the reference to feeding among the lilies). The man assumes knowledge of the woman as guardian of kids in 1:7; in the similes, all the ewes have lambs, and all of these are twins; the woman's breasts are likened to twin roes. It bears emphasizing how recently born

19. Francis Landy (*Paradoxes of Paradise: Identity and Difference in the Song of Songs* [Sheffield: Sheffield Academic, 1995], 218) discusses with a different emphasis the poem's intricate identifications of lovers, mothers, and infants.

20. The percentage would be even higher if the Hebrew wordplays on kissing and eating were included. Fox notes, for example, "Three homophonic roots are fused in RʿH: (1) desire and will (from Aramaic RʿY); (2) friendship and companionship, as in *raʿyah*, 'darling, companion,' and *reʿim*, 'companions, lovers' (a by-form of Rᶜᶜ); and (3) feeding, both as a transitive verb in the sense of pasturing flocks and as an intransitive verb meaning 'to eat' " (Fox, *Song of Songs*, 103).

are these young. They are marked as creatures chiefly by their having been begotten, quickened, incarnated, given place on the ground of these landscapes. Imbued with the tenderness with which the man responds to the woman, they praise her enterprise of good husbandry, specifically a parent's or guardian's caretaking capacity, as with the tending of the ewes. Casual references to male shepherds notwithstanding, this emphasis on a guardian's or dam's tending is an extension of the lovers' maternal cherishing and provisioning, in a passage taking for granted the woman's responsible activities in the Song's pastoral world. Moreover, the generous labor of bounty and nurture is distributed among mothers, kings, male and female lovers, animal mothers, landscapes. Indeed in the constant shepherding and gardening references we discover that creative bounty is the outcome of the labor of many beings, not of a passive, maternalized state. In this context we might consider it no small achievement that the Song celebrates fertility, abundance, and parental care without ever addressing the woman speaker's biological fertility. It is as if the poet demonstrates that there are more ways to praise the abundance of the created world than the insistent Hebraic focus on childbearing.[21] A sense of gift, hence of gratitude, circulates throughout the Song, tossed from one speaker or referent to another.

The value of such nurturant activity of the woman (and perhaps of the man also) ought not to be trivialized as *merely* maternal. Rather, we might recognize it as the poem's adducing of projects that bring the maternal into signification. In order to realize what the Song has wrought in this regard, we can turn for contrast to Irigaray's objection to Levinas. His male discourse on the beloved, she says, "relegates her to the realms of infancy, animality, or maternity."[22] This sentimental and nostalgic relegation makes impossible a positive symbolic valuation of maternal nurture as anything but (merely) natural. The Song of Songs makes nurture, in the form of the woman's tending of animals, a positive value by making it a project, something created, and something other than reproductive capacity. It provides, as Levinas (in Irigaray's

---

21. On the conspicuous absence of hopes vested in the woman's future fertility, see, for example, Trible, *God and the Rhetoric of Sexuality*, 162; on the value of childbearing in ancient Israel, see Jeremy Cohen, *"Be Fertile and Increase, Fill the Earth and Master It": The Ancient and Medieval Career of a Biblical Text* (Ithaca, N.Y.: Cornell University Press, 1989), 8–66.

22. Luce Irigaray, "The Fecundity of the Caress: A Reading of Levinas, *Totality and Infinity*: 'Phenomenology of Eros' " (1984), in *Ethics*, 185–217, at 195.

view) does not, "participation in the construction of a world that does not forget natural generation and the human being's role in safeguarding its efflorescence."[23] "Participation" is the Irigarayan term for linking natural energies and forces with human projects and orientation; "participation" is the mark of a non-violating, non-murderous intersubjectivity:

> Two subjects can advene one to the other, and an alliance between the two becomes possible.
> This is not so much a problem of mastery as the question of a creation allowing participation in the *jouissance* of the object or its cocreation: a useful work because it marks . . . the limits of energy, of the flesh and of the body, of desire and its possibilities. The creation or elaboration of the *object* becomes an architectonic of the body, of a life and a death that does not kill the other.[24]

Irigaray speaks here of the clinical relationship between analyst and analysand, but we might easily expand what she says of jouissance to the intersubjective space between lovers, and between mother and child.

Another feature of the animals of these verses emerges in the young animals' dependence on the nurturing maternal. Feeding constitutes the paradigmatic relation between dam or female guardian and offspring. The woman is enjoined to feed her kids (1:7); the ewes and their lambs together comprise the vehicle of a simile for the woman's teeth; the two young roes which are like her breasts seem also to be fawns feeding at her breasts, by a sliding of earlier verses about the man's feeding among lilies. This is the sequence:

behold, he cometh,

Leaping upon the mountains, skipping upon the hills.
My beloved is like a gazelle or a young hart . . .

(2:8–9)

Until the day breathe, and the shadows flee away,
Turn, my beloved, and be thou like a gazelle or a young hart
Upon the mountains of spices.

(2:17)

23. Ibid.
24. Irigaray, "Limits of the Transference," 113.

Thy two breasts are like two fawns
That are twins of a gazelle,
Which feed among the lilies.

(4:5)

I am my beloved's, and my beloved is mine,
That feedeth among the lilies.

(6:2)

Thy two breasts are like two fawns
That are twins of a gazelle.

(7:4)

In these verses, the book's fluid similitudes attribute to the woman the ontological plenitude of a biblical creation, the strength of the biblical mother of a household, and the material productivity of a partly urban, partly nomadic/herding economy.

I have already suggested how imagined sibship as a wished-for relationship functions in this book; the phenomenon of twinning of the animals is another disclosure of sibship. The twins suggest creative prodigality; they suggest a guarantee of successful gestation and birth. Each pair also suggests the symmetry of likeness between offspring, hence intimacy between the two young tended by the dam. All the twins expand the lambencies of the woman's cry, "O that thou wert as my brother, / That sucked the breasts of my mother." This powerful optative is the more poignant in view of the actual hostility of the woman's literal brothers in 1:6 and 8:8–9. The very superfluity of the twins serves as a claiming of the good of corporeality, as a situating of maternity within a bountiful, animated, but not trouble-free world, and as an emblem of the creative extravagance called forth by erotic love in the Song.

If the Song's network of passages on mothers, offspring, and siblings carries the force that I have indicated, then it is foundational for the utterances by the lovers, especially in the praise songs. The intuitions of maternity and filiation uttered by the lovers constitute the very ground of their relation, making possible their exalted reciprocal cherishing and seeking, even releasing in them the imaginative vigor to create their praise songs about each other. Infancy, let us say, involves the discovery of a world of objects in part through the gradual cessation of all-encompassing nurture and the emergence of responsive exchange with a maternal other. Normally these processes lie too deep for recovery by adult memory, whether repressed or simply precedent to formation of the mind's linguistic categories. With the lover-singers of the Song of Songs, however, the conditions of infant imaginative activity are reconstituted *as if* remembered, in their exchange of songs which represent each other, build on similitude, and luxuriate in the exercise of verbal play. The lovers' abounding figurative language may thus be endowed with a psychic rationale, as we shall see after turning to Winnicott and Irigaray on the emergence of the foundational I-Thou relationship through birth and parturition.

Winnicott's narrative of infant development vis-à-vis the mother traces the infant's movement from nonintegration and dependence on the environment toward increasing autonomy and complexity of exchange with the world. The newborn, exposed to the onslaughts of the world's energies, may be lucky enough to have adequate care, Winnicott's shorthand for which is "holding."[25] Gradually, in the constant flux of holding activities, the infant discovers that the mother/provider maintains its life but does not perfectly answer its demands. Gradually, the baby becomes capable of destructive rage toward this provider; gradually the baby makes the felicitous discovery that the mother survives its fantasied destruction of her. Mother and child together create a demarcated space of exchange in which the relationship comes to be characterized by imaginative makings, each in response to the other as subject. The objects exchanged with increasing skill and knowledge of the other include linguistic representations, animating forms, gestures, artifacts, fictions that elicit answering fictions.

The exercise of skill in this process is crucial to the exhilaration of play; Winnicott stresses that its pleasure lies not in instinct gratification or reduction of tension but in the precarious exhilaration of risk, created in meeting obdurately external objects. Play "is exciting *not primarily because the instincts are involved.* . . . The thing about playing is always the precariousness of the interplay of personal psychic reality and the experience of the control of actual objects."[26] If the subject has internalized an abiding sense of maternal presence or of any parental care, then the move from infant to adult experience may be creative, as for the daughter of the Song of Songs, where her verbal and affective strengths seem to derive from her capacity to summon the continuity of the

25. D. W. Winnicott, "The Theory of the Parent-Infant Relationship" (1960), in *The Maturational Processes and the Facilitating Environment: Studies in the Theory of Emotional Development* (New York: International Universities, 1965), 37–55, at 43–44.

26. D. W. Winnicott, "Playing: A Theoretical Statement" (1971), in *Playing and Reality* (London: Routledge, 1991), 38–52, at 47.

mother's presence. "Potential space" becomes the "intermediate area" in which persons encounter aesthetic artifacts, give form to creative activity, and initiate exchange. The entirely unique idiom of exchange between mother and infant, internalized by the infant over time, allows the growing person to survive, to keep herself alive, to thrive (or not). Developing his model as against Klein's fascination with the breast and the contents of the body, Winnicott veers away from the body in parts and instead works out a differently corporeal model—a formal model— of persons oriented, situated, placed, and always *verging* on each other. The "intermediate area" is demarcated, ideally reliable yet supple as its members experiment with differing degrees of nearness to and distance from each other. The space between desiring subjects and the energies with which this space may be imbued are more fundamental and more interesting to Winnicott than the alienation of objects or subjects from themselves.

It is through this notion of potential space as a site of creative exchange, including the inventiveness of language, that I read the lovers' relations in the Song of Songs under the aegis of the maternal. The lyrics of the Song, like Winnicott's model of adequate conditions for infant development, are grounded in an epistemological optimism about access to otherness and about the reliability of the disclosure of being, in love. This optimism, arising from the lovers' relation to the maternal household and the maternal apple tree, is a prime impulse of the biblical lovers' exchanges. As in Winnicott's model of the development of playing, exchange is itself the fundamental activity: exchange between lovers and more particularly exchange of created artifacts—the praise songs—which reciprocate by structuring the world as objects to be met and as a field for extension of self. Elaine Scarry admirably describes this kind of exchange in her study of acts of making in Hebrew scriptures: "what the human being has *made* is . . . this excessive power of reciprocation. . . . the total act of creating contains an inherent movement toward self-amplifying generosity."[27]

Such optimism is not naive, however. As I said in chapter 2, Winnicott has an alarming sense of how chancy it is for mother and infant to encounter each other at all; the Song of Songs tests its own optimism about access to objects. In the absence of the beloved, the anxious utterances of the woman in chapters 3 and 5 present not a speaker sub-

27. Elaine Scarry, *The Body in Pain: The Making and Unmaking of the World* (Oxford: Oxford University Press, 1985), 318.

jected to and constituted by nostalgic privation, but a questing and meeting soul whose readiness for encounter and persistence before hostility can be understood as resources accessible to her by virtue of her experience of the "potential space" of the mother's shelter, as the proximity of verses about loss, finding, and maternal household may suggest:

> By night on my bed I sought him whom my soul loveth;
> I sought him, but I found him not.
> "I will rise now, and go about the city,
> In the streets and in the broad ways,
> I will seek him whom my soul loveth."
> I sought him, but I found him not.
> The watchmen that go about the city found me:
> "Saw ye him whom my soul loveth?"
> Scarce had I passed from them,
> When I found him whom my soul loveth;
> I held him, and would not let him go,
> Until I had brought him into my mother's house,
> And into the chamber of her that conceived me.
>
> (3:1–4)

Here the movement of the lyric speaker into a maternal space is a source of her strength. It enables the creativity of figural language and an access to the ontological plenitude of the world, as these emerge in the woman's most haunted, dreamlike loss and in the form of her recovery from it. The loss is initiated by her own ambivalence, which amounts to a testing of the beloved object in Winnicott's sense:

> I sleep, but my heart waketh;
> Hark! my beloved knocketh:
> "Open to me, my sister, my love, my dove, my undefiled;
> For my head is filled with dew,
> My locks with the drops of the night."
> I have put off my coat;
> How shall I put it on?
> I have washed my feet;
> How shall I defile them?
>
> (5:2–3)

When she does open to him, she finds that he has exercised the prerogative of an agent himself, deciding to depart.

I opened to my beloved;
But my beloved had turned away, and was gone.
My soul failed me when he spoke.
I sought him, but I could not find him;
I called him, but he gave me no answer.

(5:6)

The woman's desolation is marked by the failure of language in its primal functions of call and response ("My soul failed me when he spoke. . . . I called him, but he gave me no answer"), linguistic functions among the first to be learned in infancy, and among the first to teach the infant the necessary disillusioned discovery that she does not omnipotently control others. If the biblical lovers inhabit a potential space originally made possible by the woman's specific experience of having been mothered, her loss of him leads the adult woman to venture further, and to persist, in spite of exposure and humiliation, in an adult expansion of the potential space. Her loss leads her to creative exchange with others besides the mother or the lover, thence to the specific form of a praise song, structured as a catalogue of similitudes. The items of her catalogue celebrate objects in the psychoanalytic sense as objects in the biblical sense—creatures—and her access to imagining them:

My beloved is white and ruddy,
Pre-eminent above ten thousand.
His head is as the most fine gold,
His locks are curled,
And black as a raven.
His eyes are like doves
Beside the water-brooks;
Washed with milk,
And fitly set.
His cheeks are as a bed of spices,
As banks of sweet herbs;
His lips are as lilies,
Dropping with flowing myrrh.
His hands are as rods of gold
Set with beryl;
His body is as polished ivory
Overlaid with sapphires.
His legs are as pillars of marble,
Set upon sockets of fine gold;
His aspect is like Lebanon,

Excellent as the cedars.
His mouth is most sweet;
Yea, he is altogether lovely.
This is my beloved, and this is my friend,
O daughters of Jerusalem.

(5:10–16)

The deictics of the woman's last sentence—"This is my beloved, and this is my friend"—point both to the poem that she has created out of initial distress and to the lover with whom she is reunited. The deictics form a triumphant emphasis on the happy fusion of her poem with the apparently coincidental reappearance of the beloved, in the flesh. It is as if the woman's stubborn journey from desolation *achieves* the presence and presentation of the man, but also as if the beloved's return is bestowed upon her. At any rate we need both formulations to account for the tone of erotic fulfillment and tenderness in her subsequent words: " 'My beloved is gone down to his garden, / To the beds of spices, / To feed in the gardens, / And to gather lilies. I am my beloved's, and my beloved is mine, / That feedeth among the lilies' " (6:2–3). A Winnicottian would take the loss of and search for the beloved, the praise poem, and the beloved's reappearance as the riskier, more painful willingness to suffer the constantly shifting and ambiguous operations of fantasy, reality, and illusion. The Winnicottian subject learns to value not only the desired other but also the interval or space within which actions toward the other may gather, gestures form, the mind invent.

The circumstances eliciting this praise song—the desolation of the woman, the hostility of the watchmen, the challenge of the other women—mark the woman's lyric as her high achievement, as her deprivation gives way to the inventiveness of figurative speech and a celebratory reclamation of the world's fullness. Winnicott would say that deprivation is only one of many repeated experiences of the infant's relationship to the mother, one of many roots of symbol formation. As Scarry says of the imagination: "Perhaps because it originally comes into being in the midst of acute deprivation, it continues to be, long after that original 'given' has disappeared, a shameless exponent of surfeit."[28] Winnicott would say that the capacity for imaginative surfeit arises because there is both deprivation *and* an original "given"—the internalized structure of care—that never disappears altogether. To extend Winnicott's concepts toward poetic process, *representations* of objects need

28. Ibid., 323.

not be poor substitutes for an absence but *presentations* of invention, animation, and artifice generated between two passionate speakers.

Metonymy and Winnicottian Aggression

But where is aggression in this account? In this section, I move with Winnicott closer to the ways that one kind of aggression complicates the account of potential space that I gave above; then I draw on Irigaray to link the similes of the praise songs with poetic distancing (in Vicki Hearne's words, "From my mountain of words I can see / You on your mountain").[29]

Explicitly in Winnicott and implicitly in the Song, the child forms an identification with a mother who already desires elsewhere; the daughter in the biblical book acknowledges the mother's erotic and familial history, a history that preceded the child's existence. The mother had erotic relations with a man who would become the father; she has a home and mature sons; she must live within a city; her children maintain a domestic economy of flocks and vineyards. The adult daughter acknowledges the mother's ties that place her apart from the child as needy baby, for the daughter too has ties apart, represented chiefly through the expansive movements outward from home to distant places and landscapes. The woman in the Song of Songs holds, as we have seen, an identification with her mother as provident shelterer; simultaneously she holds an identification with her mother as divided and desiring subject. To hold these simultaneously requires some expense of energy. The lines linking mother to child, which are the flexible boundaries of the potential space, are the verge that attaches two persons but also holds them apart from each other. This is the specific, nonhostile form of aggression that is definitive for the Song. A "holding" of each other at some distance opens the space for the relationship between two divided, internally heterogeneous, "good-enough" persons. The energy it takes to sustain this "plain," the "bounding turf" across which the speakers of Vicki Hearne's poem communicate, is the Winnicottian kind

---

29. Vicki Hearne, "Ana Dadach Holeach," in *In the Presence of Horses* (Princeton: Princeton University Press, 1983), 13:

From my mountain of words I can see
You on your mountain. Here is the plain
Between them, the text to be sponsored

By the bounding turf . . .

of primitive aggression that shapes the mother-daughter relationship of the Song.

The holding of an open space also characterizes many of the lovers' exchanges in the Song, evidently in their passages toward and away from each other, toward and away from open landscapes and domestic enclosures—but also in their praise songs to each other. The flamboyance, voluptuousness, and downright oddness of the praise songs constitute a poetic excess that has scandalized a wide range of readers through many centuries.[30] Clearly the two lovers as well as the poet exult in the varied symbolic actions of their piled-up similitudes. A figure often strikes out on an unexpected path, as if an invention of Robert Frost's infant, hurling paths of "vocabulary, grammar, prosody, and diary" all about. In order to address these, I want to follow Winnicott by thinking of the blazon catalogues in gestural, relational, spatial terms, not (as might seem more likely) in terms of the Kleinian vocabulary of discrete body parts, and to follow Irigaray in thinking of holding open an interval. Together these forge a link between the Song's adumbrations of mothering and its poetic structures.

The strange similes of the Song's praise songs foreground the gestures and movements in the making of them, conceived as crossing over a ground toward otherness or as making a wide sweep of the arm in hailing, praising, thanking. Thus, to turn to a most challenging instance: "Thy neck is like the tower of David / Builded with turrets, / Whereon there hang a thousand shields, / All the armour of the mighty men" (4:4). We could domesticate this simile by emphasizing that the intended meaning lies only in the transfer of grandeur from the tower to the woman's neck, or to suggest that she wears a magnificent necklace that matches the details of the simile. But perhaps the symbolic action of this verse from the Song is better described as the movement of oscillation between holding the intimate proximity of the beloved—this simile is part of a catalogue of her eyes, hair, teeth, lips, neck, breasts—and holding her *off* through the grandeur of the tower of David. To hold off in this way is to delineate the expansive terrain over which one reaches.

---

30. Nearly all commentators address the Hebrew idiosyncrasies; see *Encyclopedia Judaica* (New York: Macmillan, 1971–72), 146; Pope, *Anchor Bible Song of Songs*, 33–34. Scholars also worry over the Song's general exoticism, its catalogues, the unlikely objects of its similes. The alienation of the culture of modern scholarship and criticism from pastoral, agricultural, and animal life seems to make commentaries increasingly puzzled. See Ariel Bloch and Chana Bloch, *The Song of Songs: A New Translation with an Introduction and Commentary* (New York: Random House, 1995), 9–10.

It requires "zest" or fierceness, terms for Winnicott's primary aggression. To read the simile this way is also to honor the Song's many gestures and movements across a demarcated, increasingly animate and tender space, as in its deictics ("Look, there he stands," "This is my beloved"), in its invitations to walk, follow, arise, come away, draw in, enter, go about, or in its intensely prepositional structure ("into my mother's house," "into the chamber," "under the apple tree," "beside the shepherds' tents," "from Lebanon," "depart from the peak of Amana," "to my garden").

It is the holding of these vectors of nearness-to and distance-from very specific and literal places that I want to use as a formal model of metonymy in the farfetched similes of the Song blazons. I propose, in other words, that we provisionally lay aside attacks on metaphoric equivalence that blazon catalogues, including those of the Song, have sustained in recent years from structuralist, feminist, and psychoanalytic criticism.[31] In such critiques of the whole blazon catalogue tradition, simile becomes culpable for its economy of identification with, substitution for, and sacrifice of the object on the far side of the copula. Nouns and noun phrases bear blame as reifications of part objects of the idealized beloved. Catalogues are exposed as inventories of fetishized goods.

Poststructuralism has done a great deal to elaborate on metonymy as metaphor's other, the former based as it is on contiguity, on syntagmatic chains of signification, on differential meanings of terms. Irigaray herself deploys various aspects of Saussurean and Lacanian metonymy to map the metaphor/metonymy binarism onto an elemental physics, so that metaphor, dependent on nouns/things, is "a quasi solid" while metonymy "is much more closely allied to fluids."[32] Although this dichotomy poses certain problems in literary history that have yet to be worked out, I want to cleave to Irigaray on the movements implied by metonymy broadly understood. Early in her published work she uses

---

31. Among Nancy Vickers's influential essays see, for example, "Diana Described: Scattered Woman and Scattered Rhyme," *Critical Inquiry* 8 (1981): 265–79; see also Patricia Parker, *Literary Fat Ladies: Rhetoric, Gender, Property* (London: Methuen, 1987); Mark Taylor, "Voyeurism and *Aposiopesis* in Renaissance Poetry," *Exemplaria* 4, 2 (1992): 267–94.

In discussing the Song's catalogues for the movements, I scant their substantives, because this seems to me a first necessity in order to shift the ground of present debate (or lack of it). But it is worth thinking about the objects of catalogues generally as transformational objects in a sense I describe in chapter 5.

32. Luce Irigaray, "The 'Mechanics' of Fluids" (1977), in *This Sex*, 106–18, at 110.

the bold and controversial figure of the two pairs of lips that women have, making them a sex which is not one—to propose an economy not of metaphor but of metonymy broadly understood as contiguity. Two women, let us say mother and daughter as in Margaret Whitford's explication, would not be "*identified* in a movement of metaphoric substitution" (which is to take identification as murderous displacement) "but *contiguous*: they touch, or associate, or combine."[33] In *An Ethics of Sexual Difference*, the metonymic economy is insistently ethical; Irigaray offers it as an alternative to the bleakly powerful analyses of patriarchy offered by social theorists, and to Lacan's ineluctable logic of the name of the father.

Metonymy for Irigaray is a matter not chiefly of the temporal interval or syntagmatic chain of signifiers but of a spatial interval, even a topographical one, between subjects. Irigaray makes increasingly beautiful figures and fictions of contiguity and the interval or space linking subjects. In her lyrical practice we can see most markedly that metonymy becomes a matter not just of contiguity but of the open space, the interval, the liberation into air. Thus her unforgettable formulation "air keeping the copula from hardening up or disappearing into is," which I use here to think about the copulas of the Song's scandalous similitudes.[34] The woman of the Song would understand the fluidity and linguistic pleasure of Irigaray's formulation; the woman seems to think about and enjoy wielding metonymic simile as part of her erotic pleasure: "Until the day breathe, and the shadows flee away, / Turn, my beloved, be thou like a gazelle or a young hart / Upon the mountain of spices" (2:17). We might entertain the similes of the Song of Songs metonymically, to see what they tell us about how space structures the lovers' praise songs. If, as I think, the catalogues are *not* instances of a murderous sacrificial economy of "like" and "is"—an objection often made to the similes of catalogue blazons—then what are they instead?

They are language and desire in motion. As we have seen, the praise songs are prepositional, deictic, and expansively invitational. Even when a particular simile has no grammatical prepositions in it, it partakes of the Song's topographical dynamics and movement vectors. The

33. Margaret Whitford, *Luce Irigaray: Philosophy in the Feminine* (London: Routledge, 1991), 180. This positive ideal of association between mother and daughter revises Irigaray's earlier, darker sketch of the tormented fusions of mother and daughter in "And the One Doesn't Stir without the Other."

34. Luce Irigaray, *I Love to You: Sketch of a Possible Felicity in History*, trans. Alison Martin (London: Routledge, 1996), 149.

praise passages proceeds by topographical expansion, until the sexual encounter with the loved one opens out into figures not of penetration, depth, or solidity but of mingling with the objects of the Song's creatural and cultural world. This is certainly the case with the praise song that, as we have already seen, crowns the woman's search for the man, when the object world is presented as if returned to her imbued with relief, triumph, and new security. But it is also true of the man's most sustained song addressed to the woman, at 4:1–15. We have already seen some features of the song, the ewes coming from the river and the tower of David; they suggest that part of the catalogue's effect comes precisely from the distance among the items on the far side of the copula, sketching an extravagant terrain and creaturely, culturally mediated world. If the following passage partakes of any material element, it is an element in transition, like flesh opening to a beyond or to air as much as to encounter with another's flesh:

> Thy two breasts are like two fawns
> That are twins of a gazelle,
> Which feed among the lilies.
> Until the day breathe,
> And the shadows flee away,
> I will get me to the mountain of myrrh,
> And to the hill of frankincense.
> Thou art all fair, my love;
> And there is no spot in thee.
> Come with me from Lebanon, my bride;
> With me from Lebanon;
> Look from the top of Amana,
> From the top of Senir and Hermon,
>
> . . . .
> Thy shoots are a park of pomegranates,
> With precious fruits;
> Henna with spikenard plants,
> Spikenard and saffron, calamus and cinnamon,
> With all trees of frankincense,
> Myrrh and aloes, with all chief spices.

(4:5–14)

One could imagine that this praise song could inspire Irigaray's ideal of the process of sexual encounter in "The Fecundity of the Caress." In the biblical lyric, similitude confounds distinctions between metaphor and metonymy, and the mingling of objects' emanating fragrances means that the spaces between them matter as much as or more than discrete body parts. The caress, as Irigaray says, "would begin at a distance. Tact that informs the sense of touch, attracts, and comes to rest on the threshold of the approach. . . . The lovers would beckon to each other, at first from far away. A salutation that means the crossing of a threshold."[35]

Throughout the Song, the arcs of motion sweep its speakers' imaginations out from and then back to "the house of my mother." The mother of nursing infancy is neither displaced nor repressed, not absented or buried. Rather the feeling tones of the child and the spaces between mother and children change shape from verse to verse, as experiences elicit thought, feeling, action in the speakers. The lovers who are children of mothers test the suppleness and variability of potential space, as they evoke psychic movements between each other. Here I turn again to Robert Frost to convey both the poetic and the nuptial possibilities of this kind of metonymy—though, a good modernist, he puts it as a remark about metaphor: "The estrangement in language is pretty much due to the very word-shift by metaphor you do your best take part in daily so as to hold your closest friend off where you can 'entertain her always as a stranger'—with the freshness of a stranger."[36] To hold, and also to hold off so as to entertain her freshly: metaphor is like, and due to the commitments of, a marriage—but not in its condensing or fusing of two objects, not like a Wordsworthian wedding of mind and natural world. It is like a marriage rather in the metonymic movements and gestures it takes to hold each other off, the energies it takes to refresh the open spaces through which a marriage courses. The two lovers, who hurl the paths or playthings of "vocabulary, grammar, prosody, and diary" around and ahead, have become full-grown giants, "always hurling experience ahead of us to pave the future with against the day when we may want to strike a line of purpose across it for somewhere."[37]

The terrain that the lovers of the Song are willing to traverse is indicated by the Song's geographical scope, and its inhabitants' alternations between repose and mobility. The woman, for instance, discovers that

35. Irigaray, "Fecundity of the Caress," 207.

36. Robert Frost, preface to the British edition of *A Masque of Reason* (1948), in *Collected Poems*, 803. He is drawing on Hebrews 13:2: "Do not neglect to show hospitality to strangers, for by doing that some have entertained angels without knowing it" (New Revised Standard Version).

37. Robert Frost, "Constant Symbol" and "The Figure a Poem Makes" (1939), in *Collected Poems*, 790, 778.

the metaphoric-metonymic objects of her analogies for the loved man do indeed serve her when she wants to strike a line of purpose across them for somewhere; she marshals the achievements of a Winnicottian playing to fortify her in her purpose, when, as part of the lovers' negotiations of nearness and distance, strangeness and familiarity, she sets out to search for her lost beloved in Song 3:1–3 and 5:6–8. The woman's search is also a testing of her capacities for similitude, or rather a testing of the strength of those similitudes to sustain her during the time of trial, to incite her to action. Reaching beyond and traversing the terrain of desire are not, in these verses, easy, luxuriant, and high-spirited motions; they cause pain, ambivalence, and a challenge to her trust in affective/linguistic resources. We have seen how she takes her erotic venturesomeness from her imagined origins in her mother's life, and the question she faces is whether she will succumb to nostalgia for some plenitude at the breast, thus disavowing the gift of venturesomeness itself, or risk herself in the search for the beloved. "How do you get from an attachment to follow an attraction?" Frost asks. "It ought to be painful to you, it ought to be, if you're any good. It ought not to be easy. You ought not to do it cheerfully, lightly."[38] Poised between attachment to the mother's house and attraction to the beloved, she takes her balance from the oscillation of sweeping outward to find him, then drawing him, and his own divisions, his alterity, into "the house of her that conceived me."

Perhaps this is also the Song poet's encompassing of different classes, economies, and ways of being Israel in relation to the foreign. For this poem is also willing to take a good deal of risk in its gestures toward Solomonic trade in luxury goods with the East. Kim Hall has noted the importance of this thread of the Song to the Renaissance and its writings on colonialism, but a simultaneous fascination and discomfort with Solomon's excesses occurs in the earliest biblical narratives about him and throughout commentary, although for other political reasons than ours.[39] The Song's composer may welcome, as a technical challenge, this cultural ambivalence about the potentate, and take advantage of the

---

38. Robert Frost, "Speaking of Loyalty" (1948), in *Collected Poems*, 799–800.

39. Kim Hall, *Things of Darkness: Economies of Race and Gender in Early Modern England* (Ithaca, N.Y.: Cornell University Press, 1995), 107–16. It is probably the Solomonic exemplar that fuels Deuteronomy 17:14–19, which limits any king's possession of horses, wives, silver, gold, and general commerce with the foreign. Such cautiousness toward the foreign may have some bearing on the dating of the Song of Songs; for instance Goulder, on the premise that the Shulammite is an Arabian tribeswoman, places the Song at the time of

mixed associations about wealth, luxuriance, uxoriousness, foreignness. Furthermore, the poet fashions a conceptual distance and oscillation between the two sides of each similitude: ornamental and luxury objects or vast sweeps of topographical distance on the one side, the warm and proximate human body on the other; in arcs larger than the individual similitude, courtly wealth and ostentation on the one hand, the natural creature on the other. This would explain the precise sequence of passages in chapters 3–4 on the palanquin of Solomon, his crowning, and praise song to the woman:

> King Solomon made himself a palanquin
> Of the wood of Lebanon.
> He made the pillars thereof of silver,
> The top thereof of gold,
> The seat of it of purple,
> The inside thereof being inlaid with love,
> From the daughters of Jerusalem.
> Go forth, O ye daughters of Zion,
> And gaze upon king Solomon,
> Even upon the crown wherewith his mother hath crowned him
>   in the day of his espousals,
> And in the day of the gladness of his heart.
> Behold, thou art fair, my love; behold, thou art fair;
> Thine eyes are as doves behind thy veil;
> Thy hair is as a flock of goats,
> That trail down from mount Gilead.
> Thy teeth are like a flock of ewes . . .

(3:9–4:2)

As Frost, in his offhand allusion to Hebrews 13:2, remarks on estrangement in language, we entertain ideas much as we entertain strangers: "thereby some [of us] have entertained angels without knowing it," thus drawing them into the domestic house while acknowledging the visitor's radical mysteriousness and even wildness. To entertain a "closest friend" in this way is to extend the verge across which she

---

Nehemiah's and Ezra's actions against foreign women (*Song of Fourteen Songs*, 71). Stuart Lasine provides a survey of biblical scholarship on the Solomon narrative in "The King of Desire: Indeterminacy, Audience, and the Solomonic Narrative," in *Textual Indeterminacy*, vol. 2, ed. Robert Robinson and Robert Culley, *Semeia* 71 (Atlanta: Scholars, 1995), 85–118; see also Michael Fox, "The Uses of Indeterminacy," ibid., 173–92.

may reveal her annunciatory bearings toward mysterious further reaches.

Part of the woman's sense of transmissible, inexhaustible gift, and of her Winnicottian use of objects, is that, having apparently received nurture, bounty, and protection from her mother, the woman in the Song can give *to* mothers, specific mothers in their historical, ongoing lives. For the woman also shelters the good-enough mothers in her book, honoring their histories and complex, divided lives. The Song's apple tree, like the mother's house, amounts to a daughter's provision of *figurative* shelter for her mother—we remember Irigaray's call for daughters to mother mothers. The Song's provision of shelter is a matter of poetically envisioning or holding distance, in spaces where the good-enough mother has her own experiences.

4
The Scandal of Similitude:
The Song of Songs in Spenser's
Wedding Volume

I bewail nothing me-thinks so much, as [Spenser's] Version
of the *Canticles*. . . . never was Man better made for such a
Work, and the Song it self so directly suited, with his
Genius . . . that it could not but from him receive the last
Perfection, whereof it was capable out of its Original.
—Samuel Woodford

Well before the death of Edmund Spenser in 1599, there were rumors
that he had translated the Song of Songs. No such text has ever been
found; it and other of Spenser's "lost works" remain a mystery, or a
wish, as in Samuel Woodford's lament cited above.[1] But it is plausible
that we already have Spenser's translation in the 1595 book of sonnets,
anacreontics, and wedding ode entitled *Amoretti and Epithalamion*, often
called his wedding volume since it celebrates his marriage to Elizabeth
Boyle in 1594.[2]

The author of the wedding volume sets for himself, or discovers, an

---

1. Samuel Woodford, preface to *A Paraphrase Upon the Cantciles* (1679), cited in *Spenser Allusions in the Sixteenth and Seventeenth Centuries*, ed. William Wells (Chapel Hill: University of North Carolina Press, 1972), 273.

2. See Israel Baroway, "The Imagery of Spenser and the Song of Songs," *Journal of English and Germanic Philology* 33 (1934): 23–45.

ethical problem. He uses Petrarchan, biblical, and Graeco-Roman mythological traditions to think out problems between lovers, problems of the sort that Lynne Huffer describes as those of *address*: "How does the subject speak to the other? How does the first person account for and think the second person who would hear her, draw her up short, put her into question? How does the subject speak her relationship to a *thou*, her ethical relation to an other?"[3] The poet puts these ethical and rhetorical questions to the textual traditions that he engages. To be exact, the lover's Petrarchan and mythic traditions repeatedly lure him into imposing on his beloved the kinds of demands that a baby ruthlessly places on its mother. Imitation of the Song of Songs, chiefly of the woman's voice, leads him to a fleeting convergence with the lady. But the biblical book's sketch of the mother/daughter relationship remains out of reach to the male Renaissance lover. The sequence returns to a demonstration of the difficulty of escaping nostalgia for the mother. Spenser never abandons the Song, though, and he uses it in the *Epithalamion* to adumbrate hope for a fragile, risky ideal of erotic happiness. A major achievement of Spenser's wedding volume is thus to push against the obstacle of nostalgia for the mother within his culture. For notwithstanding Spenser's just reputation for certain kinds of poetic ease and fluency, he is always attracted to the most intractable poetic resources and forms. Or, more accurately, he represents as intractable, outmoded, yet irresistible certain forms and received traditions, as if to make a plot, parallel to the marriage plot, of the working through—and triumph over—poetic logics that have become constraints.

The speaker of Spenser's book is a man who, in the words of Vicki Hearne's poem about the Song of Songs, "wants to live in love, / Bear fruit in his hands, in a garden, / To hear the ultimate song," and whose language approaches this felicity when, more than two-thirds of the way through, the *Amoretti* becomes saturated with hues from the Song.[4] That his language takes on this coloring at all, so near the end of the set of eighty-nine poems, constitutes an ethical and affective achievement for the lover, as well as an evident aesthetic achievement. The diction, motifs, and themes informing these poems are inaccessible, even unimaginable, to the tormented, exasperated Petrarchan lover of the

3. Lynne Huffer, *Maternal Pasts, Feminist Futures: Nostalgia, Ethics, and the Question of Difference* (Stanford: Stanford University Press, 1998), 27.

4. See Vicki Hearne, "Ana Dadach Holeach," in *In the Absence of Horses* (Princeton: Princeton University Press, 1983), 13.

greater part of the sequence, entangled in labyrinthine trains of adoration, resentment, woundedness, narcissism, struggles between dominance and submission, and eventual poetico-amorous exhaustion. Among all the poems indebted to the Song, there is a narrative of two clear stages, with hints of a third more fully developed in the *Epithalamion*. The first stage encompasses sonnets 64, 71, 72, and 74, representing a period of joy and accord early in the lovers' betrothal, after the Petrarchan tempests. In these poems, love is refigured in the linguistic shelter of the Song, a gesture that clears a Winnicottian potential space where love can be refreshed, enfranchised, rectified. Here Spenser freely improvises upon the lyric strength of both woman and man in the Song. The transfiguration of the sonnet speaker's utterances, which is to say a shift of his verses' allegiance from a narrowly defined Petrarchan register to a Canticles register, elicits creative, positive responses from the beloved woman. These in turn evoke the further exercise of confident figuration from him. In the second stage, taking in sonnets 76, 77, and 78, the handling of the Song discloses the strains of the betrothal period, when the precarious poise and happiness of the previous stage gives way to a hunger within the lover for a fulfillment still inaccessible, and a defensive contraction of the spacious ground of invention. In sonnets 76 and 77—which, not accidentally, imitate the man but not the woman in the Song, as if to mark gender difference as a problem in voicing—the speaker fetishizes the beloved's breasts; in 78 he compares himself to a lost fawn and the woman to its mother, a striking transformation of the Song's exuberant young animals. When this happens, the lover finds himself trapped in the same snares that had made him unhappy to begin with.

The chief challenge to the poet-lover of the *Amoretti* is to discover or create a language sufficient to the passionate, hymeneal love he hopes to establish with the lady. To establish the poet's right relation to language would be simultaneously to establish the lovers' right relation to each other; the pain that the sonnets document marks the difficulty of discovering a voice which would make possible a marriage of true minds. No amount of twisting and turning within the narrow confines of Petrarchan sonnets (as the lover implicitly delimits that tradition) can achieve such a marriage, in part because the lady rebuffs his hopes for response from an adored goddess, and he repeatedly fails her implied challenge to invent a more adequate narrative model for their exchanges. The lady is first situated as an adored idol, which is to say that she is placed in the position of an omnipotent mother-provider with an unquestioned responsibility to nurture the man. But she continually surprises and dismays her dependent lover by resisting the job of bestowal of provision, a job the performance of which would count to him as her love for him. She steadfastly refuses and even ridicules the role of the woman who must provide *because of* her lover's claim on her, which grieves and angers him. (The woman lover of the Song of Songs, as we have seen, has made a leap beyond this claim on the mother, and has discovered a ground for her own creation of poetry, not in need but in harder-won imaginative identifications with distance from the good-enough mother.) The cumulative effect of the first sixty-odd sonnets is one of claustral entrapment within narrowly defined limits of erotic relationship derived from the larger Petrarchan tradition; the speaker suffers restless despair that venture after venture fails to win the lady.

The Problem of "as": Blazon and Simile

The Spenserian passages most markedly indebted to the Song of Songs are blazons, and in this chapter I focus on these densely allusive passages and their near relations in the wedding volume, for they analyze and critique the blazon form of the time as well as pay homage to the Song. Before turning to Spenser's blazons, therefore, I briefly raise the question of blazons generally, especially the problematic ethical matter of similitudes for parts of the female body. Many different shades of meaning and implications of linking hinge on that transparent little word "as." Blazons throughout medieval and Renaissance writing, and indeed in the Song itself, have drawn a good deal of fire in the last decade. The very idea of the blazon of the sonnet mistress has come to function as an epitome of the ways that gendered discourse systems commodify and exchange women, silence women writers, control women's agency and sexuality, and mystify masculine desire as normative. Within certain feminist critiques of representation, the blazon's dominant figure of similitude and its dominant scheme of catalogue bear culpability for a double burden of visual aggression and metaphoricity.[5] But the various traditions that converge in Renaissance blazons, including those derived from Petrarch and from Canticles, also

5. See the influential essays cited above in chapter 3, note 31. The most aggressively careless instance to date occurs in Jonathan Sawday, *The Body Emblazoned: Dissection and the Human Body in Renaissance Culture* (London: Routledge, 1995), 199–201.

afford resources for analysis, irony, and skepticism.[6] The most powerful blazons in the work of Spenser and his contemporaries anticipate and address their own ethical, aesthetic, and psychic risks; many of them are, for their sixteenth-century English Protestant writers, reclamations of poetry from antagonisms to the image-making faculties within their own theological, philosophical, and poetic cultures. In the blazons of Spenser's wedding volume, if we listen, we can hear claims about poetic utterance pressing for articulation.

The first blazon in *Amoretti*, "Ye tradefull Merchants" (sonnet 15), is clearly indebted to the Song of Songs, in motif if not in tone. Because it is so hostile and manifests aggression in the poet's display of the lady, it is easy to underread this sonnet as the blind movement of a bankrupt ideology linking gender with greed and rapacity:

> Ye tradefull Merchants that with weary toyle
>   do seeke most pretious things to make your gaine:
>   and both the Indias of their treasures spoile,
>   what needeth you to seeke so farre in vaine?
> For loe my love doth in her selfe containe
>   all this worlds riches that may farre be found:
>   if Saphyres, loe her eies be Saphyres plaine,
>   if Rubies, loe hir lips be Rubies sound.[7]

But the stern treatment of this sonnet in recent years can only be the result of hasty reading and willful disinclination to trace historical and literary-historical contexts. (One such context is the sonnet's close relationship to Desportes's *Diane* 1.32—which I scant here.) Far from being an oblivious exemplar of the worst tendencies of men's display and exchange of women, the sonnet is a frank presentation of such motives as part of the narrative movement of the wedding volume. In its context, early in the sequence, this is the poem of an aggressive Petrarchan lover still entertaining thoughts "lyke to vipers brood" (sonnet 2), a lover

6. As Murray Krieger said more than thirty years ago, "Like any convention that has staying power, Petrarchism must have a built-in skepticism against itself" (*A Window to Criticism: Shakespeare's Sonnets and Modern Poetics* [Princeton: Princeton University Press, 1964], 77). See also Heather Dubrow, *Echoes of Desire: English Petrarchism and Its Counterdiscourses* (Ithaca, N.Y.: Cornell University Press, 1995); Barbara Estrin, *Laura: Uncovering Gender and Genre in Wyatt, Donne, and Marvell* (Durham: Duke University Press, 1994); Gordon Braden, *Petrarchan Love and the Continental Renaissance* (New Haven: Yale University Press, 1999).

7. Quotations come from *The Yale Edition of the Shorter Poems of Edmund Spenser*, ed. William Oram et al. (New Haven: Yale University Press, 1989).

whose overmastering narrative of love, based on the tacit needs of a lusty, demanding baby, is shown by the sequence to fail to win the lady's esteem. It represents the tropological motions of mind that Irigaray indicts in Levinas's work: "The beloved woman . . . finds herself dispersed in the shards of a broken mirror. Do the pearls of ice or frost of her reflection put a screen to love? Made from the brilliance of her finery? Of the beloved man . . . who banishes her from the place of greatest tenderness. Calling her to freeze into the shapes that separate her from herself."[8] As Spenser's lover learns, though, this motion of mind freezes himself as well as the woman, and must eventually be abandoned. "Ye tradefull Merchants" is placed among the most bitter and resentful of the sonnets, full of the ferocious energy that comes of unrequited idealization. In sonnet 10, the woman is called a "Tyrannesse" and accused of "huge massacres"; in sonnet 11 she is cruel, greedy, unpitying, wrathful, intent on destroying the lover; sonnets 12, 13, and 14 all play out the military conceit in violent fashion.

"Ye tradefull Merchants" functions like an infant's psychic attack on the desired object that does not perfectly answer its needs. Its fierceness is that of the Winnicottian infant who wishes to destroy that on which it depends. Hence the curious tone, colloquial and formal at once, of the parallel "if" clauses: "if Saphyres, loe her eies be Saphyres plaine, / if Rubies . . . / If Pearles . . ." These conditionals carry something uneasy in the poet toward the similitudes so facilely catalogued; we may also hear a hint of conversational, cynical braggartry among men, expressive of a detached superiority toward the lady *and* toward the very poetic gesture of similitude—for example, "If it's sapphires you want, why then it is easy enough to call her eyes sapphires" or even "If it's sapphires you want, I'll give you sapphires, in spades." This is a trivialization of poetic making, in tone as well as in recourse to easy formulae, and an index to the complex fusion of poet and lover, whose very devotion to one late Petrarchan model of amorous conversation has now set him on a path to discovering its poverty. Spenser recognizes in the early tangle of grief, despair, and resentment a fuel for poetic power, while simultaneously making clear the ways that rage and destruction constrain the poet-lover. For its rage is addressed in part to the very economy of wealth implied in the catalogue of gems: that economy from

8. Luce Irigaray, "The Fecundity of the Caress: A Reading of Levinas, *Totality and Infinity*, 'Phenomenology of Eros' " (1984), in *An Ethics of Sexual Difference*, trans. Carolyn Burke and Gillian Gill (Ithaca, N.Y.: Cornell University Press, 1993), 185–217, at 194–95.

which the lover is excluded, which he desires, but which (as he is dis-covering) is bankrupt anyway, a false way of putting an economy of abundance.

Nor is it only the immediate proximity of other anxious, bitter sonnets that suggests this. Spenser was responsive not just to the Song of Songs but to the whole expansive lore about Solomon, around whom there grew an intricate set of relations among wisdom, eros, and natural his-tory, through the Song together with I Kings, II Chronicles, Proverbs, Ecclesiastes, Ecclesiasticus (Sirach), and the Wisdom of Solomon.[9] But with the exception of this sonnet, Spenser conspicuously avoids one large set of legendary Solomonic associations, the wealth and opulence of the Solomon of I Kings and II Chronicles. In this sonnet Spenser, far from embracing merchant trading, takes pains to distinguish his speaker's ferocious willingness to trade from the Song's reveling in exotic materials brought by merchants. The blazon of "Ye tradefull Mer-chants" emphasizes the "spoile" of trade; the gemmed surface of the poem engages with merchants to deal in sapphires, rubies, pearls, ivory, gold, silver. Spenser makes intertextual choices with an eye to the verses from the Song on the fragrances, perfumes, and powders of the mer-chant (e.g., Song 3:6), but anger and disappointed idealization give rise to the chilly similitudes of the sonnet blazon. Anger stands in the sequence as an analysis of the motives for one kind of praise rhetoric, and as an event in the plotting of the whole sequence.

In this context, the garden sonnet (64) "Comming to kisse her lyps" does work markedly antithetical to that of "Ye tradefull Merchants." Part of Spenser's response to the Song is to tease apart and oppose the biblical book's sensuous continuum of luxury items (gold, silver, gems: the stuff of trade) and natural items (flora and fauna), such that the com-modities figure Petrarchan terrors and the organic realm figures the

9. Spenser's relation to the Song would have involved a familiarity with its pervasive-ness in a wide range of contexts, a sense that its words and tropes were perpetually avail-able to be worked hard, and awareness of its inflections in many genres, forms, and domains. On Reformation uses of the Song, see Israel Baroway, "The Bible as Poetry in the English Renaissance," *Journal of English and Germanic Philology* 32 (1933): 447–80; John King, *Spenser's Poetry and the Reformation Tradition* (Princeton: Princeton University Press, 1990); Barbara Lewalski, *Protestant Poetics and the Seventeenth-Century Religious Lyric* (Princeton: Princeton University Press, 1979); George Scheper, "Reformation Attitudes toward Allegory and the Song of Songs," *PMLA* 89 (1974): 551–62; Gerald T. Sheppard, *Solomon's Divine Arts: Joseph Hall's Representation of Proverbs, Ecclesiastes, and the Song of Songs* (1609), with introductory essays, including E. Ann Matter's "Joseph Hall and the Tradition of Christian Interpretation of the Song of Songs" (Cleveland: Pilgrim, 1991).

lover's release from these terrors. Sonnet 64 represents, among other things, the poet-lover's triumph over his early rage:

> Comming to kisse her lyps, (such grace I found)
>   Me seemd I smelt a gardin of sweet flowres:
>   that dainty odours from them threw around
>   for damzels fit to decke their lovers bowres
> Her lips did smell lyke unto Gillyflowers,
>   her ruddy cheekes lyke unto Roses red:
>   her snowy browes lyke budded Bellamoures,
>   her lovely eyes lyke Pincks but newly spred,
> Her goodly bosome lyke a Strawberry bed,
>   her neck lyke to a bounch of Cullambynes:
>   her brest lyke lillyes, ere theyr leaves be shed,
>   her nipples lyke yong blossomd Jessemynes.
> Such fragrant flowres doe give most odorous smell,
>   but her sweet odour did them all excell.

Joseph Loewenstein rightly calls this "the richest English imitation of the sacred eroticism of the Song of Songs."[10] The greatness of the sonnet lies in the opulence of its imagery, the delicacy of the match between flora and aspects of the lady in the catalogue's adoption of native and domestic flowers, the last couplet's synesthetic homage to the lady's corporeal integrity—an acknowledgment which assists this poem's revisionary triumph over many of the less achieved inventory blazons of the period. It is the *Amoretti*'s most satisfying shift from Petrarchan discourse and Petrarchan relations, and it is the shift into the register of the Song by which it achieves its sense of buoyancy and release. In "Comming to kisse her lyps," the lover finds himself the receiver or the addressee of the woman's intimate presence. She has survived his destruction of her; the discovery of her separateness from him or of the space between them, which makes it possible for both of them to cross a verge toward each other, is what Spenser lauds in this sonnet. It is as a fellow creature that the lover now understands the beloved, not as an adored goddess or idealized provider; we might say they are level, established on the same ground, in an English garden harking back to

10. Joseph Loewenstein, "A Note on the Structure of Spenser's *Amoretti*: 'Viper Thoughts,' " *Spenser Studies* 8 (1987): 311–23, at 319–20; see also Loewenstein, "Echo's Ring: Orpheus and Spenser's Career," *English Literary Renaissance* 16 (1986): 287–302. The great lyric precursor to this sonnet, Ronsard's *Amours* 1.110, is worth considering in relation to the Song in its own right.

the Song of Songs. The achievement is marked in part by the sonnet's play of similitudes taken not only from the man's praise of the woman in the Song but also from the woman's language—for example, the praise of the man's cheeks as a bed of spices, of his lips like lilies (5:13), "My welbeloved is gone downe into his garden to the beds of spices, to feede in the gardens, and to gather lilies" (6:1).

Does the Winnicottian idea of potential space, variously contoured and traversed by the lovers, afford us any purchase on the ethical problem of blazons that feminist critique pursues in regard to this sonnet? It might seem both obvious and lamentable that the land of the garden is mapped onto the body of the beloved woman, in the glib manner that we impute to Renaissance blazons: "Her snowy browes lyke budded Bellamoures, / Her lovely eyes . . . / Her goodly bosome," and so forth. But it may be more just to the exactitude of simile and syntax to say that the first quatrain's emphasis on the fragrance of the whole garden, along with the massed flowers and stichic formality of lines 5–12, together have the force of generalizing the flowers into a floral bed emanating airs of fragrance, focusing reader attention not on discrete parts of the female body but on a potential space of reciprocal bounty and conversation between the lovers. The beloved is ascribed agency and consent, and it is her "grace" that releases warmth and fragrance. The lover feeds, as in Hearne's poem, "in spicy beds over which I watch"; he has made a transition from the nursling's needy desires to an adult erotic and formal exchange within an intermediate space. This lover feeds not at the maternalized body but "At Table With Fruit, Evening With / Roses . . . in the valley of // The text of songs."

The dynamism of Winnicottian potential space may draw attention to the way that garden security and composure follow the sea-soaked sonnet 63, "After long stormes and tempests sad assay." The weary navigator of that poem had seemed to see "fayre soyle" "fraught with store / of all that deare and daynty is alyve"—and he was right in this perception of fair soil laden with life, as the subsequent garden sonnet shows. After the misdirections and stalls of the Petrarchan poems, sonnets 63 and 64 trace the lover's movement toward the beloved: he is "Comming to kisse her lyps," a syntactic structure that draws attention to the changing space between them, and to movement. As in the Song, it is both an association of the beloved with profuse gardens *and* a passionate traversal of intersubjective space that constitute the experience of place itself.

To pursue this Winnicottian way of taking the association of beloved with land is to discover ways to read phrases likely to awaken unease in our time, among them "Her goodly bosome lyke a Strawberry bed" or "Pincks but newly spred." The flowers' "dainty odours" are thrown around the site of sensual satisfaction, so that the floral catalogue represents not so much visually discrete, bounded things as a metonymic contiguity of color, shape, and smell in the lovers' verging toward each other. With Irigaray's help, we might see the garden sonnet as a tribute to air, or a momentary harmony of earth and air. Irigaray's sustained gesture of reminding us of our debt to the encasing air gives rise to this buoyant passage:

> Is not air the whole of our habitation as mortals? Is there a dwelling more vast, more spacious, or even more generally peaceful than that of air? Can man live elsewhere than in air? Neither in earth, nor in fire, nor in water is any habitation possible for him. No other element can for him take the place of place. No other element carries with it—or lets itself be passed through by—light and shadow, voice or silence. No other element is to this extent opening itself. . . . No other element is as light, as free, and as much in the "fundamental" mode of a permanent, available "there is."[11]

Irigaray's purpose here is to charge Heidegger, standing for philosophers generally, with occluding the debt to air and to the mother who first gave it to us, in his pursuit of metaphysics: "The vacuum that they create by using up the air for telling without ever telling of air itself: chasm at the origin of their thought's appropriation?"[12] But we might see Spenser's garden sonnet as an acknowledgment of this debt, with its fragrances thrown round, the lover moving through the tender air of the garden created by the similes toward a welcoming presence.

Spenser is certainly thinking out erotic relations by means of an elemental physics, for the poem also activates a sense of earth or ground peculiar to this writer. By this I mean earth's intimations of a foundational stability and stable source of food, which Spenser frequently apprehends as features of garden beds, tables, altars, and so on. Solid surfaces that support, elevate, hold, and proffer foods or sustain profusion, spread, and growth occur many times in his work. They are part of his lifelong meditation on substrata, foundations for creativity, and his

---

11. Luce Irigaray, *The Forgetting of Air in Martin Heidegger*, trans. Mary Beth Mader (Austin: University of Texas Press, 1999), 8.
12. Ibid., 7.

representations of these substrata as markers of creatural life.[13] They arise from Spenser's capacity to seek, achieve, lose, and seek again an internalized sense of the mother-provisioner's continuous presence, a capacity of the poet to "hold" a good internalized object, she who had once sustained him.

The sonnets immediately before and after "Comming to kisse her lyps" (62 through 72) are the happiest in the *Amoretti*. As an amatory sequence they lead from a wary reparation of trust between the lovers (sonnet 62), through the man's increasing anticipation of happiness, to the lady's reciprocation of love and their betrothal (66, 67). As a seasonal sequence they mark the transition from rough weather (63) to the vernal energies of spring (70). As a liturgical sequence they move through Holy Week to the triumph of Easter Day (68). The aligning of these three time structures amounts to a sanctification of the paths to nuptial eros and a transformation of the Petrarchan amorous and poetic system, so poisonous in this sequence's construction of it, which has dominated the affair. Within this joyous movement, the anglicized Solomonic garden of "Comming to kisse her lyps" arises out of the delineating, holding, and sustaining of potential space.

Nostalgia in the Beloved's Absence

The adult lovers of *Amoretti* 62–72, like the lovers of the Song of Songs, are enfranchised by the considerable achievements of the Song's woman to claim her relationship to good-enough mothers, and the liberating

---

13. In *The Faerie Queene*, these include details from the following passages: 1.11, the Tree of Life; 2.7.51–56, 2.3, the description of Belphoebe; 2.7, the Garden of Proserpina; 2.12, the Bower of Bliss; 3.1.51, Castle Joyous; 3.4, Marinell on the strand; 3.5.39–40, Belphoebe's bower; 3.6, Chrysogonee and the sun and the Garden of Adonis; 3.9.30–31, the table in Malbecco's house; 4.1.25–26, Ate's garden; 4.2.43 and 3.3.29, the conception, rearing, and life force of the brothers Priamond, Dyamond, and Triamond; 6. Proem, with its nursery; 6.6, the Hermit's dwelling; 6.9.8, Pastorella; 6.10, Mount Acidale; 7.7, Arlo Hill; 7.7, the description of Earth. Related descriptions of altars and supporting or holding pillars include: 4.10, the altar and the statue in the Temple of Venus; 5.7, the Temple of Isis; 6.8, the altar on which Serena is placed. "Aprill" of *The Shepheardes Calender* and sonnets 63 and 65 also belong in this company.

For the notion of the substratum I am indebted to James Nohrnberg, *The Analogy of "The Faerie Queene"* (Princeton: Princeton University Press, 1976), 519–98; to Irigaray, who everywhere discusses the feminine as a "substratum" upon which masculine identity and discourse are built; and to Norman Bryson, *Looking at the Overlooked: Four Essays on Still Life Painting* (Cambridge: Harvard University Press, 1990), on representations of tables and food.

verge between them; as I argued in the last chapter, this is the chief function of her reconstructions of mothers' independent experiences. In Spenser's sonnet sequence, the founding of an ability to love reciprocally is represented as much more difficult: Petrarchan constraints keep arising for the male speaker. In the sonnets numbered in the mid-seventies, this male speaker reverts to desiring the beloved woman roughly as a needy infant desires its maternal provider, and this is complicated by the boy child's anxiety about his difference from the mother.[14] The ambivalence of the boy toward the mother, in his sharper and more traumatic differentiation from her than the girl child's, emerges in the sonnets as a trace of the infant's need to elicit provision from a woman marked as provider. Hence the intense, troubled fascination with face, lips, breast, and feeding in certain sonnets. Melanie Klein would attribute the fantasies of these body parts to babies of both genders, but Spenser attributes them to the male, by marking their difference from the woman speaker's exultant uses of the idea of maternal feeding capacity in the Song of Songs. The place of love is no longer a potential space between them on which they both stand, as in "Comming to kisse her lyps," but is the desired female body itself, on which the male lover would rest, nestle, feed, give up his adult autonomy and the essential space between.

The break comes between sonnets 74 and 75, the former containing an explicit reference to Spenser's mother, Elizabeth, as well as to Elizabeth Tudor and Elizabeth Boyle:

> Most happy letters fram'd by skilfull trade,
>   with which that happy name was first desynd:
>   the which three times thrise happy hath me made,
>   with guifts of body, fortune and of mind.
> The first my being to me gave by kind,
>   from mothers womb deriv'd by dew descent.

The coincidence of proper name celebrated in writing ("fram'd by skilfull trade") allows a transparent happiness of reception in the speaker: it is represented as remarkable but also perfectly right that he is endowed with such gifts. This sonnet celebrates an adult gratitude emergent from infant experiences of continuous internalized maternal presence.

14. There are now many analyses of male desire for and dread of the maternal body, along with anxiety about masculine autonomy, in Renaissance English culture; see the bibliographical essay.

But sonnet 75 immediately complicates the radiant naming performed by this lucky lover, with the introduction of the beloved whose words challenge the lover's sense of bounty, and a masculine ocean challenging as simple and naive his tracing of the name "Elizabeth" in the sand:

> One day I wrote her name upon the strand,
>   but came the waves and washed it a way:
>   agayne I wrote it with a second hand,
>   but came the tyde, and made my paynes his pray.
> Vayne man, sayd she, that doest in vaine assay,
>   a mortall thing so to immortalize.
>
>   .   .   .   .
>
> Not so, (quod I) . . .
>
>   .   .   .   .
>
>   my verse your vertues rare shall eternize,
>   and in the hevens wryte your glorious name.

The poem will end with brave words in the face of devouring Time, but it is notable that the woman herself utters the most powerful challenge to the lover whose blissful receptivity in the previous sonnet seems to lead to the happy, heedless creativity of writing names in sand. She does this not by refusing the lover's Petrarchan demands as she had earlier, but by speaking the barest truth about creatureliness. The poet is provoked to high claims for poetry, but subsequent poems form adult adumbrations of the lover as anxious male child, separated from the intensely desired maternal body.

Although Spenser's poet-lover has expressed devotion for his mother, and drawn eloquent parallels between mother, beloved, and queen, he claims neither an imaginative identification with nor a generative distinctness from the mother, as does the woman in the Song of Songs. Both mother and beloved remain desired others, associated with the inaccessible female body which is identified by synecdochic focus on the breast. The masculine gender of the speaker becomes relevant in the sonnets, representing a nostalgic craving for the security that could be provided by a maternal breast, a craving now extended by the adult lover to the beloved woman. The Song of Songs and its mother/child motifs continue to work in the sequence, but increasingly that work is to carry an unhappy infantilization of the speaker's feelings. The contrast between the woman lover of the Song and the man lover of the sonnets emerges forcefully. The speaker moves from amorous happiness of a kind worthy of the Song of Songs to a tension in which he projects onto the beloved a regressive craving for a maternalized body. Sibship, so central to the Song, is conspicuously absent in these late sonnets. Instead, the speaker is the weak infant and the beloved as the maternal body promising "hevens blisse" (sonnet 72), in a hierarchy of weakness and strength that prepares the way for reversions to a bitter Petrarchism in the late sonnets and to the Anacreontics.

This nostalgic craving Spenser has enlisted, in a brilliant innovation, in the service of representing something hardly addressed in any other Renaissance sonnet sequence, the betrothal period. Carol Kaske has identified this betrothal stage in the *Amoretti* and its uniqueness among sonnet sequences. The 1595 wedding volume provides, she says, "an emotional progression of not two but three stages: not just courtship and marriage but courtship (sonnets 1–67), betrothal (extending from sonnet 68, the Easter sonnet, through the Anacreontics), and marriage."[15] In the betrothal stage, the lover can afford the hope, the sensuous promise, the erotic fantasies, and the creativity that emerge in anticipation of union. He can invest the intensity of wish with the trust of future fulfillment—a fusion made possible by the Song's maternal ground of the lovers' imaginative fulfillment—even when one of the lovers departs temporarily, exacerbating the poet-lover's desire. Nervous desire mounts in the last fifteen or so sonnets. In all of this Spenser purposefully transforms the Song lovers' complex choreography of movements toward and away from each other into the wandering of a child lost and bereft of its mother.

Both the promise and the strain of the betrothal stage are visible in sonnet 76, an unnerving cousin to the blazon sonnets:

Fayre bosome fraught with vertues richest tresure,
   The neast of love, the lodging of delight:
   the bowre of blisse, the paradice of pleasure,
   the sacred harbour of that hevenly spright.
How was I ravisht with your lovely sight,
   and my frayle thoughts too rashly led astray?
   Whiles diving deepe through amorous insight,
   on the sweet spoyle of beautie they did pray.
And twixt her paps like early fruit in May,
   whose harvest seemd to hasten now apace:

15. Carol Kaske, "Spenser's *Amoretti and Epithalamion* of 1595: Structure, Genre, and Numerology," *English Literary Renaissance* 8 (1978): 271–95, at 272–73.

they loosely did theyr wanton winges display,
   and there to rest themselues did boldly place.
Sweet thoughts I envy your so happy rest,
   which oft I wisht, yet never was so blest.

Alexander Dunlop, one editor of the *Amoretti*, remarks that this sonnet
and sonnet 77 comprise "the most sensual poems of the sequence, but
that sensuality is at the same time denied by the fact that the subject of
these sonnets is not the poet but, specifically, his *thoughts*."[16] If this is one
of the two most sensual poems, it is not evident that Spenser thinks this
a good or a simple thing, and we ought to be wary of those thoughts'
mysterious "diving deep" and predatory interest in "the sweet spoyle of
beautie." The thoughts of the speaker are now addressed as if infants
themselves, free to rest and display their "wanton winges" between the
lady's breasts. Like a Kleinian baby, the speaker splits off a part of himself—his desire, figured as thoughts themselves figured as putti with
access to the intimacy of the breast, and observed by the Spenserian
child exiled from that intimacy. This envy is an aggressive action, making a claim against both the maternalized woman and the winged
infant/sibs. The infantilizing of the split-off, personified thoughts in the
third stanza function as the speaker's hopeful illusion that the deep-div-
ing, preying thoughts in the second quatrain can be made benign; this is
poetic figure representing the speaker's weak attempt at self-deception.

This account still leaves the question of the sensuousness of the first
quatrain. What has this Canticle-inspired opulence to do with the
aggressions of the greater part of the poem? Say that potential space in
the happiest sonnets, like "Comming to kisse her lyps," constitutes not
the lady's body but an airy enclave of provision and exchange between
them, roughly analogous to the mother's house in the Song of Songs.
The first quatrain of "Fayre bosome fraught with vertues richest
tresure," using lexical items from the Song, gives itself up to the implicit
temptation of blazons to nominalize; in this case to catalogue is to
reduce the expansiveness of the terrain between the lovers to ever-
smaller holding spaces. Then the disquieting element of the sonnet is a
constriction of this space to the lady's body itself, now called upon by
the frustrated, betrothed lover to answer his desire in the way that the

16. Alexander Dunlop, in Spenser, *Yale Edition of the Shorter Poems*, ed. William Oram et
al. (New Haven: Yale University Press, 1989), 646. See also Donna Gibbs, *Spenser's
"Amoretti": A Critical Study* (Brookfield, Vt.: Scolar, 1990), 113–16, for a survey of commentary on this poem.

maternal body can be called upon by the needy infant. The verge between lovers has diminished in proportion to the increase of the poet-lover's expectations. When this terrain, which had been a site of creative agency and speech for both lovers, narrows to the lady's body, her creativity is drained of agency, as natural process, beautiful in itself, takes the place of her autonomous will. Thus the lover's thoughts rest "twixt her paps like early fruit in May, / whose harvest seemd to hasten now apace." It is this twist away from the sequence's nascent acknowledgment of the lady's agency, and the mapping of potential space not onto the verge between lovers but onto the lady's body, that gives rise to both the luxuriance and the unease of the sonnet. And unease wins out over confident lyricism by the time of sonnet 84, "Let not one sparke of filthy lustfull fyre," with its nervous prohibitions and denials.

Something similar occurs in sonnet 77, "Was it a dreame," kin to the blazon poems and a strange transformation of the man's praise songs about feeding in his garden in the biblical book. The oneiric feel of this sonnet and the impossibility of declaring it either a dream or not has always been remarked; Spenser fuses this episode with the epistemological hovering characteristic of dream vision:

> Was it a dreame, or did I see it playne,
>   a goodly table of pure yvory:
>   all spred with juncats, fit to entertayne
>   the greatest Prince with pompous roialty.
> Mongst which there in a silver dish did ly
>   twoo golden apples of unvalewd price:
>   far passing those which Hercules came by,
>   or those which Atalanta did entice:
> Exceeding sweet, yet voyd of sinfull vice,
>   That many sought yet none could ever taste,
>   sweet fruit of pleasure brought from paradice
>   by love himselfe and in his garden plaste.
> Her brest that table was, so richly spredd,
>   my thoughts the guests, which would thereon have fedd.

The laden table and the food it so firmly supports and proffers are indebted to the festal, social eating of adult lovers and guests in the Song, and the breasts upon which the lover wishes to feed as a guest to the nursling/mother bond in the Song. The "twoo golden apples" of the dream or vision have generally and rightly been taken to be all but direct representations of the lady's breasts. But both apples and breasts, alloforms in the poem's dream logic, have made many readers of the poem uneasy. Most often this is articulated as a disapproval of the sensuality of the lines. But I think rather that we have not thought precisely enough about their sensuality *in relation to* the Song of Songs. Thus we might make something of the sonnet's surprising recourse to the rhetoric of the man in the Song—a switch from the sonnet speaker's general use of the woman's verses. Israel Baroway cites Song 4:10–11, 13–16 as the chief passages behind Spenser's sonnet; these biblical verses comprise part of the man's praise song to and about the woman, and catalogue some of the foods and spices so prominent in the Song.[17] I would emphatically add another, spoken by the man in tones of expansive celebration: "I am come into my garden, my sister, my spouse: I gathered my myrrhe with my spice: I ate mine hony combe with mine hony, I dranke my wine with my milke: eate, O friends, drinke, and make you mery, O welbeloved" (5:1; Geneva). In the Song, the male lover is now grandly social, now tenderly intimate about eating and sexual appetite. Remarkably, in these passages he is entirely without anxiety about ingestion and incorporation, about the role of infantile gratification in adult sexual experience, about his access to what he desires and its sufficiency. His verses' weave of food, drink, spices, regality, and erotic celebration informs Spenser's first quatrain describing the splendor of the banquet table.

But the intertextuality of this sonnet is complicated by its classical, pagan allusions to tales of golden apples, and these swiftly deplete the poem of the strengths of the Song's male lover and his feasting. The shift to golden apples of pagan myth, together with the dream's uncertain epistemological status and the negative claim of the fruit's purity ("voyd of sinfull vice"), manifest the shifting undercurrents of anxiety marking the distance of this lover from his model in the Song of Songs. For instance, it seems likely that the "twoo golden apples" are an oneiric redaction of the twin animals in the Song, or a condensation of its animal twins with its apples, by a solitary speaker without the comfort of siblings. Certainly the Song's young animals are nearby, for in the next

17. Baroway, "Imagery of Spenser," 41–42. In the Geneva translation, edited in facsimile by Lloyd E. Berry (Madison: University of Wisconsin Press, 1969), they include these: "My sister, my spouse, how faire is thy love? how muche better is thy love then wine? & the savour of thine ointments then all spices? // Thy lippes, my spouse, droppe as honie combes: honie & milke are under thy tongue . . . Thy plantes are as an orcharde of pomegranates with sweete frutes, as camphire, spikenarde, // Even spikenarde, & safrran, calamus, & cynamom with all the trees of incense, myrrhe & alloes, with all the chief spices."

sonnet he compares himself to "a young fawne that late hath lost the hynd," and the Geneva translation of the relevant verses make more of twinning than the translation of the Masoretic text cited in my last chapter. Thus Geneva has "Thy two breastes are as two yoong roes that are twinnes" (4:5 and 7:3). One might say that the Song provides Spenser's sonnet with its generosity, and classical myth with its temptation to infantile neediness and anxious envy. Most optimistically, its apprehension of tablature spreading outward can be taken as a brave attempt by a tantalized lover to recover an expanded space of bounty and creativity. One of my aims in the previous chapter was to conserve the literalness of the Song's apple tree, because it is significant for the complex sense of ground in the biblical book. But Spenser's apples show the lover discovering betrothal to be a condition of tantalization; hence all the wishes and uncertainties in the sonnet. The male lover of the Song repeatedly imagines the pleasure of entering his garden— climbing the palm tree, enjoying his lover's breasts "like clusters of the vine" (7:8); Spenser's speaker clearly aspires to this generosity of love. Instead, the elusiveness of satisfaction and the tainted eros of the golden apples coalesce in the final couplet, and the persistence of the lover's focus on the lady's breasts defeats the poem's nobler effort to move away from nostalgic yearning for the provident maternal body.

A collapse into this infantilism and its requirements of the maternal body is complete in the next sonnet (78):

> Lackyng my love I go from place to place,
>   lyke a young fawne that late hath lost the hynd:
>   and seeke each where, where last I sawe her face,
>   whose ymage yet I carry fresh in mynd.
> I seeke the fields with her late footing synd,
>   I seeke her bowre with her late presence deckt,
>   yet nor in field nor bowre I her can fynd:
>   yet field and bowre are full of her aspect,
> But when myne eyes I thereunto direct,
>   they ydly back returne to me agayne,
>   and when I hope to see theyr trew object,
>   I fynd my selfe but fed with fancies vayne.
> Ceasse then myne eyes, to seeke her selfe to see,
>   and let my thoughts behold her selfe in mee.

The lone fawn and the absent hind merge the Song of Song's celebration of animal young, its evocations of maternity, and the bride's desolate searching for her lover, by means of a domestication and generalization (field and bower) of the Song's memorable locations, especially those landscapes where wild animals wander, leap, and even approach human habitations, and by means of the increase of pathos in the sonnet's bereft, dependent fawn. We have seen throughout the Song and the *Amoretti* choreographies of movement toward and away from, and also of spatial expansion and contraction. To trace how the lover gives himself to these motions and spaces is to follow the vicissitudes of his attempts to rectify desire through engagement with textual traditions. The fawn and the lover in this sonnet venture abroad in search of the desired woman, but she carries the double burden of being both beloved and mother substitute; in the Song, as we have seen, it is the woman's imagining of good-enough mothering that allows her and her lover to seek each other not as surrogate parents but as partners. The lonely lover of "Lackyng my love" wanders, but finds that the beloved's absence precludes a desirable ease of dwelling, as the landscapes repel his gaze (lines 8–12). He is driven into the compass of his own mind, there to envision the beloved (13–14) in an unnerving hall of mirrors. One might see this move as a fragment of a *fort/da* game, with the lover feeling himself to be an abandoned child and representing to himself the lost maternal object; only instead of the energy and anger in Freud's grandson, Spenser's lover performs a gesture of retraction, much unlike the delighted movements into enlarged psychic and literal spaces of the Song and the earlier sonnets. The lonely child hungers for its mother, and withdraws into thought; the poet-lover loses heart for the bold exercise of creative faculties in the space delineated by two lovers. This sonnet is the clearest marker of the second stage in Spenser's Canticle sonnets, a stage in which love retreats into craving for an imagined plenitude of maternal presence.[18]

If this arc of sonnets coheres in light of Klein, Winnicott, and Irigaray as suggested here, then we can also make sense of the great anomaly in the 1595 wedding volume, the four Anacreontic epigrams lodged between the *Amoretti* and the *Epithalamion*. These little poems have repelled, embarrassed, or perplexed virtually all serious readers of the

18. On the other hand, the pleasures of thought in its own right and not merely as impoverished recompense for loss should not be underestimated. See Elizabeth Harris Sagaser, "Shakespeare's Sweet Leaves: Mourning, Pleasure, and the Triumph of Thought in the Renaissance Love Lyric," *English Literary History* 61, 1 (1994): 1–26. See also chapter 7 for the idea of fantasied destruction as a form of thought.

past century.[19] Dominated as they are by lascivious trifling and teasing between Venus and the infant Cupid, they nevertheless constitute a crucial link in Spenser's figurative story about the temporality of nuptial love. The betrothal stage in the sonnets includes a physical separation between the lovers, with renewed Petrarchan bitterness and torment for the lover (sonnets 83–89). The Anacreontics follow immediately as a second recourse to fantasies of satiety and merger at a bodily site both maternal and erotic. But at this late, difficult stage of the lovers' relationship, a temporary suspension between erotic promise and fulfillment, the maternal dynamics are governed by amorous and literary conventions more explicitly genital and riskily perverse than those springing either from Petrarchism or from the Song of Songs.

We have already seen the lover's envious splitting off and projection of his thoughts as winged infants free to nestle between the lady's breasts (sonnet 76). These putti occupy the place of envied siblings in a version of sibling rivalry, but they are summoned in order to focus an envy that seems to preexist them, more like a Kleinian envy of the mother as container of good things. In the Anacreontics, the lover shifts his envy from his own desirous thoughts to a new rival, the infant Cupid, "bath'd in Venus blis" (line 72). Venus herself is affectionately accessible and even lascivious toward her son. There is a good deal of amorous teasing between the two of them; the infant boy's neediness dominates this relationship; the paradisal site of the mother's body is localized not at the nurturant breast but at the lap, a site suggesting a wish to return to a fantasied merger with the mother, and a corollary negation of the rival son.[20] All of these changes comprise a bold shift on Spenser's part. His suggestion of perversity in the erotic pleasure that Venus and Cupid share marks a retreat into fantasy by the strained lover, from the grave playfulness of the achieved Canticle sonnets.

There is one more blazon in Spenser's wedding book, *Epithalamion* 148–84. In these lines the poet creates the largest and riskiest blazon of all, as if to demonstrate the restoration of the shaken, bereft lover of the late sonnets and the Anacreontics. A good part of the achievement of

19. These responses are surveyed in Robert Miola, "Spenser's Anacreontics: A Mythological Metaphor," *Studies in Philology* 77 (1980): 50–66; see also James Hutton, "Cupid and the Bee," *PMLA* 56 (1941): 1036–58.

20. On the iconography of the erotic/maternal lap, see Mary Nyquist, "Textual Overlapping and Dalilah's Harlot-Lap," in *Literary Theory/Renaissance Texts*, ed. Patricia Parker and David Quint (Baltimore: Johns Hopkins University Press, 1986), 341–72.

these two stanzas lies in their transvaluation of "Ye tradefull Merchants," that chilly and resentful sonnet, by means of the Song of Songs. The world of commerce, fleetingly glimpsed in the Song of Songs then remorselessly applied in "Ye tradefull Merchants," gives way to the related but more supple, more variously useful imagery of luxury goods. The bitter invitation of sonnet 15 to abstract merchants is now transformed into a rhetorical question to specific, local "merchants daughters" (*Epith.* 76) launching the groom's praise song. The catalogue of similes is no longer proffered as cheap ware but as the poised culmination of many Spenserian passages, in the *Amoretti* and elsewhere, dealing with issues of sexual vision, display, female agency.

> Her goodly eyes lyke Saphyres shining bright,
> Her forehead yvory white,
> Her cheekes lyke apples which the sun hath rudded,
> Her lips lyke cherryes charming men to byte,
> Her brest like to a bowle of creame uncrudded,
> Her paps lyke lyllies budded,
> Her snowie necke lyke to a marble towre,
> And all her body like a pallace fayre,
> Ascending uppe with many a stately stayre,
> To honors seat and chastities sweet bowre.
>
> (*Epith.* 171–80)

This catalogue has earned its transformation of the Song of Songs' blazons through the lover's vicissitudes in love and in poetic making. The biblical book's lavish, unthreatened way with gems and precious stones moves easily into Spenser's stanza; as in the Song, the lapidary images are warmed and balanced by organic and domestic ones. There is a striking difference in function between "Her paps lyke lyllies budded" (*Epith.* 176) and the phrase "her paps like early fruit in May" from sonnet 76; the latter collapses the necessary distinction between a garden and the beloved's body that had been so delicately sustained in "Comming to kisse her lyps." Even the catalogue's surprising shift upward— first eyes and brow to cheeks, mouth, breasts, neck, then unexpectedly "all her body like a pallace fayre, / Ascending uppe with many a stately stayre" (*Epith.* 178–79)—calls home Spenser's network of solid surfaces that lift up. Here Spenser taps the Song of Song's towers, pavilions, pillars, pedestals, and thrones of marble, ivory, cedar, and gold. Some of these occur in the similes of the praise songs (cited here from the Geneva Bible), for example, 7:4, "Thy necke is like a towre of yvorie"; others are descriptions of Solomon's famous building program: "King Salomon made himselfe a palace of the trees of Lebanon. // Hee made the pillars thereof of silver, and the pavement thereof of gold, the hangings thereof of purple, whose middes was paved with the love of the daughters of Ierusalem" (3:9–10). It is apt that such lavish foundation building is followed immediately by the culminating coronation of Solomon on his wedding day (3:11), and that this crowning involves a gesture upward from the king's floors and pillars to his head—just as Spenser's catalogue makes a sedately regal ascent to "honors seat" (*Epith.* 180).

This movement implies Spenser's willingness to let stand the fears and anxieties of both bride and groom in the wedding poem, to be part of the marriage. The blazon form's strong generic impulsion down the body creates a generative tension with the poem's unexpected upward movement; imminent sexual activity and the bride's power to elicit desire are neither refused nor simply welcomed, but acknowledged in this blazon. They are also acknowledged in the image of "Medusaes mazeful hed" (*Epith.* 190), in the recurrence of infant Cupids (357–63), in the bride's abashedness and silence throughout.[21]

To take, for example, the "little loves" reintroduced as the marriage approaches its consummation:

> The whiles an hundred little winged loves,
> Like divers fethered doves,
> Shall fly and flutter round about your bed,
> And in the secret darke, that none reproves,
> Their prety stealthes shal worke, and snares shal spread
> To filch away sweet snatches of delight,
> Conceald through covert night.
> Ye sonnes of Venus, play your sports at will,
> For greedy pleasure, careless of your toyes,
> Thinks more upon her paradise of joyes,
> Then what ye do, albe it good or ill.
>
> (*Epith.* 357–67)

In light of what I have argued in this chapter, it is easy enough to take these loves as figuring a split-off representation of the anxious groom's

---

21. I have discussed this aspect of the *Epithalamion* in *Gazing on Secret Sights: Spenser, Classical Imitation, and the Decorums of Vision* (Ithaca, N.Y.: Cornell University Press, 1990), 186–89.

desire, now that he will soon have access to the female body. The prolif-
eration and playfulness of these sons of Venus might conceivably be
read as a benign figuration of the wedding night's long intercourse.[22]
But given their implications earlier in the volume, and their proximity in
Epithalamion to other unstable signifiers of sexuality, these sons of Venus
seem to bear into the wedding poem a darker apprehension of sexuality.
They cover for, or serve as a defense against, the aggression that forms
an inevitable part of the groom's desire; they are displaced from the
place of intimacy with the woman by the groom-as-victorious-rival.
Most important, they are deployed in a breaking down of an earlier
defense against full acknowledgment of the *bride's* sexual desire. The
speaker had ventured near female desire, then swerved away from it,
three stanzas earlier:

> Behold how goodly my faire love does ly
> In proud humility,
> Like unto Maia, when as Jove her tooke,
> In Tempe, lying on the flowry gras,
> Twixt sleepe and wake, after she weary was
> With bathing in the Acidalian brooke.

(*Epith.* 305–10)

This complex allusion seems to delineate female agency and desire only
to smudge them or disavow them. In the later lines dismissing the sons
of Cupid, the lover's desire can relinquish its hold on envy and hence on
figurative siblings; the winged loves are demoted from sibling rivals to
irrelevant triflers; man and woman are embarked on real intimacies the
articulation of which owes a great deal to the Song of Songs, with room
enough and nourishment enough for the active desires of both: "For
greedy pleasure, careless of your toyes, / Thinks . . . upon her paradise
of joyes."

In many instances throughout the wedding poem, the move from biblical to classical allusion registers the anxiety of the man's desiring and
needing to depend upon a woman, and the woman's ambivalence and
inwardness. For Spenser to have made these difficulties a part of the

---

22. Thus Joseph Loewenstein, in correspondence, suggests that the little loves of the *Epithalamion* might be "a jollily decorous rendering of sheer dazzle." This is terrifically attrac-
tive, but would require a rather different argument from the one I make here.

published poem was bold and risky. But it is by virtue of the formal tension created between the biblical and the classical that his central blazon stanzas in the *Epithalamion* demonstrate the many levels of achievement in his negotiations with the Song of Songs and with maternal structures in adult sexuality.

PART THREE

Gratitude, Envy, Song

5

From Aggression to Gratitude: Air and Song in the *Parlement of Foules*

The number of successive saltations the nimble thought can make . . . [t]he habit . . . of not pausing but going on, is a sort of importation or domestication of the Divine effort in a man.

—Ralph Waldo Emerson

Chaucer among all early poets in English seems to love salience in Emerson's sense: going on, wandering, venturing forth, sallying out, taking leaps, crossing unanticipated thresholds—as in the *Parlement of Foules*, where his saltations surprisingly lead him to Dame Nature and to song.[1] In her region he engages with forms of cultural nostalgia for the shelter provided by maternal sound, insofar as the mother's singing, crooning, encompassing the child with a volume of air shaped by her voice constitute long-lived and haunting topoi. Psychoanalytic theory makes much of maternal voice. Recent theorists of song, especially of opera and its audiences, find it indispensable. But how can we have the textured richness of interior life borne on that voice, while also paying the debt to the mother, saluting her distinctness and difference from us?

1. Emerson's notions of saliency and sallying are articulated in many places in his works; the epigraph comes from "Poetry and Imagination," in *Complete Works of Ralph Waldo Emerson*, 8 vols. (Boston: Houghton Mifflin, 1903), 8:1–75, at 72.

In this third part of the book I turn to Chaucer's *Parlement of Foules* and Shakespeare's *Love's Labor's Lost*, along with their related topoi of bird-song, maternal goddess Nature, voice, mother tongue, and biblical garden of creatures. I argue that the works' movements from aggressive plot to lyric and their male protagonists' oblique, stepwise approach to the maternal together draw us into an ethical stance of welcoming our natality, the mother's otherness, *and* the pleasures of maternal sound. Topoi that seem conventional enough in subscribing to cultural fantasies of the maternal voice and nostalgia for the plenitude it offers also create narrative and lyrical spaces for alternatives to such nostalgia. They mark and celebrate (not lack or loss but) a formally distinct space between singers and speakers, between mothers and progeny.

Both Chaucer's narrative poem and Shakespeare's play link feminine voice and song to social aggression—boisterous and comic in the discussion of the birds in the narrative poem, punitive and edgy in the outbursts of ridicule and humiliation near the end of the play. Readers also suggest that Shakespeare might have written his play with the *Parlement* in mind, chiefly because of the parallel decisions of the female characters to defer a decision about marriage for a year in spite of (or because of) the insistent hopes of their wooers, and also because each work nears its end with memorable and charming seasonal songs. I take the songs near the end of each work, so different in tone from what immediately precedes them, as surprises of plot, more relevant, more achieved, and more interesting in their relation to aggression than they are often taken to be. It is easy to be charmed quite away from the specific ways that the songs emerge from and resolve urgencies of plot. How is it that songs of such simple and happy elements—Chaucer's praise of Dame Nature in "Now welcome, somer, with thy sonne softe" and Shakespeare's "When daisies pied and violets blue"—emerge from complex and erudite plot sequences? How do they help their writers and singers negotiate the larger works' concerns with creatural exposures? How is their simplicity accomplished rather than banal? How does each work's representations and figures of maternity lift aloft the changes of voice that become song? To consider these questions of genre, form, and feeling, I call on Klein's and Winnicott's work on transitional objects, gratitude, envy, and aggression, and Irigaray's on the vigor necessary to acknowledge our lives in the element of air. But I also use the airs and other movements of Chaucer's and Shakespeare's works to supplement Klein and Winnicott with ways of speaking about poetic language: naming in catalogue, onomatopoeia, topoi, vernacularity, sequence (for instance, aggressive squabbles succeeded by song). Klein and Winnicott will have little force if readers do not first feel that questions of form and feeling *are* aroused by the relations of song to story in these works, for it is these questions that lead to matters of mothers, voice, and infancy. In each work there is an implicitly plotted drive from narrative to the release of what each work gradually valorizes as a preferred kind of lyric. Within the evident plots about courtly eros, both works turn aside from the frustrations of courtly-Petrarchan amorous relations and discover the liberation of a cosmic, creative eros derived from hexaemeral and ency- clopedic traditions. This liberation takes the form of lyric naming and praise of creatures and seasons, at or near the end of each work.

Sallying Forth: The Peripatetic Dreamer

Chaucer's dream vision, spoken entirely in the first person, represents Chaucer the protagonist as an avid reader of books, seeking in them some answer to some desire that he knows is still inchoate. He tends to turn to books that seem to offer a wisdom that emerges in ancient writ- ers' commerce with one another, chiefly Cicero's "Dream of Scipio" (the sole part of Cicero's *De re publica* known to the Middle Ages, a conclud- ing dream vision which is itself an imitation of the vision of Er in Plato's *Republic*) and Macrobius's long commentary on the "Dream" (ca. 400 A.D.). In the former, Cicero tells of the dream vision of Scipio Africanus the Younger—vouchsafed to him during a visit to King Massinissa of Numidia, friend and admirer of Scipio's grandfather—in which he is visited by that same adoptive grandfather Scipio Africanus the Elder, and the two Scipios embark on a philosophical dialogue. In the latter, Macrobius uses the dream vision to launch a massive, encyclopedic sur- vey of mankind's knowledge of the way things are, through the disci- plines of astronomy, arithmetic, music, geography, and so on.[2] This is the philosophical-cum-familial romance of which Chaucer's protagonist dreams in the first part of his own dream vision, and the passion of the bibliophile for the intoxicating regress into antiquity—or back to the earliest founts of knowledge—is familiar to us as well. The first big structural surprise in the *Parlement*—to the dreamer as well as to the

---

2. See William Harris Stahl's introduction to and translation of *Commentary on the Dream of Scipio by Macrobius* (New York: Columbia University Press, 1952, 1990).

reader—is that his dream carries him elsewhere: into an eroticized, burgeoning garden clearly embedded in traditions not of classical, philosophical poetry but of love lyric, narrative topoi like pleasure gardens, and luxuriantly feminine mythic deities like Venus and Dame Nature. His final experience is to witness the mating of all the birds on Saint Valentine's Day, a ritual that includes three aristocratic birds of prey making speeches to win a female (formel) eagle as mate, the other birds' spirited debate on the general question of sexual choice, and their concluding hymn to the saint and the coming summer.

As I will suggest, the terrain on which the two realms—Graeco-Roman philosophical and vernacular erotic—can meet is the garden of creatures, a topos which joins the discursive world of classical learning, cosmology, and origins ("the way things are," as many Graeco-Roman philosophical poets put it), and the discursive world of Eden, with its commentaries on the seven days of Creation or hexaemera, its legacy to erotic narrative traditions like those of the vastly influential *Roman de la Rose*. Graeco-Roman and Judaeo-Christian speculative writing on the origins of the created world intertwine very early, and fuel a vast array of biblical commentary, scientific and natural-history encyclopedias, philosophical treatises and dialogues, and allegories of creation. So Chaucer's charming and perfect *Parlement* is remarkable not least for its invisible powers of exclusion, the cunning with which it draws on vast and intricate traditions to create a narrative line of such simplicity, cleanness, and mobility.

Here is my argument about the *Parlement of Foules*. Chaucer brings together these two grand traditions about creation: the hexaemeral and the neoplatonic-cosmological. The narrator's dream of Scipio Africanus, Venus's Temple, Nature, and the birds unfolds a plot of the dreamer's search for release into lyric utterance, but it is only the birds' roundel at the dream's end that clarifies the poem and the dreamer's walk *as* such a quest. The itinerary of the dream has three steps. To the protagonist these seem random, as in dream experience, but they are actually steps toward his becoming the poet who later writes the poem.[3] For with each step the dreamer moves into a different literary region. First is the Lati-

---

3. See A. C. Spearing, *Medieval Dream-Poetry* (Cambridge: Cambridge University Press, 1976), 33, 39–40, and passim, for the suggestion that this temporal structure of character is a legacy of the *Roman de la Rose* to later dream poems. Other temporal divisions of the "I" in dream visions are charted in E. B. Vitz, "The *I* of the *Roman de la Rose*," *Genre* 6 (1973): 49–75.

Another way to describe the complex temporality of the *Parlement* is to mark its deploy-

nate, philosophical realm where he meets Africanus and receives aus-
tere ethical direction. Next is the garden and temple devoted to Cupid
and Venus, a region of late-medieval, vernacular, courtly love poetry
represented in eerily silent vignettes. He leaves the temple to find himself within the third region, an expansive, vociferous realm of natural
eros, presided over by Dame Nature and her divine creativity, where he
sees a "daughter" of Nature, the formel or female eagle, held on
Nature's wrist as they listen to three aristocratic suitors and the birds'
raucous debate on marriage. The celebration of creatures occurs in part
through a fusion of vernacular love poetry with Graeco-Roman philosophical and scientific writing, the two traditions that the dreamer has
already encountered.[4] The roundel sung by the birds in homage to
Dame Nature is the poet-dreamer's unexpected movement into the lift
and loft of song, as well as a gift of temporal movement into an incalcu-

---

ment of related genres. Like the quest romance, with which it has many features in common, the dream vision seems to carry a dreamer into a risky, unpredictable future, the
meaning of which can only be understood by following its unfolding. In dream vision, it is
a good to be capable of awaiting surprise, and a good to be reluctant to force meaning from
events and appearances. (Thoreau would elevate the willingness to venture into life this
way into the virtue of living "open in front." One could say that Winnicott would align
himself with this sense of dream vision as a model for his hope of human freedom.) But
Chaucer's dream vision, which turns out to have a strong teleological drive perceptible
only from a vantage point after—or above—the experience of the dream, oddly shares with
continental novellas of the thirteenth and fourteenth centuries (among them those of Boccaccio, whose work Chaucer knew well) a sense of closure and plottedness providing an
intense readerly satisfaction in the act of *retrospection*. Lorna Hutson beautifully discusses
the "plots" of such novellas in humanist Renaissance culture by contrasting the knight-
errant of medieval romance (living "open in front") with the discourse of military history,
which organizes narrative so as to enable planned, prudential heroic action: "military history positions the reader as traveling captain rather than as *chevalier errans*; that is, it offers
him a vantage point from which to survey the entire narrative as a terrain to be advanta-
geously ordered as *potential for emplotment*" (92); again, "military history, the history of
stratagems appropriate to the augmentation of states, offers a figurative language for the
intellectual and emotional experience of enterprise, of prudential activity" (97). Lorna Hutson, "Fortunate Travelers: Reading for the Plot in Sixteenth-Century England," *Representations* 41 (Winter 1993): 83–103. Yet Chaucer, while relishing the temporal movements of
simultaneously reading for the quest and writing for the plot, declines the prudential kind
of closure prized by the novellas and military histories that Hutson studies. Instead, as we
will see by the end of this chapter, Chaucer prizes the dreamer who declines strong agency
and strong individualism, who simply rejoices to be absorbed into song, then awakens to
welcome renewed absorption into old books.

4. For an account of Chaucer's commitment to *translatio* as invention, see Rita Copeland,
*Rhetoric, Hermeneutics, and Translation in the Middle Ages: Academic Traditions and Vernacular
Texts* (Cambridge: Cambridge University Press, 1991), 179–202.

lable future. Furthermore, the song retrospectively releases meanings and narrative momentum in the poem's beginning and middle. As the fable unfurls into its immediate narrative future, it also gathers up and makes manifest its past—the events just laid out on the page, but also the literary past by which the dreamer and the dream came to be, and came to be for the reader. The plot of the dream is haunting because, while represented as it was presumably experienced, full of unexpected turns and surprises, it is also familiar. Much of it is familiar in the sense that Chaucer deploys the venerable topoi found in dream visions, romance, philosophical and mythopoeic poetry: Dame Nature, Venus and her devoted pairs of lovers, catalogues of trees, birdsong.

But the dream is more uncannily familiar because its perambulatory progress through literary histories awakens in the dreamer, and thence in the reader, partial recognitions of early, prelinguistic phenomena, namely, transformative fusions with or absorptions into experience. The capacity for these absorptions into experience is anterior to a subject's self-awareness; they are known but not thought, processes that constitute "the unthought known," in Christopher Bollas's helpful phrase.[5] Bollas describes the youngest infant's experience of the mother "as a process linked to the infant's being and the alteration of his being," rather than as a discrete entity; the mother is not a reified object but "a transformational object." Many events of provisioning, protecting, and interacting with the infant, laid down in complex braids over time, constitute Winnicott's state of "holding," within which occurs the unique, idiomatic dialectic of nature and nurture that structures psychic, creative, and linguistic resources. Subjects may thus do more than nostalgically seek substitutes for an absent mother, or a fantasy of preverbal merger with the mother; they may also seek external objects with their own integrity when, as Bollas says, "the object is sought for its function as a signifier of transformation. Thus, in adult life, the quest is not [invariably] to possess the object; rather the object [may be] pursued in order to surrender to it as a medium that alters the self."[6] Nostalgia to possess the fantasied object would freeze not only the object (mother) but also the self's capacity to use or encounter the mother otherwise and be thus transformed. In Donna Bassin's formulation, "the dynamics of

---

5. Christopher Bollas, *The Shadow of the Object: Psychoanalysis of the Unthought Known* (New York: Columbia University Press, 1987), 60 and passim.

6. Bollas, *Shadow*, 14. On holding, see D. W. Winnicott, "The Theory of the Parent-Infant Relationship" (1960), in *The Maturational Processes and the Facilitating Environment: Studies in the Theory of Emotional Development* (New York: International Universities, 1965), 37–55.

nostalgia prevent a true identification with the transformational aspects of maternal practice."[7]

For all the *Parlement*'s Chaucerian meandering and peripatetic relaxation, it is driven by a vigorous underground current: the pressure of the narrator's inchoate desire for transformation by praise song: "For bothe I hadde thyng which that I nolde, / And ek I ne hadde that thyng that I wolde" (90–91).[8] The vagrancy of the plot is thus undergirded by a plotted urgency that we can follow, as in Freudian dream plots, in its cunning deferrals and arousals of excitement.[9] Implicit in the plot from the beginning, the aim of lyric bestows meanings imperceptible on first reading and releases dynamics represented as gradually discovered by the protagonist. At the start of the dream there is a good deal of distance between this figure and the Chaucer who so brilliantly plots a dream logic. By the end, the protagonist and the maker are all but indistin-

---

7. Donna Bassin, "Maternal Subjectivity in the Culture of Nostalgia: Mourning and Memory," in *Representations of Motherhood*, ed. Bassin, Margaret Honey, and Meryle Kaplan (New Haven: Yale University Press, 1994), 162–73, at 163. In this essay Bassin provides examples from clinical practice of clients whose nostalgic objects—collectibles—were used as defenses against mourning, and gradually became transformational objects in Bollas's sense.

8. Passages from Chaucer are cited by line number from *The Riverside Chaucer*, 3d ed., ed. Larry Benson et al. (Boston: Houghton Mifflin, 1987).

With these lines, both haunting and seemingly offhand, Chaucer crystallizes the problematic nature of desire and knowledge of one's own desire as the riddle that the poem's sally through multiple poetic forms makes possible of solution. The earliest stage of the protagonist's dream, recapitulating Macrobian dream theory, links the content of dreams with the occupations and waking concerns of the dreamer: dreams contain the objects of desire or aversion that common sense dictates as the respective investments of social roles or persons. Thus Chaucer's dreamer thinks it no wonder that he dreams of Scipio Africanus, of whom he has just been reading. In a stanza of implicit simile, he is like dreamers whose dreams and desires seem to be easily discernible: "The wery huntere, slepyinge in his bed, / To wode ayeyn his mynde goth anon; / The juge dremeth how his plees been sped; / The cartere dremeth how his cart is gon" (99–102) and so on. (Readers of Shakespeare will recognize the similarity to Mercutio's Queen Mab speech—Shakespeare's bravura turn on the Macrobian topos—in *Romeo and Juliet*.) Moreover, Africanus promises the dreamer a reward: "Thow has the so wel born / In lokynge of my olde bok totorn, / Of which Macrobye roughte nat a lyte, / That sumdel of thy labour wolde I quyte" (109–12). But the *Parlement* will demonstrate that the dreamer's objects of desire are more elusive, more historically mediated, and more a matter of form, voice, and movement than Macrobian dreamers could imagine.

9. See Peter Brooks, *Reading for the Plot: Design and Intention in Narrative* (Cambridge: Harvard University Press, 1984), 90–112; Marshall Grossman, *The Story of All Things: Writing the Self in English Renaissance Narrative Poetry* (Durham: Duke University Press, 1998), 34–55.

guishable; the seeking dreamer overtakes and fuses with the maker. This last point has become a commonplace about the internal dynamics of dream visions, but Klein and Winnicott allow an articulation of the precise sort of dreamer-maker that Chaucer becomes. To reach the ends of release into song and new self-organization will require all the adult poet's complex craft and adult mastery, but the fusions with and transformations of literary history are represented as made possible through structuring events of infancy. The poet of the *Parlement*, through a poetic craft that includes his own psychic identifications with poetic antecedents, bestows on the dreamer a transformative process of fusion with objects in the world he dreams. These are objects like the heavenly spheres, the birds, the trees, the lovers—which are also different families of objects from different genres and traditions. As he goes deeper into subjective experience he finds freedom in becoming less conspicuous as an agent in the plot, more important as witness and then utterer of the dream, more voice than agent. The narrator's functions as witness and voice need more examination, but first I trace his steps through the gendered literary-historical landscapes of his dream.

The first part of the dream directly rehearses characters, texts, social contexts of his evening reading, but unexpectedly moves him beyond these first, apparent objects of desire. This amounts to a display of the unexpected fruitlessness, for this poet-dreamer, of much of the masculine, Latin, literary culture to which he has provisionally attached himself. Macrobius's *Commentary on the Dream of Scipio* seems to link him securely in a chain of philosophical writers extending back from Chaucer's own time and place: the narrator on Macrobius, Macrobius on Cicero, Cicero on Plato. The chain carries a good deal of ardor, evinced in the form of the stanza describing the social context of Scipio's dream (36–42). Massinissa takes Scipio "in armes for joie"; there is talk and "blysse"; in the dream, says the protagonist, Scipio meets "Affrycan so deere." The first part of his dream thus seems to be a classic wish-fulfillment based on the desire that drove his evening reading: his wish to join a learned Graeco-Roman culture of aristocratic men linked through the centuries. Africanus's appearance to him and the offer to requite the narrator's reading labors constitute a promising start, drawing the Chaucerian narrator-poet into the charismatic company of Latinate philosophers and suggesting material for elevated philosophical poetry in the same vein as that of Macrobius: "thus seyde he: 'Thow hast the so wel born / In lokynge of myn olde bok totorn, / Of which Macrobye roughte nat a lyte, / That sumdel of thy labour wolde I quyte' " (109–12).

The Chaucerian narrator is clearly taken with this kind of reading and learning, for he devotes eight stanzas to laying out the book and its "sentence" (29–84). Retrospectively, these eight stanzas may be seen as one of those cunning delays that create frustration in the plots of dreams and dream-vision poems. The noble vision of a learned Latin heritage presents itself to the narrator as grounds for his own poetry, but it generates little more than a recapitulation of Macrobius's own writing. This is the wrong kind of *imitatio*; the poet-dreamer must discover how to reap his own corn from the "olde feldes" of books (22). So Africanus, an agent for the mysterious intrapsychic composer of the dream, startlingly sends the dreamer into non-Macrobian territory; he sends the dreamer from a masculine culture of philosophical, narrative poetry into a maternal realm of Venus, Nature, and vernacular love poetry within a heterosexual erotic culture. More prosaically, the dreamer must keep walking, feeling his way step by step over an articulated terrain, then over streams of water, on his way toward the element of air.

Once the dreamer is through the gates, his itinerary depends upon the poet's journey through several genres and several vernaculars. With the dreamer's anxious crossing of the threshold, Chaucer the maker shifts his allegiances from Latin prose to medieval courtly poetry in its many languages and genres, and he seems to shift the balance of his writing allegiances from philosophical exposition to lyric, as the dreamer steps cautiously toward the welter of affect that he observes in the garden. A further shift occurs when he leaves the temple of Venus and discovers Eros in the mobile realm of Nature, a movement that will allow him to fuse philosophic and singing impulses in a narrative that embraces song. This very diversity of genre, language, and form signals the dreamer's movement from his initial dream-plot of firm identification within a social group, a genre, and a gender, to his eventual creative absorption in transformative processes. A history of genres and disciplines provides Chaucer with his adult transformational objects as well as a theory of transformation in poetry: they are the poetic and philosophic works of his predecessors, carried across the centuries and across Western Europe into fourteenth-century England.

The famous catalogue of trees that fill the new terrestrial landscape of the dream (176–82) shows one way that Chaucer's literary/topographical steps carry him from the comfortable region of the ancient Graeco-Roman tradition into the unexpected squabble of the birds in the poem's concluding episode. The intricate tissue of borrowings in Chaucer's tree catalogue has been meticulously mapped by scholars; by the late fourteenth century it had gathered such density as to exemplify the very survival of poetry through time, and to moot or defy exclusive distinctions between philosophy and poetry, or between books and nature. Hence it both complicates and makes possible the protagonist's steps toward the rich generic fusions of the poem's late episode in Dame Nature's garden, where the masculine, Latin, philosophical tradition weds with courtly, vernacular, heterosexual, lyric forms. Within the plot outlined here—the dreamer's unwitting journey toward conditions that would make lyric composition possible—the topos is also a trope for the forward momentum and generativity of lyric poetry. It is in this way that we might easily interpret the tree catalogue's elaborations of its trees' use value: as a figure for the crafting of poetic artifacts.

But the tree catalogue works in a more complicated way. Ellen Martin argues persuasively that a tree catalogue often serves a temporizing function within the narrative. Its "crucial play . . . is to convey the mind, the reader's, writer's, or protagonist's mind, from a familiar situation into a strange one, by tricking it out of recognition of what's going on. Given the mind's resistance to sudden strangeness, this amounts to carrying it over from a safe and probably pleasant situation into a strange and dicey one."[10] If the narrator is temporizing in this tree catalogue, dilating on the trees' usefulness to humankind, he is also stalling on his passage into hexaemeral territory, where objects are less useful in a prosaic sense than usable in a Winnicottian sense: as discrete, bounded objects unbroken by human impingement and enjoying some space between themselves and their observers. The tree catalogue here is a kind of pause or hesitation in the dreamer's sally as he gradually discovers what he really desires: not just Macrobius and his cohort, not just high-poetic vernacular works, not just the sighs of courtly lovers, but all of this transformed into the communal song celebrating summer, warmth, Saint Valentine.[11]

The mediating literary term, the passage by which these two literary realms work together, is cosmological poetry. The *translatio* or transformation of cosmological poetry sought by Chaucer is most salient in the

---

10. Ellen Martin, "The Shady Trope of Spenser's Trees: Inside the Catalogues of the *Parliament of Fowls* and *Faerie Queene* I.i," paper presented at the Twenty-Eighth International Medieval Congress, May 1995.

11. On the tree catalogue topos, see Martin, "Shady Trope"; Ernst Curtius, *European Literature and the Latin Middle Ages*, trans. Willard Trask (New York: Harper and Row, 1963), 194–95; Piero Boitani, "Chaucer and Lists of Trees," *Reading Medieval Studies* 2 (1976): 28–44; Charles Muscatine's explanatory notes in *Riverside Chaucer*, 997.

poem's other catalogues. The most animated of these catalogues, the list of birds (330–64) and its narrative adaptation in the birds' debate, arise from an encyclopedic impulse to name the creatures of the world. Charles Muscatine has commented on Chaucer's "lay encyclopedism" and his favoring of "enumerative, processional, paratactic" forms, of which Chaucer's emphatic working of the *voie* as walking tour in the *Parlement* is an instance.[12]

Encyclopedic and cosmological catalogues, often structured hexaemerally on the six biblical days of creation, and descended as well from ancient scientific poetry, are frequent enough in medieval writing. Stephen Barney mentions Alan of Lille and Bernardus as creators of encyclopedic catalogues behind which stand "the philosophical sciences we gather under the name cosmology: the general sciences of creation, generation, procreation, emanation, which define God's relation to the universe."[13] Chaucer clearly values the form of enumerative catalogue, virtuosically summoning attention to their precision and namings. Now, as I said in chapters 1 and 2, writers do not passively find objects scat-

12. Charles Muscatine, *"The Canterbury Tales*: Style of the Man and Style of the Work," in *Chaucer and Chaucerians*, ed. Derek Brewer (University, Ala.: University of Alabama Press, 1966), 94–95.

13. Stephen Barney, "Chaucer's Lists," in *The Wisdom of Poetry: Essays in Early English Literature in Honor of Morton W. Bloomfield*, ed. Larry Benson and Siegfried Wenzel (Kalamazoo, Mich.: Medieval Institute Publications, 1982), 297–307. On lists generally, see Jack Goody, "What's in a List," in *The Domestication of the Savage Mind* (Cambridge: Cambridge University Press, 1977), 74–111. On the encyclopedists, see also Peter Hurst, "The Encyclopaedic Tradition, the Cosmological Epic, and the Validation of the Medieval Romance," *Comparative Criticism* 1 (1979): 53–71; E. C. Ronquist, "Patient and Impatient Encyclopaedism," in *Pre-Modern Encyclopaedic Texts: Proceedings of the Second COMERS Congress, Groningen, 1–4 July 1996*, ed. Peter Binkley (Leiden: Brill, 1997), 31–45. On hexaemeral arts see Theodore Silverstein, "The Fabulous Cosmogony of Bernardus Silvestris," *Modern Philology* 46 (1948): 92–116; Rosemond Tuve, *Seasons and Months: Studies in a Tradition of Middle English Poetry* (Paris: Librairie Universitaire, 1933); and especially Diane McColley, *A Gust for Paradise: Milton's Eden and the Visual Arts* (Urbana: University of Illinois Press, 1993). Throughout this chapter I am indebted to the great studies on twelfth-century narrative-allegorical-scientific-cosmological-encyclopedic works composed in medieval France: Peter Dronke, *Fabula: Explorations into the Uses of Myth in Medieval Platonism* (Leiden: E. J. Brill, 1974); Brian Stock, *Myth and Science in the Twelfth Century: A Study of Bernard Silvester* (Princeton: Princeton University Press, 1972); George Economou, *The Goddess Natura in Medieval Literature* (Cambridge: Harvard University Press, 1972); and Winthrop Wetherbee, *Platonism and Poetry in the Twelfth Century: The Literary Influence of the School of Chartres* (Princeton: Princeton University Press, 1972). Economou's book has a useful chapter on Chaucer's *Parlement*. More recently, see Jon Whitman's splendid study of the lineage of this literary culture in *Allegory: The Dynamics of an Ancient and Medieval Technique* (Cambridge: Harvard University Press, 1987).

tered around them; they work their way to various textual traditions and the nature of objects within them. Even encyclopedias, apparently omnivorous textual containers of the natural world, are not simply compilations of objects but indices of their writers' discovered pathways through the hexaemeral plenitude of creation. As William West says, drawing on Winnicott, "Like children's play, the encyclopedic tradition mediates between the self and the world once it has become apparent that the world will not of its own accord satisfy the desires of the self."[14] West's remark about play might be extended toward the encyclopedic *Parlement* by the observation that in each catalogue, even each naming in each catalogue, Chaucer presents his working of hexaemeral and encyclopedic traditions as poetic achievements, with the feeling tone of a jubilant discovery of the externality of creatures.

To develop this point about discovering the externality of objects, I turn briefly to the Kleinian art critic Adrian Stokes, who argues that the artwork summons its audience "so that they are enrolled by the formal procedures . . . and then absorbed to some extent into the subject-matter on show"—that is, first we are drawn in by tracing formal processes, and only then by engaging content. But his corollary is that "under the spell of this enveloping pull, the object's otherness, and its representation of otherness, are the more poignantly grasped."[15] Most often, for Stokes, this otherness emerges from the artist's relief that he has repaired and restored the beloved object's wholeness. For Chaucer it proves more useful to turn to Winnicott's alternative to Kleinian guilt as a motivator for world-making: that readers and writers alike discover, again and again, the independent existence of creatures, which are the particular objects of hexaemeral textual and pictorial traditions. Stokes describes "an enticing eloquence in regard to the *varied* attachment to objects" and the "outwardness" that "spells out enlargement"; formally, the namings of Chaucer's catalogues celebrate "the hardiness latent in design and pattern."[16] This is a kind of hardiness that Winnicott, like the pragmatic Emerson, would understand as a capacity of objects to stand up to hard use and to survive without depletion, as resource. Even in Chaucer's most charming moments, he is a fierce user of textual objects;

---

14. William West, "Spaces for Experiment: Theaters and Encyclopedias in Early Modern England" (Ph.D. diss., University of Michigan, 1997), p. 34.

15. Adrian Stokes, *The Invitation in Art* (New York: Chilmark, 1965), 18, 104–5.

16. Stokes, *Invitation* 29; *Reflections on the Nude*, cited in *The Image in Form: Selected Writings of Adrian Stokes*, ed. Richard Wollheim (New York: Harper and Row, 1972), 125; *Painting and the Inner World*, cited in *Image*, 99.

this Winnicottian vigor accounts in large part for the sense of mastery that Chaucer conveys in the way he coordinates his works among texts and traditions. It makes his catalogues sturdy in their own right as they stand up to our reading practices.

The *Parlement*'s sturdiness arises in large part from hexaemeral origins. The Winnicottian infant discovers a world of particular objects through the first object's fantasied destruction and survival, and this process continues lifelong. Visual artists engaged with the biblical creation account clearly enjoy working out the formal relationships of created objects to space; this is evident particularly in pictures unconcerned with technical matters of perspective. They also enjoy the Creator's apparent pleasure in delineated, bounded creatures, and in the lines of a shape that fills up an enclave of air. We can infer from such pictures, and from hexaemeral writers like Chaucer, an implicit pleasure in the initial void of Genesis: each picture, each catalogue begins by implying, enacting, laying claim to the formless void, in the form of a blank page (the baby says, "I destroy you!"), then delineates and discovers the creatural world that its artist has always known. ("Hullo, I destroyed you! You survived my destruction of you. Therefore you have value to me; therefore you are hardy, earnest of the reliability of the world in general.") As Stokes argues repeatedly, there is "a firm alliance between generality and the obdurate otherness of objects"; both of these are central to hexaemeral representations, and they first arise in the mobile space between mother and child.[17]

As exultant perpetuators of ambitious bird catalogues in the *De planctu naturae* and in the courtly-cum-philosophical *Roman de la Rose*, Chaucer's bird catalogues celebrate a joining of courtly and philosophical genres, shift the trope of birdsong from courtly to hexaemeral lyric, and bring to English poetry a further fusion of a line of ancient scientific poetry with a line of biblical namings of creatures. The bird catalogues manifest the adult poet's joyous mastery in the fusion of elements of his art, now transformed from the infant's relatively passive, nonverbal undergoing of fusion. Insofar as the utterance of celebratory naming in lists, whether in short poems or long, is among the "roots of lyric," and insofar as it takes a further step away from the poem's early, less vivified catalogues, we may take Chaucer's bird catalogue in the *Parlement* as another important movement toward the lyric of praise near the end, as well as a further clarification of his true desire for the achieved lexical

17. Harold Boris, *Envy* (Northvale, N.J.: Jason Aronson, 1994), 36.

simplicity of lyric hymn, with its beautiful and complex fusions of gen-res.[18]

Such a focus upon the transformational process (Bollas) or the formal procedures (Stokes) first structured in relationship to the mother helps to explain the poem's turn to Dame Nature as a sponsor of creative action. It is not chiefly the mother as reified female who underlies the realm of Nature in Chaucer's poem, but the mother as structurer of the self's experience of metamorphosis through interaction with environment. When Africanus shoves the dreamer into a maternal realm, this means in part the obvious movement from an oedipal realm of strong fathers to a preoedipal realm of nurturant mothers. But we can also use Chaucer's poem to address psychoanalysis and to suggest that the modern discourse emphasizing the ruptures and exclusions separating these two realms, and the positing of their sequentiality, are inadequate to account for the complex discursive and aesthetic exhilarations achievable through relations to the maternal other than repression or abjection. The protagonist's initial, stable genre expectation of philosophic discourse in narrative verse is *too* stable and exclusionary. The Latinate landscape may easily be read as the dreamer's wish to sustain the identifications and renunciations that come with resolution of the oedipal stage. The oedipal element of this dream is complex and contradictory because it is Africanus himself who abruptly delivers the dreamer into a realm of maternal, transformative process leading to vernacular song.

Dame Nature and the Maternal Sponsorship of Sound

The birds dwell in the precincts of the garden presided over by the goddess Nature, and it is to her—the powers of her voice and her role in the protagonist's interweaving of song and narrative—that I now turn. To say that Nature is maternal is to belabor the obvious only if we think of her as a fiction generated by nostalgic cultural fantasies of maternal tenderness. Chaucer eludes the tendentiousness with which "Mother

18. On naming in poetry, see Andrew Welsh, *The Roots of Lyric: Primitive Poetry and Modern Poetics* (Princeton: Princeton University Press, 1978), 243–51 and passim. The *Parlement*'s shift of birdsong from chiefly courtly to chiefly hexaemeral and encyclopedic traditions emerges more clearly by way of contrast with the very similar lyrics of the birds in the *Legend of Good Women*—entirely without the specific genre affiliations and object relations I sketch here—and with the courtly, subtle bird-singers of the *Romaunt de la Rose*. (Even in the *Romaunt*, though, Chaucer's impulse is to expand the catalogues of the original, often doubling their size and transforming the relation between narrative and lyric in the process.)

Nature" is so powerfully naturalized for us, in part because of the obliq-
uity of his protagonist's orientation to her. The goddess Natura is often
useful to poets precisely because her maternity is not her own biological
function; Chaucer's Nature rather presides, governs, calls to order, creates occasions for conversation. It is her sponsorship of a wide range of
verbal activities and exchanges that I pursue here.

Psychoanalytic and feminist theorists have for some time discussed
the mother's voice as the "sonorous envelope" surrounding and lapping
a newborn child.[19] Didier Anzieu speaks of a "sound envelope" encompassing the earliest infant, and thinks of the sound space as "the first
psychical space," "shaped like a cavern. . . . a hollow space like the
breast or the bucco-pharyngeal cavity, a sheltered, but not hermetically
sealed, space. . . . a volume within which there are rumblings, echoes,
and resonances." These resonances create what Anzieu describes in
another figure for sound as "a first enchantment (the illusion of a space
where no difference exists between the Self and the environment and
where the Self can draw strength from and the stimulation and calm of
the environment to which it is joined)."[20] "Enchantment" suggests a
legitimate place and work for nostalgia for the maternal: sound or chant
or song associated with the mother allows the emergent person to give
himself or herself to the transforming environment (as, say, Titania gives
herself to the maternal wood when her fairy attendants lullaby her to
sleep). Theoretical work on the enveloping maternal voice tends either
to idealize it as "plenitude and bliss" or to demonize it as "impotence
and entrapment," as Kaja Silverman notes.[21] I want to emphasize, as
Chaucer does, the mother's long-term, complex agency of voice in
mediating the child's initial, formative encounters with objects in the
world, teaching the young child language and, in traditional family
structures, nursery rhyme, poetry, story. The mother structures a potential space in relationship with the child, a harbor for the growing
exchanges of language, and also teaches more directly, as the one who

19. See, for example, Didier Anzieu, *The Skin Ego: A Psychoanalytic Approach to the Self*,
trans. Chris Turner (New Haven: Yale University Press, 1989), 157–73, and the widely influential ideas of Julia Kristeva; one précis occurs in "Place Names," in *Desire in Language: A
Semiotic Approach to Literature and Art*, trans. Thomas Gora, Alice Jardine, and Leon
Roudiez (New York: Columbia University Press, 1980), 282. Kaja Silverman gives an extensive account and critique of several such proposals in *The Acoustic Mirror: The Female Voice
in Psychoanalysis and Cinema* (Bloomington: Indiana University Press, 1988), 72–140; see
also Claire Kahane, "Questioning the Maternal Voice," *Genders* 3 (1988): 82–91.

20. Anzieu, *Skin Ego*, 157, 170, 171.

21. Silverman, *Acoustic Mirror*, 73.

names, who charts linguistic pathways into the world, who transmits the "mother tongue." It is thus, as Bollas says, that "the first human aesthetic passes into the idiom of formal aesthetics, as the mother's aesthetic of care passes through her tongue, from cooing, mirror-uttering, singing, story telling and wording into language."[22] Psychoanalytic theory here extends and participates in the trope that links acquisition of the vernacular with maternal figures.

Through Chaucer's poem, I want to suggest that the *child* makes the discovery of voice in the presence and presiding of the mother, and that the "sonorous envelope" is not limited to the infant-encompassing song of the mother, for several reasons. First, while no one in the wake of Kristeva underestimates what Anzieu calls "the infra-linguistic signification found in care and bodily play, the pre-linguistic signification of general listening to phonemes,"[23] the "envelope" surrounding and supporting the dependent neonate swiftly gives way to socially mediated linguistic forms with which the specific, historical mother sustains the child's increasing experience of the world. Second, related tropes in all the arts—the mother tongue or the singing woman who orders the world or the narrative motif of the music lesson—seem to suggest that the "sonorous envelope" experienced by the infant may come to be internalized as an affective spring of that sense that certain realms of experience, fiction, and dream are *for* us, soliciting and welcoming us, because they are realms belonging both to ourselves and to the other who first gave them to us.[24] Third, an expansion of the idea of a "sonorous envelope" into an environment that encourages giving voice—as in debate or in song—helps to describe and account for the noisy self-assertiveness and empowerment that Chaucer's fowls impart to the formel and to the narrator. In this third point I depart from Silverman, who follows out a Lacanian logic so far as to take the entry into language as necrotic: "because . . . it is through the voice that the subject normally accedes to language, and thereby sacrifices its life, it is associated as well with phenomenal loss, the birth of desire, and the aspiration toward discursive mastery."[25] But acquisition of language, as Nancy

22. Bollas, *Shadow of the Object*, 35.

23. Anzieu, *Skin Ego*, 161.

24. This point is adapted from André Green, who discusses dream as "an affective matrix in which the spectator feels himself not only solicited but welcomed, as if the spectacle were intended for him." See *The Tragic Effect: The Oedipus Complex in Tragedy*, trans. Alan Sheridan (Cambridge: Cambridge University Press, 1979), 18.

25. Silverman, *Acoustic Mirror*, 44.

Chodorow observes, is not intrinsically alienating, and the possibility that language acquisition may generate rather than require sacrifice of the subject's life allows proper weight to be given to the child's discovery of voice within the volumes, caverns, and vigor of her own body.[26]

Aggression, in the culturally specific shape of the fowls' clash of views on love and marriage, frees the formel eagle to speak in her own voice, for the first and only time in the poem, and to make the decision to defer marital choice. At first she has been tongue-tied and blushing with embarrassment: "She neyther answerde wel, ne seyde amys, / So sore abasht was she" (446–47). But after the debate she articulates in thirteen eloquent lines a choice that had not been among those initially offered, and she does it "with dredful vois" (638). This creativity and resolute independence arise less from any argument so far put forward about marriage than from her *witnessing* the birds' squabbles, from the heating up of the emotional atmosphere in the vociferous debate, and from the concomitant changes in poetic devices. The debate does not simply follow the aristocrats' speeches accidentally; the debate has functions and effects specifically for the witnessing female who has the temporary breathing space of shelter in the presence of a maternal Nature. In these stanzas, far from the serene celestial harmonies contemplated in the Macrobian part of the dream, the conflict gains poetic energy from an intensification of colloquialisms, from the hurling of insults, from the onomatopoeic words evoking the bodily sounds of the most raucous birds ("Kek kek! kokkow! quek quek!" 499). This aggression changes and refreshes the verse texture, opening it up to what Chaucer would have understood as the vernacular's lower levels of diction and sound. And the narrator changes as well, perhaps as a result of witnessing the formel's witnessing. He moves closer to becoming the poet who can fashion the lyric that is vernacular but not coarse, uttered by the birds in their vivid physicality but with a sound system that moves away from the raucous gutterals and stops of the debate to the liquids, sibilants, and labials of the roundel.[27]

26. Nancy Chodorow, *Feminism and Psychoanalytic Theory* (New Haven: Yale University Press, 1989), 189–90, with thanks to Janet Adelman for this point about language acquisition.

27. The debate and the song together may be Chaucer's transposition of Augustine's neoplatonically inflected allegory on the hexaemeron in the *Confessions*: "in verborum signis vocibusque subiectis auctoritati libri tui, tamquam sub firmamento volitantibus, interpretando, exponendo, disserendo, disputando, benedicendo atque invocando te, ore erumpentibus atque sonantibus signis, ut respondeat populus: amen" (in the expressions

In the *Parlement*, Dame Nature directs and encourages a riot of talk, and herself performs a number of striking speech acts. She tells the birds where to go and what to do, she speaks "in esy voys" and "with facound voys" (382, 521); she bids all to attend to her words and insists on the importance of speech (383–85); she presides over the formalized occasion of the parliament itself; she urges the formel eagle to speak out of the authority of her own desire; she declares the waiting period for the tercels and the mating period for the other birds. In all these expressive activities, Dame Nature's realm contrasts strikingly with the two other spheres of poetic experience in the poem. First is the Temple of Venus. Though full of stationed vignettes presented to the eye, it is eerily silent, its only sounds the sighs of lovers (246–48) and the prayers of the two young people to the enigmatically unresponsive Venus (278–79). This silence accentuates the dreamer's resurgence of language, its poetic capacities as a joyful noise, upon his emergence from the temple into the precincts of Dame Nature's garden. Many commentators have linked the birds' debate with a historical parliament, and some link the birds' linguistic and social patterns to the growth of merchant and other city classes, as opposed to the aristocratic birds. Thus the duck, the goose, the cuckoo reflect in their differing ways a high valuation of the utility of language and the importance of thriftily managing time, in contradistinction to the aristocratic birds' lordly refusal to "economize time."[28] For the formel, the debate registers a movement from linguistic "use value" in its economic senses to linguistic use in its Winnicottian sense: the verbal clashes of the fowl make possible the formel's sense that she possesses language or "has a voice" precisely because she can employ it actively, as a medium with which to relate to others and to differentiate herself from the positions already outlined for her by others. It gives her agency and removes her from the realm of commodity-objects

---

and sounds of words, subject to the authority of thy book [like the fowls as it were flying under the firmament]; namely, by interpreting, expounding, discoursing, disputing, praising and praying unto thee with the mouth, expressions breaking forth with a loud sounding, that the people may answer, Amen). Augustine, *Confessions* 13.23, trans. William Watts (1631), 2 vols. (Cambridge: Harvard University Press, 1961), 2:436–37.

28. This characterization of courtly love lyric's encoding of leisure as a form of cultural capital comes from Louise Fradenburg, *City, Marriage, Tournament: Arts of Rule in Late Medieval Scotland* (Madison: University of Wisconsin Press, 1991), 125; on the *Parlement*'s representation of class distinctions on the level of style, see Craig Bertolet, " 'My wit is sharp; I love no taryinge': Urban Poetry and the *Parlement of Foules*," *Studies in Philology* 93 (1996): 365–89.

in which the male aristocrats compete for her. The courtly speeches alone could hardly have given her this sense, but the courtly speeches in conjunction with the antagonisms and overtly embodied sounds of the other birds can.

Because the formel's decision to defer her choice departs from the buildup of an epithalamic plot expectation in the courtly, competitive speeches of the males, commentary often registers it as a surprising anti-climax if not an outright failure of plot. Yet it deserves to be thought out as a surprising *achievement* of plot, not least because her decision marks her with the female autonomy that we value so highly now, and marks her refusal of the imprisoning system of specular desire that her suitors represent. But it is an achievement of plot in a further sense. Precisely how does it succeed the fowls' debate, and what does it owe to the debate? One might follow Freud on group psychology and argue for the dominance of rivalries within overlapping economies of scarcity, and Klein's refocusing of sibling rivalry as infant envy of the world's abundance. But Chaucer's avian parliamentarians show little envy or resentment in these senses; if we read for the dominance of class and estate, the debate suggests something more like the debaters' sense of the aristocrats' relative obsolescence in urban economies that no longer create wealth by the feudal processes that allow aristocrats to slight the time and labor that support them. So the sense that there are alternative economies in finance, in love, and in the psyche is an immediate gift to the formel.

The presentation of alternative economies functions as a gift to the formel because the birds arise from a textual world that owes much to the hexaemeral account of Genesis. In this tradition, before the Fall, the psychic economy of scarcity manifest in infantile envy and sibling rivalry is precluded by the primordial biblical moment of abundance. The objects created in the six days give assurance of world, because they survive destruction like the maternal psychic object in Winnicott; they survive Adam and Eve's exile from the garden; indeed they exceed Eden itself and constitute world. (One reason for the myth's persistent strength is that it founds this assurance and abundance even as it also founds primordial loss.) Aggression in this psychic economy of plenty therefore manifests itself in a Winnicottian eagerness, in delineation of form and space, in implicit gratitude. To return to Emerson's articulation that I cited in chapter 1, "By virtue of this science [knowledge of objects in the world], the poet is the Namer, or Language-maker . . .

thereby rejoicing the intellect, which delights in detachment or boundary."[29] The birds in the *Parlement of Foules* speak with a strikingly *unen-
vious* aggression that derives from hexaemeral delineations of creatures
in a world of abundance. Their linguistic energies create room for the
formel's cautiously emergent sense of a psychic economy of abundance,
which for her means breathing room in relation to the maternal Dame
Nature, the space of parturition in which she can choose and speak; she
sets this against her suitors' assumptions of scarcity in love.

Dame Nature's garden contrasts also with the Latinate region of the
poem, filled with strong father/son bonds. The poetic movement
toward song, presided over and made possible by the inclusive Dame
Nature, supersedes or embraces Macrobius's world of Roman fathers.
Macrobius's big subjects—the knowledge of the heavens, the soul's
immortality, the ethical choices following upon awareness of the cosmos, the "commune profit," the notably inaudible music of the
spheres—are deferred in favor of a poetry and poetic subjects founded
at earlier levels of discovery of the world, subjects tied to the mother
tongue. One could say that the scientific features of this kind of ancient
work, generally focused on the celestial canopy, are preserved but
brought down to earth, wedded to the realm of mutable Nature. The
movement from Africanus to Dame Nature is a recovery of Bollas's
"unthought known," the subject's relations to the maternal that shaped
cognition and language itself. This movement earns the poem's deep
narrative structure of passage from narrative to lyric, from a desire to be
among fathers and sons and their literary genres to an anterior desire
for those transformations and fusions—fusions of genre by the poet,
fusions of poet and genre together—that lead to lyric hymn and access
to the plenitude of the natural world. Paradoxically, this is not a regression but an enlargement of adult apprehension and mastery by means
of a resituating of the protagonist's nature as child.

Invisible in Good-Enough Company: The Dreamer in Nature's Household

But who *is* the speaker of Chaucer's poem, and how is he a child? Or
rather, what is his status in relation to the events and dynamics of the

29. Ralph Waldo Emerson, "The Poet," in *Works*, 6 vols. (Philadelphia: John D. Morris,
1906), 5:261–91, at 275.

dream? Where is he during the fowls' debate? Why is it that neither Dame Nature nor any of the birds attend to him? Is he invisible to them? But then why is he not invisible or inconsequential to the Roman figures in the earlier part of the dream? Why does he passively find himself in proximity to such significant objects and events? Who is responsible for the shape of the dream? I said at the start of this chapter that the narrator undergoes transformations, including the movement from being an agent to being a witness. He also sallies from waking to sleep and back to waking, and finds himself absorbed in, then into, old books. The poem demonstrates that there is no unitary subject, or more accurately that the protagonist willingly entertains transformations and discontinuities of self experience. But how, exactly? In this section I first address these questions on the level of genre and then suggest by means of our psychoanalytic terms how Chaucer complicates his genres.

Anne Middleton speaks of *Piers Plowman* and the kind of subject who absorbs its vision by way of contrasting the poem with philosophical works in the Latin visionary tradition: "In this [Latin] mode, a display of universal harmony—of the stars, of natural generation, of ideal discourse—is offered to a subject in spiritual need of a restored inner equipoise. The receiver of this privileged display is conceived primarily as a receptive mind, not as a historical actor, and it is to his contemplative gaze, not to his worldly praxis, that these ministrations are addressed." But in *Piers Plowman* the visionary harmony is always crossed by the insistences of the individual Will: "Whatever the visionary scene, whatever the identity of the instructor or expositor, whatever the philosophic question that initiates the encounter, at some point the interaction becomes charged with opposition." "The splendid sight of the regularities of the created cosmos, offered by Latin didactic vision literature from Boethius' starry harmonies through Alanus' natural fecundity, become the background, the landscape in which the subject composes himself as a historical being. He is defined by this enterprise not as a contemplative man, but as *homo faber*."[30] Such a generative tension between visionary contemplation of order and obdurate autobiographical experience clearly undergirds Chaucer's *Parlement of Foules*. One might well take the narrator's unexpected transition from the realm of Scipio Africanus to that of Dame Nature as part of this tension; the

30. Anne Middleton, "Narration and the Invention of Experience: Episodic Form in *Piers Plowman*," in *Wisdom of Poetry*, 104–5, 96–97, 102.

movement of textual traditions parallels the changes in the speaker, who moves from contemplation or reading to active fashioning of stanzas, or singing, as alternative models of claiming a poetic genealogy.

But the movement of the dreamer is more complicated than this. He passes from individual reading experience into eternal Macrobian verities, and then into communal experience; unlike Langland's Will, he leaves autobiographical uniqueness behind as he is absorbed into song. Here is a possible example of this process. One of the closest imitations in the poem, the description of the garden translated from Boccaccio, contains the brilliant, well-known image of red and silver fish.[31] These fish dwell in the river on which the garden verges; it is a river of many currents, "colde welle-stremes, nothyng dede, / That swymmen ful of smale fishes lighte, / With fynnes rede and skales sylver bryghte" (187–89). These fish contrast with the fish of the gate's inscription, fish who die in the drought of the "sorweful were" (138–39). The sorrowful weir, itself the antithesis of the well of grace in the previous stanza, may be the alluring stasis or death drive of merely courtly love. But Chaucer may also be elaborating Augustine's hexaemeral meditations in *Confessions* XIII, where Augustine allegorizes the fish as words, copulative or generative of meaning as they link texts. The fish isolated in the weir die; the fish in the flowing river of poetic tradition live on in their brilliant rhetorical colors as the dreamer moves from water to air.[32] This progression anticipates Irigaray's figure of birth and air. We have seen this passage before; it bears repeating in the context of the *Parlement*'s dream:

> Once we have left the *waters* of the womb, we have to construct a space for ourselves in the *air* for the rest of our time on earth—air in which we can breathe and sing freely, in which we can perform and move at will. Once we were fishes. It seems that we are destined to become birds. None of this is possible unless the air opens up freely to our movements.

31. The chief precursor text is Boccaccio, *Teseida* 7.51–56, but there are also echoes of the *Roman de la Rose* and Dante's *Commedia*. J. A. W. Bennett, *The "Parlement of Foules": An Interpretation* (Oxford: Clarendon, 1957), 74–106, provides detailed comparison.

32. What Chaucer adds to his translation of Boccaccio's description is the small fishes' "fynnes rede and skales sylver bryghte" (189); the colors (*argent and gules*) are those of what is just possibly Chaucer's own coat of arms. Though there is no definitive evidence that Chaucer was even granted a coat of arms, some features on the tomb of Thomas Chaucer suggest that it is possible; at any rate, in the fifteenth and sixteenth centuries the Chaucer family had ascribed to it such a coat of arms. See Derek Pearsall, *The Life of Geoffrey Chaucer: A Critical Biography* (Oxford: Blackwell, 1992), 279, 294. Grossman discusses the Augustine passage in *Story of All Things*, 63–79.

To construct and inhabit our airy space is essential. It is the space of bodily autonomy, of free breath, free speech and song, of performing on the stage of life.[33]

Chaucer seems to provide his protagonist with the birth passage by which, claiming the red and silver fish as his embryonic, readerly condition, he nonetheless dreams of walking further to begin the identification with birds, an identification that will make him a different kind of singer than his readerly self could have envisaged. Winnicott would remind us of the fierceness and aggression required in being born, and Chaucer's charm is supple and complex enough to include such fierceness. Constructing a space for oneself in the air is never easy, as Irigaray's own imperative construction implies. It is a powerful imitative practice that embraces a Chartrian Dame Nature yet transforms her, gradually dislodging her from neoplatonic cosmology and strengthening her alliance with human fabulation. The mother moves, or is refigured by the poet. But she is not absented; she is acknowledged in her autonomous activity. This is one way of paying the debt to the mother.

The large movement from contemplative to autobiographical fiction evidently needs some qualification in the case of the *Parlement*. As the dream goes on, the protagonist becomes not more but less visible and historically specific. The birds' song to summer is a communal, anonymous lyric, not the meditative shaping of a solitary speaker's self-consciousness or historicity. If we look for exaltation of an individual poetic singer in the *Parlement*, we will not find it. In fact, the protagonist seems grateful to escape some expectations that his creator, or he himself, might have entertained for him.

The display of universal harmony early in the *Parlement*'s dream unfolds for a man who is a beloved son, one on whom time, affection, and visionary experience are lavished. This son expects much of himself, chiefly the composition of a philosophical poetry that will justify the attentions of his fathers of learning. It is a daunting expectation that some part of the dreamer has of himself. When he finds himself merely reporting or repeating their vision in rime royal, that part of the dreamer who composes the dream removes the paternal pressure *and* makes possible a surprising new poetic path by sending him through the double gates and into the garden. In the garden of Nature he views, takes in, absorbs, but is not doted upon. He escapes the concentrated attentions

---

33. Luce Irigaray, "Divine Women" (1984), in *Sexes and Genealogies*, trans. Gillian Gill (New York: Columbia University Press, 1993), 55–72, at 66.

of his elders. He is as if, in Winnicott's formulation, alone in the presence of the mother.[34]

This condition Winnicott infuses with a profound sense of relief, release, and protected freedom—for mother and child alike. It is an achievement in the relationship of child to caretaker, such that the child can be protected by her, tended by her, but is free not to engage her vis-à-vis. The child may be absorbed elsewhere: in developing motor skills, in uttering the sounds that precede meaningful speech, in simply breathing, in fantasizing, in watching a mobile, in testing the reality of the cat—or later, absorbed in reading, or in taking in other members of the household, witnessing. Such taking in or witnessing may be voyeuristic, but need not be; Winnicott's concept allows for a wide range of visual hungers, a range of scopic passivities and actions. The central feature of this condition, in Winnicott's lexicon of movement and space, is that of having room to stretch, turn, reach. Being alone in the presence of the mother is the precursor to the adult's being alone *tout court*, and finding solitude safe enough because of having internalized the mother's nonintrusive structures of care. This is moreover a partial relief of focus and absorption for the mother, who continues the process of being a good-enough mother by partially withdrawing her direct engagement with the child. Crucial to Winnicott's conception here is the notion of the child as free to be passive or elsewhere engaged, without demands for responsiveness from an excessively avid mother: "When alone in the sense that I am using the term, and only when alone, the infant is able to do the equivalent of what in an adult, would be called relaxing. The infant is able to become unintegrated, to flounder, to be in a state where there is no orientation, to be able to exist for a time without either being a reactor to an external impingement or an active person with a direction of interest or movement."[35] The mother creates an enclave of air for the child, and ideally this airy envelope unfolds itself, to protect yet release the two of them to movement and light. In this condition one might grow into tolerating phases of emptiness or unintegration; as Michael Eigen says, "One can be missing. The great secret of being missing, which is so taboo, can be experienced."[36] Winnicott's and

34. D. W. Winnicott, "The Capacity to Be Alone" (1958), in *Maturational Processes*, 29–36, at 30.

35. Ibid., 34.

36. Michael Eigen, *Psychic Deadness* (London: Jason Aronson, 1996), 79.

Irigaray's pneumatology leads the subject to alarming, potentially generative states of unintegration, an emptiness which may fill up.

As readers have always noted, Chaucer frequently represents his protagonists' absorption, not to say absentmindedness, in sights and sounds before them. This absorption has many aspects, not least the Chaucerian character's repeated failures to comprehend that which is presented to him. Here, though, I emphasize the character's capacity for a transformational passivity, and suggest that his apparent invisibility to the birds and Dame Nature figures that passivity. Absorbed into the processes before him, he becomes transformed from an agent into a witness, but then, upon waking, into a glad reader and poet of energy and scope. Transformation comes through an association of the maternal with voice, but in a way strikingly different from the one that Silverman takes as representative of so much Western philosophy and art. For Silverman,

> the male subject later hears the maternal voice through himself . . . it comes to resonate for him with all that he transcends through language. In other words, through a symmetrical gesture to that whereby the child "finds" its "own" voice by introjecting the mother's voice, the male subject subsequently "refines" his "own" voice by projecting onto the mother's voice all that is unassimilable to the paternal position. . . . the boundaries of male subjectivity must be constantly redrawn through the externalizing displacement onto the female subject of what Kristeva would call the "abject."[37]

The dynamics of voice, maternity, and agency in the *Parlement* offer an alternative to this scheme in at least two particulars. First, it is not so much the sonorous envelope of the mother's voice that bestows voice upon the formel and then upon the poet-dreamer, but the raucousness, taunt, argument, song, and variously embodied sounds from many of Nature's "children." Chaucer's Dame Nature does not envelope, cradle, cuddle, croon, or resound through uterine caverns; she fosters, tutors, encourages independence of mind in her charges, knows when to hold her peace in the interest of creating a space for the formel to work out her alternatives. This is not the sonorous maternal envelope for which we might long nostalgically but a comic space of ambient noise by Nature's progeny.

37. Silverman, *Acoustic Mirror*, 81.

Second, the function of being a child in relation to the parent is transferred from the dreamer to the formel, as if the dreamer occupies a place like that of an eldest child now observing, at some distance, Mother with a new baby. But in this instance the model suggests feeling states and relationships precisely the opposite of those that inevitably characterize Freud's and Klein's representations of sibling rivalry; we can think of Chaucer as expanding the repertoire of family dynamics crystallized in the scene of mother, eldest child, new baby. To begin with, there is no *nursing* dyad for elder brother to observe, no mother/infant in massive physical contact; rather Dame Nature and the formel are in the process of negotiating a space for the autonomous action of the daughter. (In this respect it helps to think of the formal, fluid spatial relationship between Nature and the bird on her wrist; in falconry the young bird would be encouraged to mount aloft but also to return, and would at first be held by jesses that choreograph its distances and proximities in relation to the trainer.) Even the other birds, so often discussed in terms of class and estate, might function as other siblings in a vociferous family or, in Chaucer's case, the nonnatal, junior members of a large aristocratic household, as opposed to the infants of nuclear families and psychoanalytic theory, who are relatively impoverished in sibs. The dream makes available to the dreamer a surprising, unanticipated field of desires: membership in the noisy clan of Nature, absorption in their voices rather than a pressure to perform like the fathers, poetry as communal song rather than philosophical exposition.

Winnicott writes that if the infant can be entrusted by the mother to that crucial state of letting-be, entrusted to a solitude which is freedom from demands, then the infant will come to discover desire as its own, unalienated: "The stage is set for an id impulse. . . . In the course of time there arrives a sensation or an impulse. In this setting the sensation or impulse will feel real and be truly a personal experience."[38] Winnicott emphasizes the temporal gap within which the infant may own its desire, an interval dependent on that balance among mother's reliable presence, her holding off from impingement, and the infant's movements, which I am calling parturition. In pediatric consultations with children between five and thirteen months old, for instance, Winnicott would set a "shining tongue-depressor" within the infant's reach, and then ask the mother holding the baby to refrain from intervention.

38. Winnicott, "Capacity to Be Alone," 34.

Mother and doctor were to wait, with the discipline to "contribute as little as possible to the situation." Eventually the baby attracted by the spatula may accept "the reality of desire." Intervals of hesitation, which are both anxious "super-ego manifestation[s]" and a clearing in which the child claims desire, vary widely from child to child.[39] "I suggest that the hesitation means that the infant *expects* to produce an angry and perhaps revengeful mother by his indulgence. In order that a baby shall feel threatened . . . he must have in his mind the notion of an angry mother. . . . as a consequence, he has first to curb his interest and desire, and he only becomes able to find his desire again in so far as his testing of the environment affords satisfactory results."[40] Ideally, the temporal interval within which an impulse will arise also shows the infant that it can tolerate emptiness in the confidence that fullness will emerge. The time of hesitation before taking the shining object allows for the discovery of one's true rather than one's supposed, triangulated, or socially constructed desire. The *Parlement*'s dream allows this temporal dilation to its protagonist—a temporality he had not known he needed when reading in the hope of finding something.

Yet to discover his true desire is not to claim a unique, separate subjectivity. Part of his desire seems to be membership, and relative invisibility, in a large family. Another aspect of his desire is for some way to use Latinate philosophical poetry while sustaining membership in the clan, to find a relationship between a beloved learned tradition and vernacular, communal, unscholarly song. The dreamer has shifted, from the position of a son welcomed by father figures into a world that they provide for him, to an identification with the creatures who, assured and at home, welcome the summer's warmth and vitality—a position, surprisingly, of greater poise than that he had occupied in the aristocratic, Macrobian portion of the poem. The chief marker of this shift is the elevation into lyric. For the protagonist of the *Parlement* (though not

39. D. W. Winnicott, "The Observation of Infants in a Set Situation" (1941), in *Through Paediatrics to Psycho-Analysis: Collected Papers* (New York: Brunner/Mazel, 1992), 52–69, at 52, 53, 54, 59.

40. Ibid., 60. It is worth noting that Winnicott's theoretical accounting for the interval of hesitation as the child's assumption of a punitive mother occurs relatively early in his career, when he still relies on Klein and her emphasis on the dynamics of a punitive superego; "The Observation of Infants" was published in 1941. His later notion, encapsulated in the title of the paper "The Capacity to Be Alone" (1958), seems to emerge through his engagement with Lacan and his wish to revise Lacan's mirror-stage.

for its avian singers) an ascent into lyric means freedom from autobiographical specificities, a releasing absorption into air and sound. Wallace Stevens, from whom we shall hear more on mothers, identifies the
welcome nonintegration made possible for the infant when the structure
of the mother's unimpinging presence allows for it. Stevens speaks of

> A long, inevitable sound,
> A kind of cozening and coaxing sound,
> And the goodness of lying in a maternal sound,
>
> Unfretted by day's separate, several selves,
> Being part of everything that comes together as one.
> In this identity, disembodiments
>
> Still keep occurring.[41]

Simple as the Chaucerian birds' song may be in its lexical and affective dimensions, it is an intricate consequence of all the movements of
genre and affect throughout the poem. Gathering up all the poem's earlier steps through ancient philosophic contemplation of the way things
are, the medieval encyclopedic and hexaemeral traditions, the
mythopoeic works of the Chartrians, and to the courtly genres of
late-medieval continental Europe, Chaucer's lyric lodges procreative
eros under the aegis of Nature's august motherhood, and brings the
Christian endowment of "Saynt Valentyn" to the natural ways of the
mating birds and to the ambivalence of the formel eagle alike.

Though the melody, if there was one, may have preexisted the words
and was "imaked. . . in Fraunce" (677), as was the rondeau form itself,
the verses are the poet's own—even the dreamer's own, since by this
late stage the dreamer has overtaken and become one with the poet. Yet
this claim, which could easily support a proclamation of the poet's indi-
viduality, is complicated by its elusive formulation: "The wordes were
swiche as ye may heer fynde, / The nexte vers, as I now have in mynde"
(678–79). I take this as the expression of the dreamer (who is now also
the poet) of his *discovery* of the song as his true desire. The song gathers
up all the shining objects of each dream episode: fathers, Latinity, the
celestial canopy, the riddling inscriptions on the gates, the life-giving
and death-dealing traditions of courtly love, catalogues of flora and

41. Wallace Stevens, "An Ordinary Evening in New Haven" XXIII, in *Collected Poems* (New York: Knopf, 1954), 465–89, at 482.

fauna, Italian and French vernacular poets, the maternity of Nature and a kinship with the birds. Both fathers and mothers have made the parturitive space in which desire can discover itself and issue song, the fathers by moving him along, the mother by benignly disregarding him as he takes in the last shining object—an event, rather—of the formel's claiming of *her* desire.

For both Chaucer and Winnicott, the capacity to tolerate anxiety and to make use of both parents to discover desire are developmental steps. But Chaucer might not make what we would expect as a natural next step, the claiming of the singularity of the unique poet. The speaker's cagey disavowals of individual poetic mastery apropos the summer song—the odd phrasing about its words that he has now in mind, its performance by the birds, its communal, general nature—suggest that Chaucer is skeptical of the valorization of "the singularity of the ego," and this notwithstanding his undeniable psychological sophistication.[42] As Gregory Stone says in his argument for the late-medieval critique of a Renaissance "fall into naïveté, into a dark age of individualism":

> Late medieval anonymity . . . is not to be explained away as a symptom of immaturity, ignorance, or naïveté but rather is a deliberate, mature rejection of the new Renaissance model of the self-determining singular ego, a model with which the late Middle Ages is already quite familiar yet regards as a lie, as an untenable violation of the truth of anonymity. The Middle Ages consciously insists that *I* am *they*: that the individual subject is never singular, is always in some essential sense general, collective, objective.[43]

On this view, the Chaucerian dreamer might well agree with Lacan's assertion that "I identify myself in language, but only in losing myself in it like an object."[44] This "losing" would mean something like "finding myself in a relation of absorption by song." And to lose oneself in this way, "like an object," would mean for the Chaucerian dreamer to come into his own mature subjectivity, which is both singular and general.

Chaucer engages a late medieval distrust of nascent Renaissance subjectivity through the form of communal, general lyric. But the lyric

42. The phrase is from Gregory Stone, *The Death of the Troubadour: The Late Medieval Resistance to the Renaissance* (Philadelphia: University of Pennsylvania Press, 1994), 4.

43. Ibid., 4. William Flesch, *Generosity and the Limits of Authority: Shakespeare, Herbert, Milton* (Ithaca, N.Y.: Cornell University Press, 1992), has good discussions of generality in Renaissance writers, providing a nice complement to Stone's work on medieval poets.

44. Jacques Lacan, "The Function and Field of Speech and Language in Psychoanalysis," in *Écrits: A Selection*, trans. Alan Sheridan (New York: Norton, 1977), 30–113, at 86.

makes this kind of sense within the narrative only because of the disregarding, obliquely maternal mother (that is, she is a mother, but not *my* mother, because she is mother of all); squabbling, aggressive, quasi-sib birds; the formel eagle who releases the dreamer into anonymity and is herself released into voicing her own desire. How do such familial structures of affect and percept, structures that permit maturity yet also a medieval anonymity, fare in the great dramatic/vernacular achievements of the English Renaissance? This question I take up in the next chapter, along with challenges from feminist theory to the ways we use the notion of the "mother tongue."

6

Feasting on Language: *Love's Labor's Lost* and the Debt to the Maternal

It is Nature he finds, Nature who, unknown to him, has nourished his project, his production. It is Nature who now fuses for him with that glass enclosure [of discourse], that spangled sepulcher, from which—imaginary and therefore absent—she is unable to articulate her difference. Thus she allows herself to be consumed again for new speculations, or thrown away as unfit for consumption. Without saying a word.

—Luce Irigaray

The lords of *Love's Labor's Lost*, deflecting a frustrated appetite for women onto infatuation with the glass enclosure of Petrarchan poetic discourse, find that the ladies who represent Nature to them refuse to be consumed or thrown away, as in Irigaray's scenario.[1] If this is an old story, Shakespeare makes it new with his play's pressure of movement toward the rueful, radiant lyrics of Winter and Spring at the conclusion. How does this happen, and how does such movement refresh the old story about mothers and sons?

In *Love's Labor's Lost*, aggression overtly circulates among men; it is

1. Luce Irigaray, "Volume-Fluidity" (1974), in *Speculum of the Other Woman*, trans. Gillian Gill (Ithaca, N.Y.: Cornell University Press, 1985), 227–40, at 228.

hostile; it seems to have little to do with the kind of Winnicottian aggression that we have seen earlier and little to do with the mother. In this chapter I argue that envy, a Kleinian form of aggression, dominates the aggressive aristocrats of Shakespeare's play; that their envy, directed against women and against males of lower standing, evinces an anxious wish to evade acknowledgment of the cost of maternal burdens to those who carry them; that the famous seasonal lyrics at the end of the play form the end point of a path that the lords could walk to own their debt to the mother. I argue also that these elements are possible because Shakespeare studied the linked formal and thematic plots of Chaucer's *Parlement of Foules*. "Our wooing doth not end like an old play" (5.2.874), laments a rueful Berowne near the end of the play. But it does end, as readers have suggested, like the *Parlement*.[2] Perhaps Shakespeare valued most of all the Chaucerian contrasts between courtly and hexaemeral/encyclopedic traditions of representing nature. This structure would fuel Shakespeare's constantly ramifying explorations of maternity, birth, and the condition of offspring. In this chapter, I link the play's handling of genre and poetic mode with the movement of the *Parlement* traced in the last chapter: an impulsive narrative unexpectedly finding elevation, closure, and composure in one family of lyric, that which catalogues creatural life.

It is easy enough to discern the need for composure of some sort among the anxious, nervy male aristocrats of the play, caught up as they are in exchanging ridicule, contempt, and superiority through a virtuoso range of verbal attacks and games. But composure may also be seen as the goal of the genre plot: how to come to rest and ease in some poetic stance that offers release from the restless Petrarchism and exaggeratedly pretentious, learned, humanist modes. Of course, the play is in an overt sense lyric from its opening lines, filled with poems and set pieces composed by the characters. But in the context of the *Parlement of Foules*, I emphasize how the deservedly famous concluding songs of Winter and Spring—so incongruous and yet so right, as readers have long attested—provide just the release that the overwrought poets within the play require.

Navarre's tendentiously masculine "little academe," devoted to bookish philosophy, fasting, and sequestration from the company of women, holds a place in the plot analogous to the early Macrobian episode of

2. See, for example, Ann Thompson, *Shakespeare's Chaucer: A Study in Literary Origins* (New York: Barnes and Noble, 1978), 78–80, 85.

Chaucer's dream. An idealized, noble, male company of learners—Berowne refers to "these earthly godfathers of heaven's lights" (1.1.88)—Navarre's academy is immediately waylaid by the vigorous intrusions of Costard, Armado, Moth, and their companions, and by the charms of the ladies who plant themselves in the wide expanse of the fields, like Dame Nature, apart from the cloistered court of philosophy.[3] When the young men do venture forth from the site of their vows (vows effectually to remain immature, as if the lords are schoolboys, as Berowne suggests at 1.1.97–109), they try to create with the ladies a kind of court of Cupid, filled with "revels, dances, masks, and merry hours" (4.3.376), along the way composing idealizing love lyrics and acting out many other forms and conventions of medieval and Renaissance courtship. This repertoire Shakespeare knew in part from his knowledge of the Thynne editions of Chaucer, with their representation of Chaucer as poet of courtship.[4] The various attempts of the lords at flirtation in their exchanges with the ladies actually stall the action they think should follow from such witty disguises and banter, since the women's caustic refusals block the men's marital plot expectations.[5] These encounters among the aristocrats constitute the equivalent of Chaucer's regions of Cupid and Venus in the *Parlement*: "Saint Cupid, then! and,

3. All references to Shakespeare are taken from the *Riverside Shakespeare*, ed. G. Blakemore Evans et al. (Boston: Houghton Mifflin, 1974).

4. William Thynne's great edition of Chaucer's works was printed in 1532, the result of a commission by Henry VIII, who gave Thynne permission to search the libraries of Britain for manuscripts. The most widely available printed editions of Chaucer throughout the sixteenth century were developments of Thynne's edition; their most interesting changes to Thynne come in the dedicatory material and in the ever expanding number of works attributed to Chaucer, many of which we now take to be apocryphal. See Joseph Dane, *Who Is Buried in Chaucer's Tomb? Studies in the Reception of Chaucer's Book* (East Lansing: Michigan State University Press, 1998); John Watkins, " 'Wrastling for this world': Wyatt and the Tudor Canonization of Chaucer," in *Refiguring Chaucer in the Renaissance*, ed. Theresa Krier (Gainesville: University Press of Florida, 1998): 21–39, and my introduction to the volume, pages 6–9. Many studies of the fortunes of Chaucer's individual works in later writing situate Thynne's edition and those stemming from his.

5. Peter Brooks's formulation of plot sequence, derived from *Beyond the Pleasure Principle*, characterizes the drive to narrative closure in terms of male sexual experience: "It is characteristic of textual energy in narrative that it should always be on the verge of premature discharge, of short-circuit. The reader experiences the fear—and excitation—of the improper end, which is symmetrical to—but far more immediate and present than—the fear of endlessness" (*Reading for the Plot: Design and Intention in Narrative* [Cambridge: Harvard University Press, 1984], 109). Whether or not this idea suits narrative generally, it is germane to the ways that Shakespeare toys with the lords and the plot that they believe themselves to enact.

soldiers, to the field!" (4.3.363). Eros in this courtly vein is not so much wrong as it is jejeune; Cupid "hath been five thousand year a boy" (5.2.11); if Shakespeare is indeed thinking of the *Parlement*, with its eerily quiet lovers in the Temple of Venus, then part of his response must be the joke of making his disciples of Love so verbose.

The finer resolution of the aristocratic plot lies in the turn that has most reminded readers of the *Parlement*: the crucial choice of the ladies to defer marital commitment for a year, during which the men will find themselves tested. It is in large part this breach of dramaturgic decorum (as the lords would see it) that leads to the unexpected ending of the Winter-Spring lyrics, just as, in Chaucer's poem, it is the contentious social energies of the birds and the formel's consequent choice to defer her choice that leads the poem into the song welcoming summer.[6] Lyrics pointedly not in the Petrarchan mode but in a vein cataloguing the continuities and vicissitudes of the seasonal world offer Shakespeare's stalled lovers a new framework of attitudes toward eros and adulthood. Like the dream that unfolds specifically for the Chaucerian character who dreams it, the play's songs of the locals may be said to exist as if they could function as a transformational matrix for the witty courtiers, whose penitential acts should draw them into the temporal processes and embodied poverties of their fellows. In terms of the textual traditions on which the two writers meditate, the courtiers are offered encyclopedic alternatives to the Petrarchan genres in which they have encased themselves.

Events leading up to the songs have created a need for some resolution other than a set of four weddings: the exacerbations of the plot have created too much hostility for some swiftly achieved marital harmony.[7] In this play, laden with emulative combativeness from the start, social aggression has reached a pitch with the extended exposures and humiliations of the lords, the subsequent punitive turn of the lords against the locals during the Pageant of the Nine Worthies, and Costard's exposure and humiliation of Armado. These things threaten to escalate into a brawl, and though the disconcerting entrance of Marcade with his news of the old king's death diverts this physical violence, social dissonance

6. Though Shakespeare certainly knew Chaucer's use of the motif of a female's deferring marital choice for a year, or a year and a day, he would have known other instances of it as well. Malory uses it, for example, in the courtship of Gareth and Lyonesse in the *Morte Darthur*.

7. On a theory of Shakespearean comedy based on curative exacerbation, see Ruth Nevo, *Comic Transformations in Shakespeare* (London: Methuen, 1980).

remains. To my mind, Shakespeare has understood the boisterous social combat of the birds' debate in Chaucer's *Parlement* dramaturgically, as a motivated and psychically compelling impulsion into the release and fresh composure of seasonal lyric. (So he is also thinking about how to motivate lyric in a drama.) Vigorous winds of attraction, aggression, envy, sharp wit, and malice fly about in "the great feast of languages" for which the play is best known. And these energies and linguistic forms parallel, in plot functions, the movements of Chaucer's poem from vernacular poetic and amatory traditions, through the debate of the fowls, to the hexaemeral and encyclopedic matrices of the summer lyric. This is one of the endlessly inventive ways that Shakespeare represents as immature the Petrarchan ardors of the young men, and offers a hard-won, adult alternative in encyclopedic nature lore.

Shakespeare's articulation of his precise role in the genre-historical issues raised by Chaucer marks not only the temporal distance of two intervening centuries but also the genre difference between staged comedy and narrative of a dream vision with its claims for writing and the worth of the vernacular; this is one thing that emerges from the play's preoccupations with writing. Throughout this play and culminating in the catalogues of the seasonal songs, Shakespeare contemplates his place as dramatist in *poetic* genre history: he opens a space which the catalogues demarcate as specifically literary.[8] He carries a step further the complex Chaucerian argument for the vernacular as the vehicle through which Latinity may be carried into his own culture, for lyric as a vehicle through which philosophy may be transformed and preserved, for a comic Dame Nature who preserves the wealth of lore over which an earlier Latinate Natura presided. *Love's Labor's Lost* assays to carry the encyclopedic, cosmological, and hexaemeral traditions from twelfth-century, learned, and Latinate works further into the vernacular (and from dream vision into comedy); hence, for instance, his dramatic inclination to highlight the performative aspects of the songs. Not only do

---

8. This phenomenon of situating himself within a long literary tradition, and anglicizing its classical aspects, is familiar, e.g., from the floral catalogues of *The Winter's Tale* 4.2, with their affinities to Ovid and Spenser and, more generally, to pastoral. A good recent discussion occurs in Julia Reinhard Lupton, *Afterlives of the Saints: Hagiography, Typology and Renaissance Literature* (Stanford: Stanford University Press, 1996), 197–206. The relationship between catalogue and lyric in *The Winter's Tale*, apparently picking up issues from *Love's Labor's Lost*, requires more detailed attention than it receives here; for instance, Autolycus's songs, some of them catalogues, complicate the traditions I discuss by his situating them within his rough market economy and detaching them from encyclopedic traditions.

they emblematize song and a history of song; they also fictionalize a central condition of song: the Winnicottian aggressive, mobile life force that insists on exchanges with the world in the exercise of breath and voice.

The play's manifold developments of such linguistic topoi make clear why notions of the maternal are at stake in representations of inventive language.[9] Holofernes—a learned, but not Petrarchan, schoolmaster as well as a playwright and composer—enunciates a number of linguistic issues. Thus one of the many contests staged in the play is that between the humanist, Latinate, written and pedantic style championed by Holofernes, in part because it affords him a sense of superiority over his companions, and the native, vernacular, unlettered speech which is the only mode available to a character like Dull. Hence Holofernes versifies extempore and thinks in letters as much as in words. As Terence Hawkes demonstrates, for Holofernes "the resonant world of speech is comically opposed to the silent world of writing."[10] This is true enough, but such a binarism is complicated by the fact that in Holofernes' speech, and for that matter in that of Armado, Moth, Costard, and Nathaniel, Latinity evinces a positive pressure to become part of the spoken vernacular. Holofernes is an extreme and parodic case, but the stylistic habit of interleaving Latin tags with English was at this time being transformed into a racy, colloquial prose style, by Thomas Nashe, among others; this style informs the drama as well as all genres of written prose. It is perhaps Nashe's greatest contribution to his mother tongue that Shakespeare, Nashe's greatest student, evidently ponders Nashe's gifts (as well as his person, perhaps, in the character of Moth) throughout this play.[11] Latin enters spoken English, transforming not

9. These topoi have been a favorite topic of criticism of the play, see especially Rosalie Colie, "Criticism and the Analysis of Craft: *Love's Labour's Lost* and the Sonnets," in *Shakespeare's Living Art* (Princeton: Princeton University Press, 1974).

10. Hawkes, *Shakespeare's Talking Animals: Language and Drama in Society* (London: Edward Arnold, 1973), 54. Many of the linguistic issues and relationships that coalesce in Holofernes are developed by David Schalkwyk in " 'She never told her love': Embodiment, Textuality, and Silence in Shakespeare's Sonnets and Plays," *Shakespeare Quarterly* 45, 4 (winter 1994): 381–407. See also William Carroll, *The Great Feast of Language in* Love's Labour's Lost (Princeton: Princeton University Press, 1976), and especially Carla Mazzio, "The Melancholy of Print: *Love's Labour's Lost,*" in *Historicism, Psychoanalysis, and Early Modern Culture,* ed. Carla Mazzio and Douglas Trevor (New York: Routledge, 2000), 186–227.

11. The scholarship has a long tradition of looking for topical parody in the character of Holofernes: does he send up Thomas Nashe, John Florio, Gabriel Harvey? Among many studies of the play's topicality regarding the hostilities between Nashe and Harvey, see Nicholl, *A Cup of News: The Life of Thomas Nashe* (London: Routledge and Kegan Paul, 1984),

simply the lexicon but phrasings, sentence rhythms, range of allusive resonance:

Hol. The deer was, as you know, *sanguis*, in blood; ripe as the pomewater, who now hangeth like a jewel in the ear of *caelo*, the sky, the welkin, the heaven; and anon falleth like a crab on the face of *terra*, the soil, the land, the earth.

Nath. Truly, Master Holofernes, the epithetes are sweetly varied, like a scholar at the least: but, sir, I assure ye, it was a buck of the first head.

Hol. Sir Nathaniel, *haud credo.*

Dull. 'Twas not a haud credo. 'Twas a pricket.

Hol. Most barbarous intimation! yet a kind of insinuation, as it were *in via*, in way of explication; *facere*, as it were, replication, or rather *ostentare*, to show, as it were, his inclination, after his undressed, unpolished, uneducated, unpruned, untrained, or rather unlettered, or ratherest unconfirmed fashion, to insert again my *haud credo* for a deer.

Dull. I said the deer was not a haud credo; 'twas a pricket.

(4.2.3–21)

As A. L. Rowse first suggested to the scholarly world, Dull hears this *haud credo* as "awd [old] grey doe," and I think the Latin/English pun is more than a lamentable Shakespearean quibble.[12] Among recent scholars to trace tropes of the mother tongue, Dolores Warwick Frese argues for a Chaucerian topos that puns on the name of Grisel/Griselda—"old grey"—as a figure for the mother tongue as ancient, lowly vernacular.[13] Moth uses another of many such tropes in his homespun invocation to the Muses: "My father's wit and my mother's tongue assist me" (1.2.90). It is lore so familiar by Shakespeare's time that we might take Dull's mistaken "old grey doe" (emphatically distinct from the "pricket" killed

---

208–20. See also Joan Holmer, "Nashe as 'Monarch of Witt' and Shakespeare's *Romeo and Juliet*," *Texas Studies in Literature and Language* 37 (1995): 314–43. Other writers were working out negotiations between Latinity and English, but the Nashe/Harvey documents, *Love's Labor's Lost*, and *Romeo and Juliet* seem to be unique in the characterization of aggressive "princoxes" of linguistic swaggering.

12. A. L. Rowse, letter to the *Times Literary Supplement*, 18 July 1952; cited in Richard David's New Arden edition of *Love's Labour's Lost*, 2d ed. (London: Methuen, 1987).

13. In "Three Men and a Baby: Boccaccio, Petrarch, Chaucer and the Making of Patient Griselda," the Grellet-Simpson Lecture in Medieval Literature, Mary Washington College, 1995, Dolores Warwick Frese argues that Boccaccio's Griselda is "the heroine of a marriage between noble *Latinitas* and the ancient Mother Tongue" and that her children are "subtle figures for the emergence of vernacular fiction." A more literal reading of Griselda is provided by Allyson Newton, "The Occlusion of Maternity in Chaucer's *Clerk's Tale*," in *Medieval Mothering*, ed. John Carni Parsons and Bonnie Wheeler (New York: Garland, 1996), 63–75.

in the hunt) as one of these figures for the mother tongue, brilliantly naturalized in a comic dialogue embodying the very contest of Latinity with native English.

This suggestion carries more force when the old grey doe is aligned with other references to maternity and female genealogy throughout the play. There is Moth's appeal to the generativity of his father's wit and his mother's tongue. Holofernes taps the same figurative fund when he characterizes the source of his linguistic gifts in a trope of pregnancy:

Hol. This is a gift that I have, simple, simple, a foolish extravagant spirit, full of forms, figures, shapes, objects, ideas, apprehensions, motions, revolutions. These are begot in the ventricle of memory, nourish'd in the womb of *pia mater*, and delivered upon the mellowing of occasion. But the gift is good in those in whom it is acute, and I am thankful for it.

(4.2.65–72)

On the nomenclature of the *pia mater*, Thomas Vicaray says this: "Why it is called Pia mater, is, for because it is softe and tender over the brayne, that it nourisheth the brayne and feedeth it, as doth a loving mother unto her tender childe or babe; for it is not so tough and harde as is Duramater. . . . this Pannicle doth circumvolve or lappe all the substaunce of the brayne."[14] This passage interlaces etymology with what it takes to be a natural maternal affection and the action of feeding, just as Holofernes does. Holofernes speaks from a highly articulated sense of the inward plenitude of the brain-space, of its protection and encompassing by a containing structure, and of its active capacity to incorporate nourishment. Freud, Klein, and Winnicott would all be happy with Holofernes' formulation of an economy of plenty.

14. Elizabeth Sacks, *Shakespeare's Images of Pregnancy* (New York: St. Martin's, 1980), 112–13, citing Thomas Vicaray, *The Anatomie of the Bodie of Man* (1548; reprint, 1577), ed. Frederick Furnivall and Percy Furnivall (London: N. Trübner, 1888), 30. On the association of matter and *mater* in Renaissance writing, see Margaret Ferguson, "*Hamlet*: Letters and Spirits," in *Shakespeare and the Question of Theory*, ed. Patricia Parker and Geoffrey Hartman (London: Routledge, 1985), 292–309; and Elizabeth Harvey, "Matrix as Metaphor: Midwifery and the Conception of Voice," in *Ventriloquized Voices: Feminist Theory and English Renaissance Texts* (London: Routledge, 1992).

Thomas Nashe also links the *pia mater* with his native tongue, as David observes in his note to Holofernes' speech. Thus Nashe: "Therefore what did me I, but having a huge heape of those worthlesse shreds of small English in my *Pia maters* purse, to make the royaller shew with them to mens eyes, had then to the compounders immediately, and exchanged them foure into one, and others into more, according to the Greek, French, Spanish, and Italian?" *Christs Teares over Jerusalem*, in *Works*, ed. Ronald McKerrow, 3 vols. (Oxford: Basil Blackwell, 1958), 2:184.

Does Kleinian Gratitude Pay the Irigarayan Debt to the Mother?

Holofernes' formulation famously participates in his culture's appropriations of birthing figures for men's achievements in writing and other arts.[15] What psychic conditions would make Holofernes' use of this trope dramatically apt, suited to his complacence? Winnicott might call Holofernes' lines an expression of holding: the schoolmaster, secure in his treasury of knowledge, experiences his own spirit as held, and has the capacity to hold his own spirit in a generative way. (He is one of the composers of the pageant and the songs.) But I defer the Winnicottian notion of self-holding until chapter 8; here I look at Holofernes' gratitude in light of Melanie Klein on gratitude, not least because his gratitude is central to the grateful songs that conclude the play and to the lords' envy that leads to the songs. Holofernes ends his disquisition with an expression of gratitude: "the gift is good in those in whom it is acute, and I am thankful for it"; he proposes that the clergyman Nathaniel say grace at table in the evening (4.2.148–49); the entire scene is dense with elaborations of feeding—literally in the evening's anticipated dining, figuratively in the "dainties that are bred in a book" (4.2.23–24). Klein argues that gratitude is innate in the newborn; the infant internalizes the "good breast" as a good object, and identifies with it so as to feel that he possesses goodness of his own, thus founding a capacity for a later, generous mode of relating, and a capacity to transform envy—also innate—into gratitude.

> A good [internal] object is established, which loves and protects the self and is loved and protected by the self. . . . Through processes of projection and introjection, through inner wealth given out and re-introjected, an enrichment and deepening of the ego comes about. In this way the possession of the helpful inner object is again and again re-established and gratitude can fully come into play.[16]

Although Holofernes is a minor character, he embodies the dynamic in which the capacity for gratitude develops through the introjection of a good, replenishing maternal figure. We say it is complacency, and so it is, but it is also this character's way of acknowledging provision. "It is not enough for [the baby] to be gratified," says Harold Boris in his study

15. See, for example, Jay Halio, "The Metaphor of Conception and Elizabethan Theories of the Imagination," *Neophilologus* 50 (1966): 454–61; Katharine Maus, *Inwardness and Theater in the English Renaissance* (Chicago: University of Chicago Press, 1995), 182–209.

16. Melanie Klein, *Envy and Gratitude: A Study of Unconscious Sources* (1957), in *Writings*, ed. Roger Money-Kyrle, 4 vols. (New York: Free Press, 1975), 3:188–89.

of envy; "he must also know that he is *being* gratified. This knowledge is a necessary precursor of knowing that there is a person there who is providing the gratification. Only with that realization—or acknowledgment—can gratitude become linked with what previously stimulated only envy. And only then can admiration grow up to become a reason for identification."[17]

But is it *de facto* a good thing to be always at play with the mother tongue? Counter to Holofernes stands Navarre, who enacts a more aggressive appropriation of an implicitly maternalized fullness in writing. The Princess says that in his letter he has fit

> as much love in rhyme
> As would be cramm'd up in a sheet of paper,
> Writ a' both sides the leaf, margent and all,
> That he was fain to seal on Cupid's name.

> (5.2.6–9)

"Cram" is a word that Shakespeare elsewhere associates with the phenomena of pregnancy and more broadly with the perceived plenitude of the filled body, a perception that variously creates bemusement, envy, nostalgia in the onlooker.[18] All the lords of *Love's Labor's Lost* unleash, in act 5, onslaughts of envy that contrast with Holofernes' gratitude and bespeak their anxious sense of exclusion from the repletion that they imagine would be supplied by access to the ladies. Navarre's copious love letter may encroach upon the fecundity of the mother tongue without acknowledgment of the debt that all speakers of native languages owe to the maternal cultures that teach it. Klein enables us to entertain the thought that Navarre's crammed pages might enunciate a love infused with envious aggression.

17. See a rich alternative account of biblical creation by Julia Reinhard Lupton, "Creature Caliban," *Shakespeare Quarterly* 31 (2000): 1–23; see also Regina Schwartz, *Remembering and Repeating: Biblical Creation in "Paradise Lost"* (Cambridge: Cambridge University Press, 1988).

18. In *The Winter's Tale* the happily pregnant, erotically alive Hermione requests that Leontes "cram's with praise, and make's / As fat as tame things" (1.2.91–92); see chapter 9 for a discussion of these lines. On the connection of literary copiousness with pregnancy and fatness, see Patricia Parker, "Literary Fat Ladies," in *Literary Fat Ladies: Rhetoric, Gender, Property* (London: Methuen, 1987); and Valerie Traub, "Prince Hal's Falstaff: Positioning Psychoanalysis and the Female Reproductive Body," *Shakespeare Quarterly* 40 (1989): 456–74. For a powerful different approach to generosity and gratitude in Shakespeare, see William Flesch, *Generosity and the Limits of Authority: Shakespeare, Herbert, Milton* (Ithaca, N.Y.: Cornell University Press, 1992), chap. 2.

Irigaray, following Hélène Rouch, calls writers to task for unexamined celebration of the mother tongue. Rouch describes her objections to her particular target, Michel Serres:

> In my study I took Michel Serres's book *The Parasite* as an example of this blindness; I thought it paradigmatic of male relationships with the mother tongue. In this book, Serres on the one hand rails against man, the parasite of fauna and flora, who takes all and gives nothing; on the other hand, he vaunts the delights of his relations with the mother tongue, which gives him everything and yet which he still finds "intact and virginal" after he (and several friends) have endlessly feasted with her. . . . he speaks, consumes a language that is inexhaustible and never stops being miraculously renewed. . . . instead of acknowledging every human being's debt, he would rather forget and speak: to speak of and with a language that has the maternal body's gifts of generosity, abundance, and plenitude, but to which nothing is owed. The materiality of the relationship to this maternal body having disappeared, language remains an inexhaustible "womb" for the use that's made of her.[19]

This is a charge of some force to bring against writers—one which Irigaray takes up in all her subsequent challenges to philosophers—and most of the poems I discuss in this book take its ethical claim seriously and mount a response to it. If Holofernes, for instance, is complacent in his ease with the *pia mater* and the classical dramatic compositions it makes possible in the form of the pageant, Shakespeare never takes the mother tongue for granted; his feast of language everywhere acknowledges its debt to the maternal body.

One way he does so in this play is to have his female characters articulate figures of female lineage. Taken alone, each is an instance of Shakespeare's brilliantly tantalizing way of offhandedly naturalizing literary traditions and tropes. Taken together, they form a delicate but strong thread joining maternity with the play's apprehension of being

19. Hélène Rouch, interview by Luce Irigaray, in "On the Maternal Order" (1987), in *Je, Te, Nous: Toward a Culture of Difference*, trans. Alison Martin (London: Routledge, 1996), 42–43. To take language as Rouch charges Serres with taking it, and to identify language with the maternal body available for our play or consumption, implies an impoverished sense of how figuration (and perhaps language itself) works. As Maggie Kilgour says in another context, "One problem with images of eating . . . is that they seem to have a tendency to consume the mediating power of figures, subverting the possibility of a free communion between individuals, by drawing extremes into a catastrophic meeting that is less 'face to face' than mouth to mouth" (*From Communion to Cannibalism: An Anatomy of Metaphors of Incorporation* [Princeton: Princeton University Press, 1990], 17).

grounded in the mother tongue. Maria is, in a bawdy exchange, her mother's daughter (2.1.201–2); the Princess is on an embassy as her father's daughter; Katherine had a sister who "might 'a' been a grandam ere she died" if it were not for lovesickness (5.2.17). In what Richard David laments as a "grievous pun," Boyet interrupts Moth's attempt to deliver a memorized paean to the ladies with a reminder of female affiliations:

> Moth: "Once to behold with your sun-beamed eyes
> —with your sun-beamed eyes"—
> Boyet: They will not answer to that epithet;
> You were best call it "daughter-beamed eyes."

$$(5.2.169-72)^{20}$$

These daughters who have dazzled the lords' eyes have a link back to Chaucer's *Parlement*, if we take seriously Boyet's deceptively frivolous compliment upon the first appearance and lodging of the ladies: "Be now as prodigal of all dear grace / As Nature was in making graces dear / When she did starve the general world beside / And prodigally gave them all to you" (2.1.9–12). This dame Nature also provides lodging for these ladies: since Navarre will now allow them within his court, they effactually establish an alternative court in "the wide fields," with a roof "too high" to belong to the mortal Navarre (2.1.91–94).

The ground outside the lords' court is base, as the Princess notes. But the negative sense of baseness—of personal honor, of language, of love—is confounded throughout the play, largely through its link with the women. Consequently what Holofernes calls "the face of *terra*, the soil, the land, the earth" (4.2.6–7) is drawn into the orbit of mother-tongue imagery, and makes possible the mutual enrichments of Latinity with native English, while acknowledging the burdens borne by the maternal-feminine in the construction of this figurative network. Thus Armado's letter, read aloud by Navarre, incidentally reveals Armado's devotion to earth and includes a Shakespearean bow to medieval English roots with its archaism "ycliped": "I . . . betook myself to walk: the time When? About the sixt hour, when beasts most graze, birds best peck, and men sit down to that nourishment which is called supper. . . .

20. David's phrase is part of his note in the New Arden edition to the play (p. 136), where he laments, "This grievous pun occurs about a dozen times in Shakespeare. . . . There is one painful example . . . in that most beautiful of sonnets (xxxiii)." But why is the pun grievous and painful?

Now for the ground Which? which, I mean, I walk'd upon: it is ycliped thy park" (1.1.234–40). Armado's ideas about language cause him to condemn the "base and obscure vulgar" (4.1.68–69), but in his practice of speech, as of love, he adores the base with a touching gallantry. Thus he loves Jaquenetta in her very "lowliness" (4.1.80), and gestures grandly that he will "profane my lips on [her] foot" (4.1.84–85). In the pageant, Armado's grandiloquent self-abasement ("I do adore thy sweet grace's slipper," he says in an access of gratitude to the Princess who is kind to him when the lords have reviled him) becomes a moving devotion to human acts of heroism and imagination, which as he sees are grounded in corporeal mortality: "The sweet war-man is dead and rotten, sweet chucks, beat not the bones of the buried. When he breathed, he was a man" (5.2.660–62). It is not inappropriate that this particular sinner in love commits himself to three years at the plough: he will become literally the georgic figure that he has been in figurative speech.[21]

In the delirium of synonymy afflicting so many speakers in this play, Armado has named Jaquenetta "a child of our grandmother Eve, a female . . . a woman" (1.1.263–64). Female lineage takes us back once more to the biblical mother of mothers, and to the play's park, a garden where women are got with child, apples and servants named for apples fall, deer are hunted and killed. The ground or earth of which we are so often reminded in the play bears a great deal of the lords' vaunting action, chiefly through offhand references to horses and their burdens. The Princess asks a forester, "Was that the King, that spurr'd his horse so hard / Against the steep-up rising of the hill?" (4.1.1–2); Holofernes, in a literary excursus, airily dismisses cheap kinds of imitation: "*Imitari* is nothing: so doth the hound his master, the ape his keeper, the tired horse his rider" (4.2.125–27). Terms of horsemanship come easily to all of Shakespeare's aristocrats (as in this play at 5.2.482–83 and 5.2.649–50), but not more often than references throughout the plays to horses'

21. Armado's extravagation of bowing before and elevations of ladies contrasts with double entendres attributing to the schoolmaster literal, sexual subordinations of local girls. In a balance of clauses that defies our recent focus on the gendered exclusions of the late Elizabethan classroom in its possible mingling of girls and boys, Nathaniel is grateful to Holofernes on behalf of his parishioners, "for their sons are well tutored by you, and their daughters profit very greatly under you"; Holofernes responds graciously, "if their sons be ingenious, they shall want no instruction; if their daughters be capable, I will put it to them" (4.2.77–79). Different productions will play this in different ways; I think that Holofernes is innocent of sexual exploits, though susceptible to the lesser sin of linguistic bathos.

fatigue at the burdens they bear for humans. These equestrian burdens we need to add to the famous, ever expanding image pattern of *bear* (verb), *bears, bare, burden, bourne, barne, born, birth,* and so on, which Stephen Booth and others have pointed out.[22] This network is probably the most sensational instance of Shakespeare's lateral, associative thinking; we need to keep a steady focus, as Booth does not, on its frequent function as the writer's acknowledgment of bearing and birthing (as with the bear who bears Hermione's rage in *The Winter's Tale*), creating the ground of experience on which humans come into language through their cultural forms of mothering. Of the instances that involve bears and horses, it seems to me that Shakespeare registers the size or volume of creatures who tap an inchoate sense of being small in relation to mother, or even being inside the volume of mother. A psychoanalyst would say that the mother forms, provides, or is the envelope of identity (on the analogy of the sonorous envelope discussed in the last chapter); a philosopher—say, the Aristotle of Irigaray's interrogation—can posit space only by occluding the mother: "The maternal-feminine also serves as an *envelope*, a *container*, the starting point from which man limits his things. The *relationship between envelope and things* constitutes one of the aporias, or the aporia, of Aristotelianism and of the philosophical system derived from it."[23] Even more strongly, as Irigaray argues of Plato's cave myth, the male philosopher abjects the feminine-maternal *in order to* create the masculine economy of thought, then to be haunted by nostalgia and longing for, and fear of, the banished maternal order. Shakespeare's pervasive language of "bearing" witnesses to its saturation of his culture's imaginary. But Shakespeare acknowledges the debt we owe to the one who provides the maternal or bearing envelope, with his

22. See Stephen Booth, "Exit, Pursued by a Gentleman Born," in *Shakespeare's Art from a Comparative Perspective*, ed. Wendell Aycock (Lubbock: Texas Tech Press, 1981), 51–66; Margreta de Grazia, "Homonyms before and after Lexical Standardization," *Jahrbuch der Deutschen Shakespeare-Gesellschaft West* (Bochum, Germany: Kemp, 1990, 143–56). On bears in Shakespeare's culture, see also Meredith Skura, *Shakespeare the Actor and the Purposes of Playing* (Chicago: University of Chicago Press, 1993); Michael Bristol, "In Search of the Bear: Spatiotemporal Form and the Heterogeneity of Economies in *The Winter's Tale*," *Shakespeare Quarterly* 42 (1991): 145–67; Caroline McManus, "Childbirth, Bears, and the Negotiation of Shame in *The Faerie Queene* Book 6 and *The Winter's Tale*," paper presented at the 1995 meeting of the Shakespeare Association of America, Chicago.

23. Luce Irigaray, "Sexual Difference" (1982), in *An Ethics of Sexual Difference*, trans. Carolyn Burke and Gillian Gill (Ithaca, N.Y.: Cornell University Press, 1993), 5–19, at 10; see also "Place, Interval: A Reading of Aristotle, *Physics* IV" (1984), ibid., 34–55; "Volume-Fluidity," 227–40.

insistence in *Love's Labor's Lost* on the horse and elsewhere on the bear, those voluminous creatures who bear burdens.[24]

Ruth Nevo recognizes the play's link to older poetico-philosophical representations of Natura obliquely in her discussion of *Love's Labor's Lost*: "Great creating Nature (Jaquenetta two months gone), time and the seasons ridicule the pretensions and presumptions to transcendence of carnal and finite creatures."[25] Riding hard, degrading what is low or near to ground, and vaunting are all expressions of such presumption, which in this play arises through the confusions of envy. If, as Irigaray says in a moment of amused indulgence about the mother-infant pair, the mother "is magnanimous toward the little one," it comes about "that man continually wants woman to be a mother and only a mother, loves her as if he were still very small while esteeming what is very great, possibly inventing it, becoming proud to the point of forgetting who he is." The first part of that "as if" clause—"as if he were still very small while esteeming what is very great"—is subject by the very processes of separation and maturity to the psychic reversals of "possibly inventing it, becoming proud."[26] The thought that one has invented what one esteems for being very great (relative to one's own smallness) is a defense against recognition that the esteemed one does not belong to oneself; it is part of the mechanism of Kleinian envy, which cannot bear to be dependent on the source of nurture and that source's apparently limitless access to plenitude. Because Irigaray's sketch of this prideful masculinity is comic as well as ethically serious, we can make use of it to pinpoint the failings of Shakespeare's superior lords in the matter of acknowledging an ethical obligation to the maternal-feminine.

Berowne's own idiom hints at such acknowledgment when he finds himself ridiculed for his fantastical humor, late in the play. Long before this, only one hundred lines into the play, Berowne has shown himself capable of sanity in his lovely lines on the just season, which function as a kind of ethical ballast for his character in their evocation of native traditions on the seasons, birth, and bearing:

24. Shakespeare characteristically complicates the binary gender division I have just sketched, however. In the matter of the killing of the deer, it is not a lord but the Princess who kills the deer, and this seems to be the very deer over whom arises the debate about its gender—a pricket or an old grey doe? And though the Princess speaks a word of reproach about the King who rides his horse so hard, there is some admiration and erotic attraction in her observation as well.

25. Nevo, *Comic Transformations*, 84–85.

26. Luce Irigaray, "Wonder: A Reading of Descartes, *The Passions of the Soul*" (1984), in *Ethics*, 72–82, at 76.

King: Berowne is like an envious sneaping frost
That bites the first-born infants of the spring.
   Ber.: Well, say I am, why should proud summer boast
Before the birds have any cause to sing?
Why should I joy in any abortive birth?
At Christmas I no more desire a rose
Than wish a snow in May's new-fangled shows;
But like of each thing that in season grows.

(1.1.100–107)

The fulfillment of these lines occurs in the play's final movement into seasonal lyric and lyric catalogue; the final steps leading up to that turn into song may make new dramatic sense in this context. The play makes it clear that the lords need to come down off the high horse of humanist aspiration and to stand firmly on "the soil, the land, the earth" of their vernacular, "sans 'sans' " (5.2.416)—without claiming a proprietary self-esteem for their inventiveness. But this is a painful tuition; at the ladies' hands they suffer ridicule, exposure, insult, and shame, all very public. The courtesy of the play requires that their response to these sufferings be similarly public, matching in wit and high spirit, but that the aggression they find awakened in themselves not be directed at the ladies. In his lines about the proper generative cycle of the seasons, Berowne has been unjustly accused of envy, which Klein understands as the impulse to spoil and degrade the goodness of the envied object. Envy is aimed at spoiling the envied one's creativity in particular, precisely because creativity is felt not to be within oneself. If Navarre's envy was suppressed or deflected in his crammed letter to the Princess, it is given free rein against the locals in the pageant. Refused a kind of nourishment by the ladies (it is significant that the locals seem to enjoy abundant access to food and meals), they turn against the offspring of the local's *pia mater*, manifested in those "forms, figures, shapes, objects" that make up the Pageant of the Nine Worthies. Berowne is lucid about this displacement of envious aggression in himself and his friends, and intuits its relation to birth and burdens: "Their form [the pageant] confounded makes most form in mirth, / When great things laboring perish in their birth" (5.2.519–20). This is not only wittily nasty; it is also a ferocious turning against the seasonable linguistic generativity that he had articulated early in the play. Furthermore these lines about the perishing of birthing forms come as a response to the King's embarrassment at the ladies' hands:

King: Berowne, they will shame us; let them not approach.
Ber.: We are shame-proof, my lord; and 'tis some policy
To have one show worse than the King's and his company.

(5.2.511–13)

Envy is internally riven because, as Hanna Segal says, it is "aimed at the object of love and admiration."[27] Shakespeare shows us, in the spoiling attacks of the lord, an adult derivative of primal envy, in which envy of the ladies and the bounty they are felt to possess is displaced onto others, whose despoiling would be less of a threat to the lords than a spoiling attack on the ladies would be. Holofernes, Nathaniel, and their associates are a safer target because they are not idealized by the lords; but they are also a worthwhile target in that they are persistently creative, throughout the play but most grandly in the pageant.

The lords fail to know that they *are* being provisioned, and by the locals, and so their envy cannot be transformed to gratitude, their self-cleansing projections transformed to admiration and then identification. In this play with so many adumbrations of the garden of Genesis, it is one of the cruelest manifestations of the lords' envy against the Worthies that it escalates from a purposeful misnaming or mistaking of the names Judas Iscariot and Judas Maccabeus, ending with a pun on "Jude-ass" (5.2.595–628). The massed verbal attack on Holofernes' face ("a cittern-head," "the head of a bodkin," "a death's face in a ring," and so on) is finally and justly rebuked by the victim himself: "This is not generous, not gentle, not humble" (5.2.629). In this "not generous" we can hear an indictment of the lords' failure in gratitude; in "not humble" we are reminded that the lords still need to learn something like Armado's commitment to earth, to a style and deportment low or humble, *humilis*, which would also be to relieve some of the unacknowledged burden on the mother tongue.[28]

27. Hanna Segal, *Melanie Klein* (Middlesex, England: Penguin, 1979), 146.
28. Philippa Berry (*Shakespeare's Feminine Endings: Disfiguring Death in the Tragedies* [London: Routledge, 1999]) argues throughout that Shakespeare links his period's vitalism to the vernacular, for example: "This gross, but simultaneously philosophical, interest in nature's recycling of the 'waste' or surplus that remains after death is intimately related to a newly expansive sense of the richly fecund 'matter' of the vernacular tongues, as they established new semantic relationships with one another as well as with the classical languages. . . . what is produced is a . . . sedimentary layering of 'earthy' figurative meanings" (10–11).

The aggressions of this moment are variously and swiftly developed in the next ninety lines. Armado appears as Hector (a formalization of aggression in role playing); Costard reveals Jaquenetta's pregnancy and Armado's part in it (an "infamonizing" of Armado); they prepare to fight (aggression made physical); Armado is further humiliated by the discovery of his wool shirt, bespeaking his poverty; Marcade enters with news of death. With the exception of Marcade's entry, these discords are all articulations of envy. But they also open up a space in a tense scene for the creaturely vulnerabilities of all the mortal subjects: Hector buried, Jaquenetta pregnant, Armado impoverished, the Princess bereaved, her father dead. This is the crucial plot link between the dead-end of lords' amatory plot and the disarray of the Worthies, on the one hand, and the closure of the final songs on the other. The interruption of the pageant is the disintegration of the locals' last attempt at a performative identification with classical antiquity; their devotion to this tradition makes all the more striking their composition of the vernacular songs.

Lyric Catalogues

Love's Labor's Lost makes much of naming, proper names, nomenclature, and nicknames; the cruelty of the lords' jests on names and faces is redeemed in the translucent simplicity of the names of humans, birds, and flowers in the songs. And the songs accommodate many other elements of the whole play, as many commentators have shown.[29] Thus, for instance, the prospect of cuckoldry, which has created so many nervous jokes in the play, is acknowledged, given room, stabilized lyrically; the ubiquitous apples of the play recur in the roasted crabs of the Winter song; the recurring motif of earth and Armado's commitment to the plough are rectified and fulfilled in the ploughman's clocks of the Spring song; the labors of bearing that the lords have occluded find their acknowledgment in the work of winter survival; the compositional labors of sermons by parsons shows obliquely what is at stake to those whose everyday lives move freely between Latinity and vernacular. Because the catalogue form is relevant to my argument, as it has been in previous chapters, I quote the songs in at length:

---

29. See, for example, Carroll, *Great Feast of Language*; C. L. Barber, *Shakespeare's Festive Comedy: A Study of Dramatic Form and Its Relation to Social Custom* (Princeton: Princeton University Press, 1959), 113–18.

Spring: When daisies pied, and violets blue,
   And lady-smocks all silver-white,
And cuckoo-buds of yellow hue
   Do paint the meadows with delight,
The cuckoo then, on every tree
Mocks married men; for thus sings he,
       "Cuckoo;
Cuckoo, cuckoo"

. . . . . .

When shepherds pipe on oaten straws,
   And merry larks are ploughman's clocks;
When turtles tread, and rooks and daws,
   And maidens bleach their summer smocks,

. . . .

Winter: When icicles hang by the wall,
   And Dick the shepherd blows his nail,
And Tom bears logs into the hall,
   And milk comes frozen home in pail;
When blood is nipp'd, and ways be foul,
Then nightly sings the staring owl,
       "Tu-whit, tu-who!"—
A merry note,
While greasy Joan doth keel the pot.

When all aloud the wind doth blow,
   And coughing drowns the parson's saw,
And birds sit brooding in the snow,
   And Marian's nose looks red and raw;
When roasted crabs hiss in the bowl,
Then nightly sings the staring owl.

                             (5.2.894–926)

In the *Parlement*, Chaucer had emphasized his lyric's fusion of French and English elements: "The note, I trowe, imaked was in Fraunce, / The wordes were swiche as ye may heer fynde" (677–78); Shakespeare's songs take us from a putatively French setting to an emphatically English one—a geographical transposition achieved partly by means of the proper names Tom, Dick, Joan, and partly by means of the floral nomenclature taken from John Gerard's 1597 *Herball*.[30] As befits a composition by Holofernes and Nathaniel, lovers of Latin and of movements

30. J. W. Lever shows that the *Herball* was Shakespeare's source for the names; see "Three Notes on Shakespeare's Plants," *Review of English Studies*, n.s., 3 (1952): 117–29.

between Latin and English, the two seasons are named twice: "Hiems, Winter" and "Ver, the Spring" (5.2.891), the Latin names gesturing toward the borderline personification and medieval *débats* that so often vivify Shakespeare's work. The pieces are sung, but prior to singing was their "compiling" by "the two learned men" (5.2.886). So the songs are, among many other things, a triumphant vindication of their idiosyncratic, locally mediated devotion to humanist pedagogical practice, and testimony to the capacities of a lore humbler than that of the courtiers' love-discourse.[31]

The nomenclature of the floral catalogue rectifies the abuses of naming earlier in the play; moreover, its lexical history demonstrates the same commitment to the vernacular, and an even keener interest in shifting an entire literary history into what are used and represented as the simplicities of a homely native speech, that Chaucer shows in the *Parlement*. J. W. Lever cites a passage on the cuckoo-bird from Gerard that demonstrates the herbal's project of drawing Latinity through continental vernaculars into English, and even into British regionalisms. Indeed Gerard makes it as local as possible, bringing the name to his birth county and even the village "where I had my beginning" and claiming a native right to "christen": "They are commonly called in Latine *Flos Cuculi* . . . it is called in the Germaine toong *Wildercress*: in French *Passerage sauuage*: In English Cuckowe flowers: in Northfolke, Caunterburie bels: at the Namptwich in Cheshire where I had my beginning, Ladie smockes, which hath given me cause to christen it after my countrie fashion."[32] This geo-linguistic pattern obtains in the composition of the whole book. For Gerard's *Herball* began as a translation from the herbal *Pemptades*, by a Dutchman named Dodoens. This work had already been put into English once, by Henry Lyte. When the next English translator Dr. Priest died and the project came to Gerard, he endowed it with the local Elizabethan air for which gardeners have long loved it.[33] The Dutch Dodoens was himself part of a scholarly movement

31. For the kind of ancient and medieval lore on the cycle of seasons tapped by Holofernes and Nathaniel, see Theodore Silverstein, "The Art of *Sir Gawain and the Green Knight*," *University of Toronto Quarterly* 33 (1964): 258–78; and Rosemond Tuve, *Seasons and Months: Studies in a Tradition of Middle English Poetry* (Paris: Librairie Universitaire, 1933).

32. Lever, "Three Notes on Shakespeare's Plants," 120.

33. This information relies on Frank Anderson, *An Illustrated History of the Herbals* (New York: Columbia University Press, 1977), 225, and on Marcus Woodward, *Gerard's Herball: The Essence Thereof Distilled* (London: Spring Books, 1964). Gerard also had the help of the Flemish botanist L'Obel, who made over a thousand corrections to Gerard—what amounts to a collaboration between the Dutch and the English speakers.

away from the taxonomies of Mediterranean antiquity and toward the documentation of local—northern European—flora: "They . . . shattered the traditional notion that the plants of Europe made by one indivisible flora, all perfectly known and described by the ancients."[34] This shift of encyclopedic geography and the vernacularizing of herbal lore create a space within which the debt to the mother might be acknowledged. I think this is what accounts for the tone of glad gratitude underlying both Gerard and the lyric productions of Holofernes and Nathaniel.

Gratitude got much less attention from Melanie Klein than envy did. Michael Eigen reverts to Genesis to suggest Klein's own lack of receptivity or openness to space and breath proffered by a formative textual tradition:

> Melanie Klein's *Genesis* reads: "In the beginning was splitting, and splitting divides good from bad: good and bad objects, good and bad instincts, good and bad affects, good and bad egos." Other readers of Genesis wonder if she missed earlier elements of creation—the formlessness, chaos, nothing, breath, emergent life and world—and perhaps missed Eden before the apple is eaten.[35]

These elements of breath and emergent world, so central to Winnicott and others influenced by him in contradistinction to Klein, are anticipated by the Chaucerian and Shakespearean lyrics that bring some shapeliness of closure to their restive, inconclusive amatory plots. I said at the start of the last chapter that the nature lyrics of the *Parlement* and *Love's Labor's Lost* come to be framed *as* lyric in relation to their historical affiliations and in relation to the pressures and dynamics of the narrative surrounding them; this is why their alternative to courtly/amatory lyric carries so much affective force. The stance toward the givenness of the natural world in the lyrics is regularly one of gratitude—full-throated in the *Parlement*, alternately contented and wry in *Love's Labor's Lost*. The gratitude is earned through the unpredictable, often odd stresses and movements within each work. The aim of the singers is, as Chaucer's protagonist says, to be "Thankynge alwey the noble goddesse of kynde" (672).

The seasonal topics of the songs, as well, speak to the issue of gratitude. While we can see well enough that these lyrics, like lyric within narrative so often, slow the temporal momentum of the plot or draw it

---

34. Anderson, *Illustrated History*, 173.
35. Michael Eigen, *Psychic Deadness* (London: Jason Aronson, 1996), 29.

toward closure, the Chaucer and Shakespeare lyrics discussed here honor what Milton would call "grateful vicissitude"—the very processes of temporality and movement. Tom's, Dick's, and Joan's emblematic motions are all manifestations of that Winnicottian aggressive life force or motility marked at birth by the first breaths of air, henceforward the infant's pattern of taking in and expelling the world through a vigorous expansion of tissues. Tom, Dick, and Joan turn this aggression or mobility to the most elemental survival—warming, eating, bearing burdens. A similar point might be made about the songs' mention of milking, coughing, cooking, winter's cold penetrating the blood, laundry bleaching in the sun, and so on. In them humans meet the rough weather and elemental objects of the world and find themselves sturdy enough. They also find the world's objects sturdy and discrete, as if the sun, the muddy earth, the warmth or bitterness of the air, the natural eros pricking the birds are all subjects ready for encounter with the human.

If the aggressive, envious lords listen well enough, they may find in Tom, Dick, and Joan's sturdy survival of the cold transformative expansions of their identities—something more than contempt and amusement in observing the lower social orders, a new attention to the low elements they have disdained. And the locals who compose and perform the songs might find in them a temporal space in which to encounter the lords with poise and assertiveness or a Winnicottian aggression, an insistence on the worth of their vernacular artifacts—as Dull insists on his vernacular understanding of "haud credo" as "old grey doe." If catalogues offer a temporizing pause, a hovering as characters or listeners move between a safe, familiar place to a strange or risky one, then Shakespeare's catalogues create an interim that transforms the harshness of the preceding dramatic events. The space is marked formally by the movement from the blank verse, rhymed couplets, and prose of the dramatic plot into stanzas and refrains.[36]

The items of the songs' catalogues are metonymic in the simple sense, in that each is an emblem for the season that generates it and each movement from one item to the next involves a tiny turn or refining of the sea-

---

36. The lords' courting poems show that they know how to build in sonnets pretty rooms, of course, but the confined quality of their amatory verse is familiar to us from two decades of critique—not to mention the criticisms that the lords, chiefly Berowne, level at other characters' poems. Here I want to focus on the expansive movement from such closed lyric, as the play represents it, to its representation of an anglicized song tradition with roots in hexaemeral, encyclopedic, and herbal lore.

son's representation. But the catalogues are metonymic in an Irigarayan sense too, in that they hold open a space in which listeners may imaginatively engage in a choreography of distance from or nearness to the named natural objects; thus far, they are like the objects in the Song of Song's praise catalogues. In Shakespeare's lengthening chain of metonymies for the seasons, the temporal becomes the (imaginatively) spatiotemporal, as the songs come to hold us safely in an imaginatively entertained village or hall; and we are held safely in weather alternately kind and rough. My sense is that the lyrics of this play function in a maternal-acoustical way. It is not that they are *envelopes* from which we must eventually be expelled, envelopes to which we nostalgically hope to return through other objects of desire; that is what courtier-poets might like to think, viz., that women should love them by giving unstintingly of a presumed abundance. It is more that these songs are like the good-enough mother who has nurtured us but also left us to our own devices in her presence, so that we learn through repeated sallies within this space (the space of the lyric, the place of hall and village) that we are strong enough to meet the energies of the world. The lyrics voice a rueful appreciation of the seasons for being always changing yet always the same: extended figures for a matrix of transformation, at least for those strong enough to turn from aggressive envy and entrust themselves to mutability. Of course this means finding some way of moving into winter, age, and death, as well as summer, song, and the verdant seasons, as the Winter song suggests. This challenge the lords *may* take up as the play ends, and I will address it at more length in the next chapter, on Lucretius and his project to release us from the fear of death. Here it is enough to emphasize that in *Love's Labor's Lost*, entrusting oneself to mutability involves working through a range of discourses on maternity.

The trope of birdsong has a surprising relation to gratitude, understood as a creative generosity antithetical to envy. This we can see not only in Chaucer, Shakespeare, and other high-poetic writers, but clearly in Thomas Nashe, who personally knew as much about envy, anxiety, aggression, and their relations to written style as anyone could. In *Summers Last Will and Testament*, which plays out many of the same dynamics among lyric, plot, and seasonal temporality that I have studied here, envy is coupled with a failure of birdsong:

> At a solemne feast of the *Triumviri* in Rome, it was seene and observed
> that the birds ceased to sing, & sate solitarie on the house tops, by reason of

the sight of a paynted Serpent set openly to view. So fares it with us novices, that here betray our imperfections [in performing the Summer pageant]: we, afraid to look on the imaginary serpent of Envy, paynted in mens affections, have ceaed to tune any musike or mirth to your eares this twelvemonth, thinking that, as it is the nature of the serpent to hisse, so childhood and ignorance would play the goslings, contemning and condemning what they understand not.[37]

This passage contains no discrete elements that Nashe could not have known through reading in widely accessible ethical and poetic works from antiquity to his own time. But perhaps the avian thematic cluster of gratitude, envy, oral performance, vernacularity, and seasonableness is a particularly Chaucerian bequest to late-sixteenth-century writers. Assuming that Nashe and Shakespeare used either the 1532 edition of William Thynne or one of the many Chaucer editions based on Thynne, they would have found another treatment of birdsong and birds' marital choices on Saint Valentine's Day in the poem immediately following *The assemble of foules*, *The floure of Curtesy*. This poem also ends with a "balade symple," although it remains in the courtly complaint mode.[38] Birdsong, bird catalogues, lyric praise of the natural world, marital choice, Saint Valentine's Day, and the love of old books recur in various combinations, each telling a different drama of genre, in (using Thynne's titles) *The complaynt of mars and venus*, *The legende of good women*, the *Romaunt of the Rose*. If Nashe and Shakespeare could understand Chaucer to be a courtly and amorous poet, then the ethical issues of envy and gratitude, worked out through the poems' engagement with literary forms, would strike writers like Shakespeare and Nashe, attuned to inflections of voice, as a central feature of that courtly poet.

The prolific and vigorous representations of great creating Nature throughout Shakespeare's career arise in part because of the place he creates for himself between a specifically poetic history and the rapidly developing institution of the theater. He holds a place in which the mythopoeic, philosophic, infolded density of Dame Nature—the maternal Natura of Chaucer and his medieval continental predecessors—is naturalized into the ladies of *Love's Labor's Lost*, who hold off from any poet-lovers who have yet to discover their debt to the maternal. Retaining the emblematic, authoritative richness of the Franco-English god-

37. Nashe, *Works*, 3:234, lines 30–40.
38. See *Geoffrey Chaucer: The Works, 1532*, ed. D. S. Brewer (Ilkley, England: Scolar, 1969), fol. cclxxxiiii[v].

desses, the ladies take on as well the poise and wit that would be Shakespearean endowments to comic heroines for centuries.

One function of such heroines is to complicate the endings of their
works, to make their endings possibly happy, possibly amorous, and
certainly risky. Nonetheless, characters and reader or audience alike
have the gift of the lyrics. This is not a simple gift, though; how are we to
take them? Do we *want* to take them if we have been invested in the hope
of epithalamic endings? This is a particularly vexing question in the *Parlement of Foules*, and especially in regard to the last stanza of the poem:

> I wok, and othere bokes tok me to,
> To reede upon, and yit I rede alwey.
> I hope, ywis, to rede so som day
> That I shal mete som thyng for to fare
> The bet, and thus to rede I nyl nat spare.

(695–99)

It is commonplace to take this stanza as expressing frustration, dissat-
isfaction, or lack: the narrator's resolution to continue reading is supposed to vitiate the experience of the dream, or of the dream's closing
lyric, and therefore (the reasoning goes) the dream is a disappointment,
or fails to give what it should have given.[39] But why? Why, first of all,
should the protagonist's desire to continue reading imply disappointment in his dream? And why would he, or we, be looking to his dream
for some final satisfaction or repletion? What would count as good
enough satisfaction in dreaming? And why would reading and dream
be antithetical, as critics often assume, rather than contiguous phenomena? To take the stanza as testimonial of lack or failure seems tantamount to *our* making exorbitant demands on the dream, as if we had
been offered a gift and turned it down petulantly because, having it, we
still experienced desire. This failure in gratitude for song is *not* characteristic of Chaucer's protagonist; the entire stanza follows upon the
lyrics in much more interesting ways if it expresses gratitude for dreaming as well as for books that provoke wayward dreams and unanticipat-
able songs. R. A. Shoaf has even suggested that it is the particular, positive relation of the poet to the maternal-transformational element in this

---

39. One happy exception is David Lawton, *Chaucer's Narrators* (Woodbridge, England: D.
S. Brewer, 1985), 44–45: "Rather than bathos, Chaucer's return to his library is, in its quiet
way, as positive an event as the preceding roundel. Rather than contradicting the dream,
the narrator corroborates it."

poem that makes the poem's closure possible at all, and reminds us that the very fact of a real concluding stanza should startle us, given Chaucer's manifold ways of *not* concluding.[40] The Chaucerian protagonist, Shakespeare's Holofernes, and even Armado and Moth would have felt faith in and gratitude for the facts figured in the lines from the *Parlement* that appear on the title page of the 1598 Chaucer edition, presided over by Thomas Speght:

> Out of the old fields, as men sayth,
> Commeth all this new corn, fro yere to yere:
> And out of old books, in good fayth,
> Cometh al this new science that men lere.

40. R. A. Shoaf, in a response to my paper based on this material presented at the Thirtieth Congress on Medieval Studies, Kalamazoo, Mich., 1995.

PART FOUR

Death Is the Mother

7

Distinctions of Birth: Hunger for Immortality in Lucretius's *De Rerum Natura*

———————

If from the earth we came, it was an earth
That bore us as a part of all the things
It breeds and that was lewder than it is.
Our nature is her nature. Hence it comes,
Since by our nature we grow old, earth grows
The same. We parallel the mother's death.
She walks an autumn ampler than the wind
Cries up for us and colder than the frost
Pricks in our spirits at the summer's end,
And over the bare spaces of our skies
She sees a barer sky that does not bend.

—Wallace Stevens

In this part of the book I turn from biblical to Graeco-Roman traditions on the earth that bore us, and to Lucretius, whose resolute refusal of mythic creator gods allows him to entertain the pull on the imagination of feminine maternal creative processes. Lucretius's unrelenting purpose in *De rerum natura* is to free his reader from the fear of death, and this involves him in the task of facing the indifference of the natural world and of the mother, as Wallace Stevens does in the lines that I cite above.[1] We find Lucretius's aims bearable, perhaps, only because part of his therapeutic method is to invoke the splendor of the phenomenal world—its plant and animal life, its elements, lights, colors, sensations, and passions—with an attachment as deep as his depictions of death are fierce or even aggressive. To Lucretius's sensuous passages I will turn in a moment, following the long arcs of his movements with necessarily substantial quotations. Then I consider Lucretius's representations of the maternal: literal and mythic mothers, but also tropes within his arguments about matter, bodies, boundaries, flowings and fixed objects, creation and destruction. This great Lucretian physics takes me next to the poem's large-scale oscillations of creation and destruction and to the way that psychic destruction becomes the condition for discovering and welcoming the externality of the world (which means, for Lucretius, the possibility of a poetics of praise). Finally, I consider how he confounds what counts as life and death, chiefly in passages about dismemberment or loss of bounded bodily integrity. When I turn to Spenser and *The Faerie Queene*, book 4 in the next chapter, it will be to argue that he deploys all these Lucretian matters to probe chivalric romance's fascination with death—its nostalgia for a chthonic, deathly mother—and to create brilliant narrative escapes from this narrative black hole with Lucretius's praise poetry. In the process, I hope to represent the unexpected ease and fluidity of one of the most knotted and laborious romances ever written—*Faerie Queene* 4.3.

Floribund Ascetic: The Philosophical Speaker

The strenuous aim to bring to consciousness, acknowledge, then defeat the universal fear of death entails an exorbitant definition of what counts as reading a poem. Lucretius demands of his listener Memmius a willingness to cleave to the vertiginous arguments of the Epicurean teacher, a willingness to bring to light and abolish deep-rooted anxieties about our primordial exposure, a willingness to undergo the agonies evoked by sustained contemplation of suffering, to move with Lucretius's habit of eliciting the strongest possible intuitive and emotional objections to his arguments in order to defeat them. We are exhorted to muster resources of energy, intellectual scope, courage to stand open to the arduous Epicurean schooling, and the fierceness to

---

1. Wallace Stevens, "Anatomy of Monotony" I, in *Collected Poems* (New York: Knopf, 1954), 107–8.

embrace the famous Epicurean dictum: "Nil igitur mors est ad nos" [Therefore death is nothing to us] (3.830).[2]

But the speaker also intends the reader to form a right relation to the living world, by developing a sense of present pleasure in and gratitude for the gifts of the senses:

> deinde animi ingratam naturam pascere semper
> atque explere bonis rebus satiareque numquam,
> quod faciunt nobis annorum tempora, circum
> cum redeunt fetusque ferunt variosque lepores,
> nec tamen explemur vitai fructibus umquam,
> hoc, ut opinor, id est, aevo florente puellas
> quod memorant laticem pertusum congerere in vas,
> quod tamen expleri nulla ratione potestur.

> [Then to be always feeding an ungrateful mind, yet never able to fill and satisfy it with good things—as the seasons of the year do for us when they come round bringing their fruits and manifold charms, yet we are never filled with the fruits of life—this, I think, is meant by the tale of the damsels [the Danaids] in the flower of their age pouring water into a riddled urn, which, for all their trying, can never be filled.]

> (3.1003–10)[3]

Critical discussion of these lines often assumes a split between Lucretius the poet and Lucretius the philosopher, a split that he cannot help.[4] By these lights attachment to mutable life and the seasons belongs to the poet, and is attacked by Lucretius the philosopher. But Lucretius, it seems to me, *wants* to heighten our attachment to life and to the phenomenal world, as well as our awareness of the costs of such attach-

---

2. Epicurus's statement that "death is nothing to us," *Principal Doctrines* 2, can be found in Epicurus, *Letters, Principal Doctrines, and Vatican Sayings*, trans. Russel Geer (New York: Macmillan, 1985), 60. On address and form in Lucretius, see Gian Biagio Conte, *Genres and Readers: Lucretius, Love Elegy, Pliny's Encyclopedia* (Baltimore: Johns Hopkins University Press, 1994), 1–34.

3. I use the text and commentary of Cyril Bailey, *Titi Lucreti Cari De rerum natura libri sex*, 3 vols. (Oxford: Clarendon, 1947) with W. H. D. Rouse's translation as revised by Martin Smith in the Loeb edition (1924; Cambridge: Cambridge University Press, 1992).

4. See, for example, Martha Nussbaum, *The Therapy of Desire: Theory and Practice in Hellenistic Ethics* (Princeton: Princeton University Press, 1994), 221–22; Phillip DeLacy, "Process and Value: An Epicurean Dilemma," *Transactions of the American Philological Association* 88 (1957): 114–26; William Anderson, "Discontinuity in Lucretian Symbolism," *Transactions of the American Philological Association* 91 (1960): 1–29; Diskin Clay, *Lucretius and Epicurus* (Ithaca, N.Y.: Cornell University Press, 1983).

ment. Acknowledging death, Lucretius also orients us toward the animation and motility of processes, flows, turbulences, seasonal cycles, constantly changing showers of light and color, the ephemeral objects that he loves the most.[5] He gives himself over to exaltations as he envisions the borders of light, the glittering air, the processions of the sky, the fecundity of spring; he breaks into praise of the peacock's splendor; he is unexpectedly moved by the memory of red, yellow, and purple theater awnings; he has sudden upsurges of fear and urgency about the implications of atomism; he tenderly contemplates the deaths of poets and philosophers. He is repeatedly drawn to opulent myths that he rejects and then reclaims. These myths include a wide array of characters and plot motifs from the Greek: Phaethon's burning chariot, Epicurus's heroic journeys, the Olympians generally. Like Wallace Stevens's ascetic character in "Landscape with Boat," Lucretius "brushed away the thunder, then the clouds, / Then the colossal illusion of heaven."[6] But like Stevens he is ambivalent in his attitudes toward myth and its power to mediate between devotion to and detachment from the mutable world; he repeatedly summons myth into his philosophical poetry.

Lucretius's speaker is, to borrow a phrase from Wallace Stevens, a "floribund ascetic," one whose very commitment to sensation makes him unwilling to break entirely with the fictions and hymns of myth, particularly those of a maternal earth, Stevens's "archaic queen."[7] Both spurned and craved, she is repeatedly reduced to the perceptible objects of earth. But the poet also finds himself composing hymns to this grandest of all "fragrant mothers."[8] The Lucretian speaker's paradoxical status as floribund ascetic in relation to the matter which is also *mater* crystallizes many of the argumentative difficulties, cruxes, and challenges of the *De rerum natura*.

Lucretius's two ethical aims—achieving gratitude toward life and

5. The most passionate writer on Lucretius as a poet of flux is Michel Serres, *La Naissance de la physique: Dans le texte de Lucrèce: fleuves et turbulences* (Paris: Minuit, 1977); for an English translation of one chapter see "Lucretius: Science and Religion," in *Hermes: Literature, Science, Philosophy*, ed. Josué Harari and David Bell (Baltimore: Johns Hopkins University Press, 1982), 98–124. To Serres, Lucretius represents the path not taken by an excessively rational Western physics.

6. Stevens, *Collected Poems*, 241.

7. Wallace Stevens, "The Candle a Saint," in *Collected Poems*, 223.

8. Wallace Stevens, "To the One of Fictive Music," in *Collected Poems*, 88. I borrow more Stevensian phrases for the title of the next section. "Milky matters" appears in "Academic Discourse at Havana" III, and "ruinous waste" comes from "The Doctor of Geneva," in *Collected Poems*, 144, 24.

(somehow, therefore) a right relation to death—generate the paradox that fuels his whole poem. Can study of the nature of things make the reader face death with composure and yet receive life with exaltation? We are creatures primordially exposed to the enormous energies and violence of the physical world:

> tum porro puer, ut saevis proiectus ab undis
> navita, nudus humi iacet, infans, indigus omni
> vitali auxilio, cum primum in luminis oras
> nixibus ex alvo matris natura profudit,
> vagituque locum lugubri complet, ut aequumst
> cui tantum in vita restet transire malorum.

> [Then further the child, like a sailor cast forth by the cruel waves, lies naked upon the ground, speechless, in need of every kind of vital support, as soon as nature has spilt him forth with throes from his mother's womb into the regions of light, and he fills all around with doleful wailings—as is but just, seeing that so much trouble awaits him in life to pass through.]

> (5.222–27)[9]

Then how can we protect ourselves otherwise than with the defensive action of seeking a godlike detachment? Yet temporal process also offers great gifts, and they too are gifts of generation. Then how can we forego the entailments of accepting such gifts as birth? Given Lucretius's eerie brilliance in evoking primitive agonies about dissolving into oblivion, falling apart forever, being crushed, suffocated, dismembered, putrefied and so on (especially in book 3), how can the reader find herself in the unexpected position of choosing, not the immortality of the serene gods, which would also mean death for humans, but the mortality of creatures in the phenomenal world—which means cleaving to the organic life of the body? I approach these problems by charting the poem's representations of maternity and its consequent, surprising paths to aggression, or Winnicottian destruction, on which the speaker embarks. He grows up and away from birth, as it were, in the poem's progress. This is clear enough in the darkening of his positions and in the large-scale movement from initial celebration of the creatrix Venus to the horrors of the plague which conclude the poem. But he grows away from birth insofar

---

9. On the range of possible ideas of birth, the young child, and maternity, see the bibliographical essay; see also Norman O. Brown, "Rome—A Psychoanalytic Study," *Arethusa* 7 (1974): 95–101, for the ways that maternity informs the very idea of Rome.

as his mytho-philosophical representations of maternity come to acknowledge mothers' separateness or otherness. A subtle, constantly shifting interplay of proximity and distance characterizes both the representations of maternity and the relationship between speaker and elements of the phenomenal world.

From Milky Matters to Ruinous Waste: The Sequence of Mothers

Sown thickly throughout the *De rerum natura*, references to mothers, maternal qualities, and birth govern its great arcs of affect. The grand and responsive *alma Venus* invoked at the start is closely allied with a maternal Natura (e.g., 3.931–62), with the fecund earth who acts most spectacularly in the creation narrative at 5.772–836, and with the Magna Mater whose cult and person, described at 2.600–644, follow one of the many paeans to the ceaseless generativity of earth (2.509–99). There is a detailed description of a cow who has lost her calf (2.352–66). The maternal earth appears frequently as womb and tomb, often with the tender implication of her cradling action: Lucretius speaks of "eos . . ./ morte obita quorum tellus amplectitur ossa" [those who have encountered death, whose bones rest in earth's embrace] (1.134–35).[10] This maternal earth is often autochthonous in her generative actions, but Lucretius is equally willing to use the different model of the *hieros gamos* or sacred marriage:

> Denique caelesti sumus omnes semine oriundi;
> omnibus ille idem pater est, unde alma liquentis
> umoris guttas mater cum terra recepit,
> feta parit nitidas fruges arbustaque laeta
> et genus humanum.

> [Lastly, we are all sprung from celestial seed; all have that same father, from whom our fostering mother earth receives liquid drops of water, and then teeming brings forth bright corn and luxuriant trees and the race of mankind.]
> (2.991–95)[11]

Throughout the poem, forces less overtly maternal than the mother's are knit into the fabric of a maternal lexicon.[12] The Muses' honey links

10. See also the tenderness of the womb/tomb of earth at 3.1035, 3.1037–38, 5.258–59.

11. Lucretius here imitates lines from Euripides' *Chrysippus*; Clay demonstrates that Lucretius moves from Greek to Roman worlds in such a way as to diminish the mythic sense of divinity in the passage. See *Lucretius and Epicurus*, 240–42.

12. Patrice Villani ("L'hymne à la naissance," in *Analyses et réflexions sur Lucrèce: De la nature. L'hymne à l'univers* [Paris: Ellipses, 1990], 27) cites Govaert's counts of words related to procreation: *genus* appears 113 times, *genitabilis* 17, *gigno* 59, *orior* 26, *origo* 15, *natura*

the poetry that ameliorates bitter philosophical truth to the sphere of mother's milk, food, nurture, and bountiful poetic gifts. Even the sea, as Charles Segal cautiously suggests, represents one kind of maternal presence, threatening oblivion and loss of differentiation, as in the shipwreck caused by "infidi maris insidias virisque dolumque" [the treacherous deep, with her snares, her violence, and her fraud] (2.557).[13]

The poem's well-known invocation praises the Venus *genetrix* from whom Lucretius hopes for an intimacy like that already enjoyed by Mars:

> tu sola potes tranquilla pace iuvare
> mortalis, quoniam belli fera moenera Mavors
> armipotens regit, in gremium qui saepe tuum se
> reicit aeterno devictus vulnere amoris,
> atque ita suspiciens tereti cervice reposta
> pascit amore avidos inhians in te, dea, visus,
> eque tuo pendet resupini spiritus ore.

> [You alone can delight mortals with quiet peace, since Mars mighty in battle rules the savage works of war, who often casts himself upon your lap wholly vanquished by the ever-living wound of love, and thus looking upward, with shapely neck thrown back, feeds his eager eyes with love, gaping upon you, goddess, and, as he lies back, his breath hangs upon your lips.]

$$(1.31–37)[14]$$

At the start of the poem, the speaker identifies with Mars's place in the lap of the goddess. Lucretius situates himself as a child held by a mother in an embrace both erotic and maternal, in whose visage he seeks responsiveness. And she provides it: she is smiling; without her, "neque fit laetum neque amabile quicquam" [nothing joyous and lovely is made] (1.23); his epic invocation is optimistic: "te sociam studeo scribendis versibus esse / . . . / quo magis aeternum da dictis,

---

(which has "birth" as one of its meanings) 236, *semen* 108, *creo* 97, *cresco* 50. Villani reminds us of the Indo-European root **g'n*, which gave rise to one lexical line conserving the notion of parenthood (*gigno, gens, genetrix*, etc.) and another conserving the idea of birth: *nascor, natus, natura, nativus* (which has "mortal, perishable" as one of its meanings).

13. Charles Segal, *Lucretius on Death and Anxiety: Poetry and Philosophy in* De rerum natura (Princeton: Princeton University Press, 1990), 83–93. Segal also joins to this oblivion/maternity pattern the description in book 3 of fainting, death, and loss of consciousness as forms of drowning.

14. On the cult of Venus Genetrix promoted by Julius Caesar, see Roger Ulrich, *The Roman Orator and the Sacred Stage: The Roman "Templum Rostratum"* (Brussels: Latomus, 1994), 128–30.

diva, leporem" [you I crave as partner in writing the verses. . . . Therefore all the more grant to my speech, goddess, an ever-living charm] (1.24–28).

Venus presents one aspect of a fortunate Winnicottian infant's mother. In Winnicott's transformation of Lacan's mirror stage and the role of illusion in it, the infant studies mother's face, and the mother—animate, not merely reflective—gives back to the infant a dynamic, subjective sense of self. Winnicott wishes to articulate not the illusion of bodily integrity and power that the Lacanian infant gains; the mechanisms by which the infant could achieve this identification would be more complex than any that the Winnicottian infant could deploy. Rather the mother bestows a gradually cohering animation and sense of feeling real made possible in part by what she receives (or thinks she receives) in exchanges with the baby: "What does the baby see when he or she looks at the mother's face? I am suggesting that, ordinarily, what the baby sees is himself or herself. In other words the mother is looking at the baby and *what she looks like is related to what she sees there.*"[15] If an infant repeatedly discovers its capacity to elicit the facial and affective responsiveness of Mother, this makes for the flourishing of creative capacity. It requires action by both: Baby regards Mother and Mother regards Baby in the vocative mood, a calling-forth of further exchange. This process over time is characteristically Winnicottian in its articulation of the interim, an open-ended period of such subtle exchanges that the theorist must live with the anxiety of not predicting its nuances and effects on either participant. Mother and child seek mutual responsiveness, and even acknowledgment. The conversation grows to encompass the mother's questions "Am I real to you, baby? Do you recognize me? How will you take my existence, once you discover it?" and the baby's "Will you respond to my initiating gestures as if I am a subject to you? How will you allow yourself to be changed by my existence?"

On the other hand, if infants have repeated experiences "of not getting back what they are giving," "mother's face is not then a mirror. So perception takes the place of apperception, perception takes the place of that which might have been a beginning of a significant exchange with the world, a two-way process in which self-enrichment alternates with the discovery of meaning in a world of seen things" (113). This mere "perception" alienates the child from a proper sense of its own reality

15. D. W. Winnicott, "Mirror-role of Mother and Family in Child Development" (1967), in *Playing and Reality* (London: Routledge, 1971), 111–18, at 112.

and from contact with the world. "Perception" seems to be Winnicott's courteous or carefully offhanded way of defining the Lacanian mirror stage as a pathology or a misfortune for the child who is thus alienated.

Lucretius is emphatically not alienated in this way at the start of the *De rerum natura*. He sees the face of *alma Venus* everywhere, as if, having internalized the linked experiences of nurture and animated maternal regard, he now disperses that internal fund of goodwill in his own grateful adult regard of the world, which fills up with Venus and takes on the aspect of a face:

> Aeneadum genetrix, hominum divumque voluptas,
> alma Venus, caeli subter labentia signa
> quae mare navigerum, quae terras frugiferentis
> concelebras, per te quoniam genus omne animantum
> concipitur visitque exortum lumina solis:
> te, dea, te fugiunt venti, te nubila caeli
> adventumque tuum, tibi suavis daedala tellus
> summittit flores, tibi rident aequora ponti
> placatumque nitet diffuso lumine caelum.

> [Mother of Aeneas and his race, darling of men and gods, nurturing Venus, who beneath the smooth-moving heavenly signs fill with yourself the sea full-laden with ships, the earth that bears the crops, since through you every kind of living thing is conceived and rising up looks on the light of the sun: from you, O goddess, from you the winds flee away, the clouds of heaven from you and your coming; for you the wonder-working earth puts forth sweet flowers, for you the wide stretches of ocean laugh, and heaven grown peaceful glows with outpoured light.]

> (1.1–9)

Clearly for Lucretius the internalized representation (the good object) of the mother is not so much a fixed imago in the picture plane of the mind; rather the face is a configuration of changing processes and transformative events, both physiological and psychic—smiling, acknowledging, blessing, eliciting, asking, inspiring. The varied actions of the poem's internalized mother will later make possible her other qualities, including even indifference to the early, seeking infant.

This is so because the therapeutic path of Lucretius's poem requires, like Winnicottian therapy, a more strenuous form of acknowledgment between subjects: between mother and child, between poet-philosopher and reader: *As I stand open and exposed before you, lay yourself open to me.* Further still, both therapies call for a gradually developed hardiness to lay oneself open to the fact of one's own primordial exposure to the enormous energies of the world. In this poem, it is Lucretius's capacity to see the benign Venus first and his assumption of her participation in his creative activity which permit his later ability to bear the indifferent mother. Even in the earliest intimacy of poet and smiling goddess, the term *genetrix* is a rather more august term than, say, *mater*; the genetrix of Aeneas carries some aura of the heroic. The very winds and clouds, elsewhere so destructive, flee before her: Lucretius acknowledges her might and her larger, sometimes alarming history.

The Venus who inspires the poet with bounty and joy throughout book 1 never abandons the poem, but cedes representational dominance to other kinds of mothers and other conditions of proximity or distance. The movement from book 1's invocation to the vignettes of the bereaved heifer and Magna Mater in book 2, for instance, is a movement from intimacy with a presiding goddess to acknowledgment of more distant maternal characters—in particular, mothers of other species. The Lucretian speaker evinces a measure of compassionate gravitas by his relative proximity to or distance from the maternal vignettes he contemplates. Thus, if book 2 opens with his disturbing complacence in the safety of distance—"Suave, mari magno turbantibus aequora ventis, / e terra magnum alterius spectare laborem" [Pleasant it is, when on the great sea the winds trouble the waters, to gaze from shore upon another's great tribulation] (2.1–2), nonetheless he begins to realign distance with a capacity for compassion.[16] In the vignette of the heifer whose calf has been sacrificed by superstitious humans (2.352–70), the speaker's distance provides occasion for sympathy and fellow feeling, not for superiority.[17] The cow wanders, seeks, surveys; she moans, yearns, revisits the stall, will not be comforted. The philosopher's detachment is, as before, a topological distance allowing him to scan many locations: altars, green glens, leafy woods, the stall, rich pastures, and flowing streams. Across this distance his mobile compassion reaches. Thus a movement from sites of desolation to *pabula laeta* highlights by way of contrast the cow's isolated suffering. Or again, the speaker expresses grief for the heifer and also pleasure in his topographical sketch of new life in the spring—

16. See DeLacy, "Epicurean Dilemma," for the poem's ideal of philosopher as spectator who can achieve *ataraxia* or detachment and its conflict with the notion of the compassionate subject immersed in experience. I think this not a weakness but an intentional strategy of the poem, as if Lucretius is challenging himself as well as the reader.

17. On this apparent digression and its pertinence to the poem's aims, see Charles Segal, "*Delubra decora*: Lucretius II.352–66," *Latomus* 29 (1970): 104–18.

something that requires sophisticated and ethical developments of the ability to distinguish self from other, and to be productively split within oneself. Just after this passage, the speaker insists upon the value of every distinct member of a species, and his examples, grains of corn and shells on the shore, are located with a gentleness that stem directly from the vignette of the bereaved heifer: "telluris gremium" [the lap of the earth] and "litoris incurvi" [the curving shore] (2.375–76).

The lengthiest description of a maternal figure in book 2, the Magna Mater goddess and her cult, places her not chiefly in a landscape but in the minds of her followers; because the speaker feels a good deal of ambivalence about her, distance and proximity function in more oblique and complicated ways. Suspension between scorn of and fascination with the goddess, and a simultaneous pleasure in the crafting of his representation of the Magna Mater, make sense if the passage models the child's early oscillation of creative reach from and periodic retrenchment to the maternal shelter, movements that occur in conjunction with the mother's dual actions of holding and pushing away. At first Lucretius pays homage to the maternal powers of the containing, nurturing earth with one of his many survey catalogues of locations and forces (2.589–97). Although he mentions fires and volcanoes, he focuses on the creations of earth that nurture humankind:

> tum porro nitidas fruges arbustaque laeta
> gentibus humanis habet unde extollere possit,
> unde etiam fluvios frondis et pabula laeta
> montivago generi possit praebere ferarum.

> [Then further, she contains the means to raise up bright corn and fruitful trees for the races of mankind, the means to produce rivers and leaves and fruitful pastures for the mountain-ranging brood of wild beasts.]

> (2.594–97)

Gratitude gives way to Lucretius's indictment of the Magna Mater's cultic excesses, as if they were an affront to the maternity of earth. But at the midpoint of the hostile passage, quiet in the midst of the obnoxious horns, drums, and wild dancing, one five-line sentence seems to attribute agency and goodwill to this majestic Mother, as if she were real to the speaker or had suddenly fused in his mind with the fruitful earth:

> ergo cum primum magnas invecta per urbis
> munificat tacita mortalis muta salute,

aere atque argento sternunt iter omne viarum
largifica stipe ditantes ninguntque rosarum
floribus umbrantes Matrem comitumque catervas.

[Therefore as soon as she rides through mighty cities, silently blessing
mankind with unspoken benediction, they bestrew the whole path of her
progress with silver and copper, enriching it with bounteous largess, and
snow down rose-flowers in a shower, over-shadowing the Mother and her
escorting troop.]

(2.624–28)

As Diskin Clay emphasizes, Lucretius argues that human beings mistakenly attribute qualities of divinity to their mortal experiences. Yet in
these lines the speaker's own attributions of qualities to the Mother
show the precarious balance between real and fantasized, or external
and internal. It is not only the Mother's majesty that moves him, for he
seems to take the ancient Greek iconographic details about the goddess
positively, on the whole:[18]

Hanc veteres Graium docti cecinere poetae
sedibus in curru biiugos agitare leones,
aeris in spatio magnam pendere docentes
tellurem neque posse in terra sistere terram.
. . . .
muralique caput summum cinxere corona,
eximiis munita locis quia sustinet urbis.

[She it is of whom the ancient and learned poets of the Greeks have sung,
that seated in a chariot she drives a pair of lions, thus teaching that the
great world is poised in the spacious air, and that earth cannot rest on
earth. . . . And they have surrounded the top of her head with a mural
crown, because embattled in excellent positions she sustains cities.]

(2.600–607)

Nonetheless, this goddess is no mother of responsive regard; she has
other interests and orientations than does the *alma Venus* of book 1.

18. On the fusions of Cybele, the Roman Tellus, and a maternal earth, see J. Perret, "Le
'mythe de Cybèle': Lucrèce II, 600–660," *REL* 13 (1935): 332–57; Anthony Esolen, "Spenserian Chaos: Lucretius in *The Faerie Queene*," *Spenser Studies* 11 (1990): 31–51. Lucretius is not
alone in ambivalence toward the goddess; DeLacy calls the Magna Mater a "frightful lady"
who heads "the cosmic household." "Distant Views: The Imagery of Lucretius II," *Classical
Journal* 60 (1964): 53.

Indeed the speaker is reluctant even to hold this Great Mother in his own mind, and buffers her internalized image in his thought, as it were, with her misguided followers. It is they who fabricate this fiction, they who rationalize their bizarre beliefs, they whose cult is alien and distant. They function as containers to receive the projection of his representations:

> hanc variae gentes antiquo more sacrorum
> Idaeam vocitant matrem Phrygiasque catervas
> dant comites, quia primum ex illis finibus edunt
> per terrarum orbem fruges coepisse creari.
>
> . . . .
>
> tympana tenta tonant palmis et cymbala circum
> concava, raucisonoque minantur cornua cantu,
> et Phrygio stimulat numero cava tibia mentis,
> telaque praeportant violenti signa furoris,
> ingratos animos atque impia pectora vulgi
> conterrere metu quae possint numine divae.

[She it is whom different nations in their ancient ritual acclaim as the Idaean Mother, and give her troops of Phrygians to escort her, because men declare that first from that realm came the corn, which then spread over the round world. . . . The taut tomtoms thunder under the open palm, the hollow cymbals sound around, horns with hoarse-echoing blare affright, hollow pipes prick up the spirits with their Phrygian cadences, martial arms show a front of violent fury, that they may amaze the ungrateful minds and impious hearts of the vulgar with fear through the goddess's majesty.]

(2.610–23)

These characters allow the speaker to distance himself from both the excesses of the cult and the religious awe throughout the passage. The internal mother is safe to contemplate because so clearly marked as a fiction, and one belonging to others: "Quae bene et eximie quamvis disposta ferantur, / longe sunt tamen a vera ratione repulsa" [But well and excellently as all this is set forth and told, yet it is far removed from true reasoning] (2.644–45). And yet: "Concedamus ut hic terrarum dictitet orbem / esse deum matrem, dum vera re tamen ipse / religione animum turpi contingere parcat" [let us grant him (anyone who wants to use the names of the gods) to dub the round world Mother of the Gods, provided that he forbears in reality himself to infect his mind with base superstition] (2.659–60). This "him" is not only hypothetical; it is also the speaker, who goes on throughout the rest of the poem to call the earth "mother." The fictive goddess and her cult fascinate the speaker; the passage as a whole functions as Lucretius's enlargement of the idea (or internal object) of the mother. Through it he entertains notions of mother's wildness, which includes her orientation away from the mother/infant dyad. If a nurturant Venus structures the horizon of the early parts of the poem by regarding him, curving over him like the sky, the Great Mother is more august and more stern. Like Stevens's hard maternal earth, she sees "a barer sky that does not bend."

The pattern of movement from a benignly regarding creatrix mother to a more complicated, less nurturant mother occurs also on a larger scale, as in the transformations between books 5 and 6. Book 5, Lucretius's book of creation, is dense with figures of birth, most strikingly in the long account of the world's creation near its center (5.780–876). It begins in the realm of *alma Venus*: "nunc redeo ad mundi novitatem et mollia terrae / arva, novo fetu quid primum in luminis oras / tollere et incertis crerint committere ventis" [I now return to the world's infancy and the soft fields of earth, to tell what first they thought fit to bring forth into the regions of light with new birth-throes and to commit to the wayward winds] (5.780–82). Those final birth-throes and wayward winds launch the creature away from the tender mother, into exposure to the enormous energies of the world. Soon Lucretius contemplates the earth's aging and loss of procreative power. This loss is anticipated by faulty creations—mutations—for instance creatures born without mouth or eyes, or with limbs adhering to their bodies; he considers the extinction of species; he considers monsters formed in imagination, like the centaur and chimaera; he considers the prehistory of humankind and its relation to a maternal earth. This prehistory places Lucretius and his contemporaries further and further from a nurturant mother earth. The last 250 lines of book 5 finally ponder the violence of nature in thunderbolts and tempests, a topic developed as a line of thought leading to the ever greater violence of natural forces in the first half of book 6, a book of destruction. In the middle of book 6 the speaker turns from the violence of sky and sea to the indifferent destructions of that rocky, noxious earth whose maternalizing has proven so irresistible throughout the poem:

> et in primis terram fac ut esse rearis
> subter item ut supera ventosis undique plenam
> speluncis multosque lacus multasque lacunas

in gremio gerere et rupis deruptaque saxa;
multaque sub tergo terrai flumina tecta
volvere vi fluctus summersaque saxa putandumst.
undique enim similem esse sui res postulat ipsa.

[And in the first place, be sure to consider the earth below as above to be
everywhere full of windy caverns, bearing many lakes and many pools in
her bosom with rocks and steep cliffs; and we must suppose that many a
hidden stream beneath the earth's back violently rolls its waves and sub-
merged boulders; for the facts themselves demand that she be everywhere
like herself.]

(6.536–42)

These lines launch a disquisition on explosions, eruptions, winds, earth-
quakes, and other powers of air and fire, and they pivot between the
completely nurturant and the distant mother. The last clause, for
instance, is not mere tautology but forges a causal link between earth's
benign fecundity—as in the middle of book 5—and her destructiveness,
by way of the notion of containers. To say that she must logically be like
herself is to acknowledge that the very inner recesses that make the
earth a container, womb, or genetrix of life-forms are the same rocky,
windy caverns that bring havoc to creatures. This Lucretian argument
proceeds by a strategy typical of the whole poem: accepting *alma Venus*,
we soon find ourselves obliged to accept the other mother who has
destructive proclivities.

To put it more strongly, Lucretius repeats the pattern of confirming his
speaker and reader in the strengths made possible by an initially nurturant mother and an authoritative mother *in order that* they be capable of
bearing the terrible destructions of book 6. There is not just a sequence
but an urgency from representations of the benign Venus to those of an
august, authoritative, and slightly alarming mother to those of a hard,
indifferent mother. To bear the burdens of book 6, not least the historical
Athenian plague with which we are challenged at the end of the poem
as we have it, is to have grown through enough births and separations
from *alma Venus*, to have grown up to the detached Lucretian compassion that marks adult ethical responsibility. After repeated encounters
with the mother at various distances and in various modes of regard
have enrolled us in an ethical subjectivity, the last two books demonstrate how history itself calls such a subject into ethical acknowledgment, in the form of the plague. The Athenian plague ends the poem's

flows of thought in a shocking historical narrative, and this strong switch in genre, while baffling to readers, is an achievement on the speaker's part. He has been moving toward this contemplation of a terrifying Natura from the start.

Nonetheless, the bleakness of this large movement from *alma Venus* to the plague is tempered by the poem's smaller-scale processions from fragrant mother to indifferent mother. Each time this process occurs—and it happens many times in the poem—there is an ethical development in the speaker, who moves from a floribund to an ascetic child of a mother. Yet Lucretius refuses to rest with any asceticism that is merely desolate; his education in facing death is also an education in gratitude, as in those passages of exaltation praising natural phenomena. How does this paradoxical speaker come about?

Destruction, Creation, and the Fixed Mother

Destruction, so frequent an event in Lucretian physics and poetry, can be fantasized, undergone, mastered, and represented, then generate new forms, precisely because of his notion of a "fixed mother" who survives fantasied destruction. In this section I argue for the link between the "fixed mother" and destruction, a link that makes the fixed mother necessary to Lucretius's argument; and I engage potential feminist critiques of this deployment of the maternal by a philosopher.

Apart from the perceivable mothers whom we have seen, a kind of mother exists for Lucretius in the atomistic composition of created bodies. Each object in the world is an intricate, unique structure of matter and void; it is the precise movements and distances among the atoms—or fixed seeds (*seminibus certis*)—which constitute objects:

atque eadem magni refert primordia saepe
cum quibus et quali positura contineantur
et quos inter se dent motus accipiantque;
namque eadem caelum mare terras flumina solem
constituunt, eadem fruges arbusta animantis,
verum aliis alioque modo commixta moventur.

[And it is often of great importance with what and in what position these same first-beginnings are held together, and what motions they impart and receive mutually; for the same beginnings constitute sky, sea, earth, rivers, sun, the same make crops, trees, animals, but they move differently mixed with different elements and in different ways.]

(1.817–22)

Lucretius recurs insistently to this sense of objects internally structured by space and motion.[19] The threat of destruction—as that which is without distinction—makes clear how much is at stake in the atomistic structure of objects: "denique res omnis eadem vis causaque vulgo / conficeret, nisi materies aeterna teneret, / inter se nexus minus aut magis indupedita" [Again, the same force and cause would destroy all things without distinction, unless everlasting matter held them together entangled more or less closely in their interlacing bonds] (1.238–40).

A crystalline, deeply knit and branching structure is guaranteed by the certain stability of the "mother" of each thing:

> quippe ubi non essent genitalia corpora cuique,
> qui posset mater rebus consistere certa?
> at nunc seminibus quia certis quaeque creantur,
> inde enascitur atque oras in luminis exit
> materies ubi inest cuiusque et corpora prima;
> atque hac re nequeunt ex omnibus omnia gigni,
> quod certis in rebus inest secreta facultas.

[Seeing that there would be no bodies apt to generate each kind, how could there be a constant unchanging mother for things? But as it is, because every kind is produced from fixed seeds, the source of everything that is born and comes forth into the borders of light is that in which is the material of it and its first bodies; and therefore it is impossible that all things be born from all things, because in particular things resides a distinct power.]

(1.167–73)[20]

The Lucretian "fixed mother," perhaps the most abstract instance of Stevens's "abstract, archaic queen," seems to participate in that unfortunate abjection of the feminine for which Irigaray, among others, repeatedly indicts philosophy. Is the maternal only a ground or substratum upon which philosophical knowledge can be built? Is maternity dispersed into tropes and postulates that preclude acknowledgment of a

---

19. See also 1.907–12, 2.444–46.

20. Cf. 2.700–709, where Lucretius argues that the rarity of monstrous mutations is evidence of "fixity" in seeds and mother; at 707–9 he says "quorum nil fieri manifestum est, omnia quando / seminibus certis certa genetrice creata / conservare genus crescentia posse videmus" [But that none of these things happen is manifest, since we see that all things bred from fixed seeds by a fixed mother are able to conserve their kind as they grow]. Translators often shy from the explicitness of the feminine "fixed mother"; Bailey's translation of *certa genetrice* is "of a fixed parent."

debt to the mother? Many passages in the *De rerum natura* are open to this line of critique; as Lucretius repeatedly insists,

> omnia sint a principiis seiuncta necessest,
> immortalia si volumus subiungere rebus
> fundamenta quibus nitatur summa salutis;
> ne tibi res redeant ad nilum funditus omnes.

> [All these (accidental qualities) must be kept apart from (the essential qualities of) the first-beginnings, if we wish to lay an imperishable foundation for things upon which the sum of existence may rest: or else you will find all things passing back utterly into nothing.]

> (2.861–64)

In all Lucretius's descriptions of the fixed mother, Irigaray might object as she does in *Speculum*, "even in the mother, it is the cohesion of a 'body' (subject) that he seeks, solid ground, firm foundation. Not those things in the mother that recall the woman—the flowing things."[21]

To arguments like this, one might respond that Lucretius's "fixed mother" at least shares the poem with other mothers, represented in their otherness and indifference, as we have seen. So *merely* abjecting the maternal is not what Lucretius is about. This does not eliminate the force of the objection, however. In order to show how the idea of the fixed mother in Lucretius does indeed acknowledge a debt to the maternal, I want first to recur to some notions from Klein and Winnicott, then to use them in following the track of the Lucretian speaker's unrelenting insistence on that fixed mother in the structure of matter, and in the destruction of matter.

For an extended period of time the human infant experiences fluctuating boundaries of itself relative to the world, especially to a maternal caretaker. Depending on the field of imaginary relations in which it finds itself, now it may be part of mother, or distinct from her and frustrated by an environment that allows it to suffer its hunger, or it may be excited by the formation of a nascent skin ego. The spectrum of variable, fine gradations in an infant's experience of its relation to mother— alliance, merger with, space between, protection by, disappearance before the threat of, distinctness from, and so on—forms its earliest sense of part-to-whole relations, in fact of the possibilities of metonymy

21. Luce Irigaray, "Volume-Fluidity" (1974), in *Speculum of the Other Woman*, trans. Gillian Gill (Ithaca, N.Y.: Cornell University Press, 1985), 227–40, at 237.

and synecdoche as fluent models for self-other relating.[22] There must be complex, layered, and overlapping experiences along this spectrum, and accompanying affects of complexity, confusion, excitement, anxiety, and contentment; and all of these must subtend values and anxieties circulating around integrity of bodily form, wholeness, and boundaries.[23] An extended period of such ambiguous, fluctuating emotion and epistemology now needs to be added to my earlier account of Winnicott on that destruction of the object that yields discovery of the externality of the world, and on the child's eventual ability to be alone in the presence of the mother. The baby may well say, as in Winnicott's account, "Hullo object!" "I destroyed you." "I love you." "You have value for me because of your survival of my destruction of you." But distinctions between internal and external continue to be negotiated throughout life, evoking complex affect constellations. Winnicott thinks of good internal objects as making possible the infant's gradual untethering from mother; he refers to possible substitutes for mother or, better, diffusions of her presence, through everyday objects like "a cot or a pram or the general atmosphere of the immediate environment."[24] This general world is unpredictable from the infant's prior experience: "In health the infant is helped by being given (by ordinary devoted Mum) areas of experience

22. James Grotstein posits a "dual-track theory" to account for the infant's experience: one of initial separation, which launches "the early infant" onto the path of becoming "the continuing infant," and another of postnatal oneness or fusion with the mother, an experience to which the subject may later regress. "Who Is the Dreamer Who Dreams the Dream and Who Is the Dreamer Who Understands It? A Psychoanalytic Inquiry into the Ultimate Nature of Being," *Contemporary Psychoanalysis* 15 (1979):110–69.

23. Many disciplines converge on the matter of bodily boundaries; see, for example, Mary Douglas, *Purity and Danger: An Analysis of Concepts of Pollution and Taboo* (New York: Praeger, 1966); Peter Stallybrass and Allon White, *The Politics and Poetics of Transgression* (Ithaca, N.Y.: Cornell University Press, 1986); Caroline Walker Bynum, *Fragmentation and Redemption: Essays on Gender and the Human Body in Medieval Religion* (New York: Zone Books, 1992) and *The Resurrection of the Body in Western Christianity, 200–1336* (New York: Columbia University Press, 1995); Gail Kern Paster, *The Body Embarrassed: Drama and the Disciplines of Shame in Early Modern England* (Ithaca, N.Y.: Cornell University Press, 1993). For bodily boundaries in antiquity, see R. F. Newbold, "Boundaries and Bodies in Late Antiquity," *Arethusa* 12 (1979): 93–114; Segal, *Lucretius on Death*, chaps. 3–7. Boundary-formation as a developmental issue is addressed extensively within psychoanalysis; a useful survey of this concern as a modernist and postmodernist phenomenon can be found in Kathleen Kirkby, *Indifferent Boundaries: Spatial Concepts of Human Subjectivity* (New York: Guilford, 1996), esp. 68–96.

24. D. W. Winnicott, "The Capacity to Be Alone" (1958), in *The Maturational Process and the Facilitating Environment: Studies in the Theory of Emotional Development* (Madison, Conn.: International Universities Press, 1965), 29–36, at 30.

of omnipotence while experimenting with excursions over the line into the wasteland of destroyed reality. The wasteland turns out to have features in its own right, or survival value, etc., and surprisingly the individual child finds total destruction does not mean total destruction."[25]

Indeed the materials of the wasteland become matter for inventiveness and feeling real. Christopher Bollas has described such destruction as part of a dialectic in the inexhaustible activity of the unconscious:

> Unconscious mental life operates according to an oscillation that ensures its continuous—indeed ceaseless—function, as on the one hand unconscious work brings together through condensation otherwise disparate ideas, and on the other hand the process of free association then deconstructs these condensations. . . . Both processes, however—bringing together and cracking up—are important features of the unconscious and constitute its dialectic; each time a condensation is created, its saturation with meaning guarantees that it will break up in subsequent moments of elaboration, and each unit of meaning, compacted in the condensation, now follows its own destiny.[26]

Manifestations of this dialectic include, for Bollas, not just psychoanalytic but also our poetic and intellectual projects. Historical construction, for instance, whether performed by analysts and patients or by historians, "collects in order to retrieve the self from its many meaningless deaths—the amnesial 'gone'—and then it generatively destroys these details and saturates them with new meaning created through the very act of retrieval, which has given them the imaginative and symbolic energy to make this past available for the self's future" (145). For Bollas, the debris trails of destruction become unconscious or preconscious disseminative paths to new condensations of saturated meanings. A Winnicottian ruthless, pre-ruth energy destroys objects so that they may be recreated and rediscovered in a new time. This is one form of what is called thinking.

Bollas takes this process as characteristic of everyday unconscious life. If we take it as characteristic of thinking, then it brings out the

25. D. W. Winnicott, "D. W. W.'s Dream Related to Reviewing Jung" (1963), in *Psycho-Analytic Explorations*, ed. Clare Winnicott, Ray Shepherd, and Madeleine Davis (Cambridge: Harvard University Press, 1989), 228–30, at 230. See also Winnicott, "Aggression in Relation to Emotional Development" (1950), in *Through Paediatrics to Psycho-Analysis: Collected Papers* (New York: Brunner/Mazel, 1992), 204–18.

26. Christopher Bollas, *Cracking Up: The Work of Unconscious Experience* (New York: Hill and Wang, 1995), 52–53.

urgencies of Lucretius's pedagogy. In Lucretius there would be three terms continually displacing one another: condensation, dispersal, destruction. Condensations would be manifest in his repeated hymns to natural fecundity, the sensuous, exalted proems, the descriptions of maternal figures and of material phenomena, as well as the most succinct statements of the atomistic argument. These arguments always expand into longer discursive streams of interwoven argument, example, and evocation of affect. These streams of thought in turn become dispersals. They are more rational, conscious, and philosophically explicit than Bollas's notion of dissemination, but they too are sustained by primary process: surges of feeling, association, and wordplay. They lead again and again to the spectacular cosmic and terrestrial destructions represented in the poem. "To shape—to re-present—is perhaps not just a pleasure but a demand," says Bollas; in Lucretius there is a marked demand to represent destruction, and to follow the dispersing implications of this destruction with a Winnicottian fierceness understood in the poem as fidelity to the truths of atomism and mortalism.[27] If, as Lucretius's passages on birth suggest, birth is both a gift and a catastrophe to the infant's ongoing sense of being, then his repeated representations of destruction permit mastery of the catastrophe through repeated thinking. The paradox that our fear of death compels us to seek death repeatedly would make sense if, for Lucretius, birth itself is the first "destruction," an event that befalls us but which we cannot encompass or symbolize when it befalls. As Winnicott would say of the fear of breakdown, our fear of death is a fear of that which has already happened.[28] Lucretius's therapeutic method, akin to Winnicott's, is first to evoke repeatedly the disaster in a survivable present, then to make bearable the dispersals entailed in the disaster, even to welcome forms of emptiness like the void, which inevitably gather toward new condensations and objects. In the words from Winnicott that I cited at the beginning of this book, "Emptiness is a prerequisite for eagerness to gather in.

27. Ibid., 44.

28. D. W. Winnicott, "Fear of Breakdown" (1963), in *Psycho-Analytic Explorations*, 87–95, at 92. Winnicott does not define birth as essentially catastrophic, but he does link Freud's death drive with specific early, once unassimilable traumas: "this thing of the past has not happened yet because the patient was not there for it to happen to." See also Françoise Davoine, "Potential Space and the Space in between Two Deaths," in *The Facilitating Environment: Clinical Applications of Winnicott's Theory*, ed. M. Gerard Fromm and Bruce Smith (Madison, Conn.: International University Press, 1989), 581–603.

Primary emptiness simply means: before starting to fill up."[29] Lucretius makes us see how harrowing such emptiness can be.

At the end of the chapter we shall return to the sense of birth as a destruction to be mourned. Here, a few instances of the varying sequences of condensation, destruction, and disseminations taken from books 1 and 2 will show this pattern at work in the smallest as well as the largest units of the poem. Within discursive verse paragraphs there may be oscillations from clause to clause, as if to elicit the reader's suppleness in the psychic movements necessary to the eventual aim of contemplating death with composure:

> Huc accedit uti quidque in sua corpora rursum
> dissoluat natura neque ad nilum interemat res.
> nam si quid mortale e cunctis partibus esset,
> ex oculis res quaeque repente erepta periret.
> nulla vi foret usus enim quae partibus eius
> discidium parere et nexus exsolvere posset.
> quod nunc, aeterno quia constant semine quaeque,
> donec vis obiit quae res diverberet ictu
> aut intus penetret per inania dissoluatque,
> nullius exitium patitur natura videri.

> [Add to this that nature resolves everything again into its elements, and does not reduce things to nothing. For if anything were perishable in all its parts, each thing would then perish in a moment snatched away from our sight. For there would be no need of any force, to cause disruption of its parts and dissolve their connections. But as it is, because the seed of all things is everlasting, nature allows no destruction of anything to be seen, until a force has met it, sufficient to shatter it with a blow, or to penetrate within through the void places and break it up.]

> (1.215–24)

Immediately after this conditional but vivid destruction, the world arises again, in a series of rhetorical questions about earth's reassuringly regular cycles of growth and nourishment:

> praeterea quaecumque vetustate amovet aetas,
> si penitus peremit consumens materiem omnem,
> unde animale genus generatim in lumina vitae

---

29. Winnicott, "Fear of Breakdown," 94.

redducit Venus, aut redductum daedala tellus
unde alit atque auget generatim pabula praebens?
unde mare ingenui fontes externaque longe
flumina suppeditant? unde aether sidera pascit?

[Besides, if time consuming all the material utterly destroys whatever by
lapse of years it removes, whence does Venus restore living creatures to the
light of life each after its kind, or, when they are restored, whence does the
wonder-working earth nourish them and make them grow, providing food
for each after its kind? Whence is the sea supplied by the springs within it,
and by the rivers without, flowing from afar? Whence does the ether nourish the stars?]

(1.225–31)

There is more of this oscillation, envisaging combinatory possibilities
then dispersing ones, for yet another verse paragraph; this train of
thought leads to the poem's first great *hieros gamos* and its remarkable
catalogue praises of natural fecundity—only to return swiftly to death:

postremo pereunt imbres, ubi eos pater aether
in gremium matris terrai praecipitavit;
at nitidae surgunt fruges ramique virescunt
arboribus, crescunt ipsae fetuque gravantur;
hinc alitur porro nostrum genus atque ferarum,
hinc laetas urbis pueris florere videmus
frondiferasque novis avibus canere undique silvas;
hinc fessae pecudes pingui per pabula laeta
corpora deponunt et candens lacteus umor
uberibus manat distentis; hinc nova proles
artubus infirmis teneras lasciva per herbas
ludit lacte mero mentis perculsa novellas.
haud igitur penitus pereunt quaecumque videntur,
quando alid ex alio reficit natura nec ullam
rem gigni patitur nisi morte adiuta aliena.

[Lastly, the raindrops pass away, when father Ether has cast them into the
lap of mother Earth; but bright crops arise, the branches upon the trees
grow green, the trees also grow and become heavy with fruit; hence comes
nourishment again for our kind and for the wild beasts; hence we behold
happy cities blooming with children and leafy woods all one song with the
young birds; hence flocks and herds, weary with their fat, lay their bodies
about the rich pastures, and the white milky stream flows from their

swollen udders; hence the young ones gambol in merry play over the delicate grass on their weakly limbs, their tender hearts intoxicated with neat
milk. Therefore no visible object utterly passes away, since nature makes
up again one thing from another, and does not permit anything to be born
unless aided by another's death.]

(1.250–64)

The whisper of dissolution at the end of this passage is a turning point.
Only a few lines later, the speaker leads his interlocutor Memmius to
envisage the destructive furor of wind and water: the wind beats upon
the ocean and overwhelms ships; hurricanes strew trees and flog mountains; flood waters wreck forests and break bridges (1.271–97).

By the end of book 1 it is evident that the speaker has discovered the
joy of mastering and riding such rhythmic sequences of thinking creation, destruction, and dispersal. The destruction concluding book 1
culminates two hundred lines of exaltation. First there is the book's second great proem, 1.921–50, in which the speaker is heady with the
power of his art as with the mountain air of the Muses, their honey and
their clear dark springs. Next the philosopher moves from this plenitude
of earth and its feeding of the poet's mind to engage the question of the
universe's extent: is it infinite or has it a boundary (1.951–1051)? Finally
Lucretius entertains the possibility of other, misguided views on the
construction of the world, in part for the peculiar satisfactions of imagining destruction (1.1052–1113). If these philosophies were true,

> ne volucri ritu flammarum moenia mundi
> diffugiant subito magnum per inane soluta
> et ne cetera consimili ratione sequantur
> neve ruant caeli tonitralia templa superne
> terraque se pedibus raptim subducat et omnis
> inter permixtas rerum caelique ruinas
> corpora solventis abeat per inane profundum,
> temporis ut puncto nil exstet reliquiarum
> desertum praeter spatium et primordia caeca.
> . . . .
> óóse turba foras dabit omnis materiai.

[(There is danger) lest the walls of the world suddenly be dissolved and
flee apart after the fashion of flying flames through the void, and the rest
follow in like manner, the thundering regions of the sky rush upwards, the
earth swiftly slip from under our feet, and amidst the commingled ruin of
sky and all things, letting their elements go free, utterly depart through the

empty profound, so that in one moment of time not a wrack be left behind except desert space and invisible elements. . . . the whole mass of matter will disperse abroad.][30]

(1.1102–13)

To get at the peculiar element of *savor* in this entertaining of the possibility of destruction, we turn to an account by Winnicott of a dream he had after writing a review about Jung, a review in which he had clarified his thought that "Jung seems to have no contact with his own primitive destructive impulses." In the dream,

> 1. There was absolute destruction, and I was part of the world and of all people, and therefore I was being destroyed. . . .
> 2. Then there was absolute destruction, and I was the destructive agent. Here then was a problem for the ego, how to integrate these two aspects of destruction?
> 3. Part three now appeared and *in the dream* I awakened. As I awakened I knew I had dreamed both (1) and (2). I had therefore solved the problem, by using the difference between the waking and sleeping states. Here was I awake, in the dream, and I knew I had dreamed of being destroyed and of being the destroying agent. There was no dissociation, so the three I's were altogether in touch with each other. I remembered dream I(2) and I(1). This felt to be immensely satisfactory although the work done had made tremendous demands on me.[31]

In Winnicott's dream about the uses of suffering and overcoming splitting, the unconscious supplies the character who blurs distinctions among destroying and destroyed versions of the protagonist, making possible his elation at moving freely among them. He discovers the energy released not so much in destroying as in *making a destruction*. This energy the Lucretian speaker also releases, through his sequences of identification with what is destroyed, identification with the

---

30. Rouse's translation borrows from Prospero's revels speech in *The Tempest* 4.1.146–58, "not a wrack be left behind." But Prospero's reverie creates a much more remote feeling tone than I think Lucretius presents here in his fierce, intent envisaging of destruction. Bailey's translation adopts Rouse's allusion. Rolfe Humphries' translation has "in one flick of time / Nothing be left but desert, chaos, darkness" (Lucretius, *The Way Things Are* [Bloomington: Indiana University Press, 1968]); Frank Copley's translation is "to leave, in a second, no remnant of themselves / except blind atoms and abandoned space" (Lucretius, *The Nature of Things* [New York: Norton, 1977]). Just before this passage there is a textual lacuna; it seems likeliest that the theories Lucretius depicts are those of the Stoics and the Peripatetics.

31. Winnicott, "D. W. W.'s Dream," 228–29.

destroyer, then a kind of new and unpredictable consequence of these two stages, which is the discovery that representations of destruction are not merely annihilative but also generative. There is a good deal of aesthetic risk in repeating world destructions so often as Lucretius does. The surplus of energy evident in his exalted intentness when he wins the risk can be seen in part as an ascetic joy that results from plunging into, rather than evading, the poem's anxieties about nothingness and entropy.

Winnicott's dream also demonstrates how both the destroyed and the destroyer may survive destruction; the dream of multiple selves leads him to an awareness not of self-alienation but of the self's hardiness. In a parallel way the Lucretian speaker welcomes with relief the return of the quotidian world, when his destructions lead through paths of argument into regenerative motions. It is not only that destructions in Lucretius lead to generation of new forms; it is that the destructions guarantee the survival of the world, its everyday phenomena, and himself. The poem repeatedly stages destruction or nonexistence, or entertains the possibility of monstrous creatures, in order to assure itself of the firm, fixed externality of the world (and, standing before the world, the "fixed mother"). The very structure and boundedness of objects is guaranteed by destructive onslaughts allowing us to know objects as external: "corpuscula materiai / ex infinito summam rerum usque tenere, / undique protelo plagarum continuato" [the small bodies of matter hold together the sum of things from infinity with an uninterrupted succession of blows from all sides] (2.529–31).

This limited and fixed order obtains insistently in book 2, where Lucretius frequently considers the threatening possibility that atoms could be infinite in number of shapes. This is false, false, it must be false. In Lucretius's repeated formula, "quare etiam atque etiam" [therefore again and again (I insist)]. If it *were* true that shapes were infinite,

> iam tibi barbaricae vestes Meliboeaque fulgens
> purpura Thessalico concharum tacta colore,
> aurea pavonum ridenti imbuta lepore
> saecla, novo rerum superata colore iacerent

> [Then, I tell you, barbaric vestments, and blazing Meliboean purple, dyed in the colour from Thessalian shells, and the golden generations of peacocks steeped in laughing grace, all would sink, outdone by some new colour in the world.]

>   (2.500–503)

The sudden reversion from logical argument about the necessary shapes of atoms (2.478–99) to percept, to this sweep of color and motion in the earth's dying generations, makes devastatingly clear how much is at stake in the argument about fixity. All the phenomena to which Lucretius can be attached in love—the arts and manufactures and sensory pleasures and categories by which we know the world—anthropological, geographical, ethological, mythological—all these things could be lost if the shapes of atoms were infinite. Worse, they could be *outdone*, and we humans could have importunate demands to respond with ever more intense and draining emotion made upon us by new objects. In an economy of excessive objects and enormous onslaughts of energies from the world, human subjects are depleted and mortal beauties cheapened:

> et contemptus odor smyrnae mellisque sapores,
> et cycnea mele Phoebeaque daedala chordis
> carmina consimili ratione oppressa silerent;
> namque aliis aliud praestantius exoreretur.

> [the odour of myrrh and the savour of honey would be despised; the swan's melody and Apollo's music set to the wonder-working art of strings would in like manner be vanquished and silent; for one thing more splendid than another would continually arise.]

> (2.504–7)

More splendors would mean more losses, and vice versa; this would be unendurable, we would be inadequate to the occasion either of the peacocks, grace or of the new objects in the world. It is with tremendous relief that Lucretius can arrive at the logical necessity of the fixity of things: "quae quoniam non sunt, sed rebus reddita certa / finis utrimque tenet summam, fateare necessest / materiem quoque finitis differre figuris" [Since this is not so, but a certain limit is set for things, which shuts in the sum from both sides, it must be confessed that matter also has a limited number of different shapes] (2.512–14). These high stakes of Lucretius's love of the phenomenal world and a precariously achieved poise of emotional response to it pervade much of the argument for atoms and their nature, themselves without color, texture, or any accidental properties at all, in the ways that their combinatory structures yield phenomena that command our hearts: "proinde colore cave contingas semina rerum, / ne tibi res redeant ad nilum funditus omnes" [forbear therefore to steep in color the seeds of things, lest you find that all things come back utterly to nothing] (2.755–56).

Once we are equipped through the practice and pleasure of thinking to face this kind of destruction, the ancient mother can return, young and passionate, in book 5, where she has purposes other and larger than feeding the speaker or even humankind generally. The force of her new distinctness from the speaker is precisely a function of his views on matter; he could not arrive at this sense of the otherwise occupied mother had he not worked through the implications of the "fixed mother." In book 5 the polarities of destruction and creation have developed into ceaseless processes of generativity, in which the dissolution of one form is the birth of another. Destruction has become positively consolatory, insofar as it permits recurring discoveries of the world's generality. The long account of earth's creative actions in book 5 is punctuated by frequent reminders that the earth is justly called mother: "linquitur ut merito maternum nomen adepta / terra sit" [it remains, therefore, that the earth deserves the name of mother which she possesses]; "Quare etiam atque etiam maternum nomen adepta / terra tenet merito" [therefore again and again the earth deserves the name of mother which she has gained] (5.795–96, 821–22).

In its pairing with book 6 (which I scant here) book 5 moves the speaker gradually from heady celebrations of immense fertility and bloom, through recognition of a distance from this summery mother, to earth's apparent indifference to the concerns of humans. Periodically there are those more representational mothers: Venus, Magna Mater, bereaved heifer. Lucretius's elaboration of the fixed atomistic mother, mother earth, and mothers generally is tightly interwoven with his speaker's movements of creation and destruction, and his sense of external, bounded objects. This is most emphatically and anxiously true of living bodies, chiefly human bodies, which are alarmingly vulnerable, for all their boundedness.

Yet another of Lucretius's core arguments about the human body—and physical bodies generally—is that we cannot escape a comfortable sense of the abidingness of things, and we therefore need to be made alarmed about the fleetingness of even the most durable of physical bodies. By book 5, the speaker who has been so excessively insistent on the logical necessity that created bodies take their forms by atoms internally fixed in relation to one another, and who had been so haunted by inevitable dispersals and destructions, struggles oddly against an intuitive assurance in the world's fixity. This assurance he assumes in his interlocutor, but it has its hold on himself as well. There is a hint of his sense of the world's generosity or sturdiness throughout the poem, in passages about the bounty of the phenomenal world; in book 5 it is explicit:

principio maria ac terras caelumque tuere;
quorum naturam triplicem, tria corpora, Memmi,
tris species tam dissimilis, tria talia texta,
una dies dabit exitio, multosque per annos
sustentata ruet moles et machina mundi.
nec me animi fallit quam res nova miraque menti
accidat exitium caeli terraeque futurum,
et quam difficile id mihi sit pervincere dictis.

[Observe first of all sea and earth and sky: this threefold nature, these three masses, Memmius, these three forms so different, these three textures so interwoven, one day shall consign to destruction; the mighty and complex system of the world, upheld through many years, shall crash into ruins. Yet I do not forget how novel and strange it strikes the mind that destruction awaits the heavens and the earth, and how difficult it is for me to prove this by argument.]

(5.92–99)

The speaker in this book, with its opulent accounts of nature's ceaseless creativity, is disturbed by the very epistemological assurance upon which Lucretius had to insist in the early books. In book 5 Lucretius addresses readers who, it seems, may all too easily forget, deny, or repress their birthright sense of the precariousness of existing at all. For Lucretius, to deny or forget that acknowledging the world's external thereness is an *achievement* is to rest with a false nostalgia. Through myth and sentiment, we unphilosophically protect our fantasy that refusing with mother would be to gain wholeness, density, and stability of bounded identity. This fantasy needs protecting—as we think, for we cannot bear the contemplation of death. Adult humans will put any resource into evasions of knowing our radical poverty and exposure through fragmentation, dispersal, dissemination, death. Yet this fantasy of a once and future fusion with mother needs dismantling, because such a fusion would obliterate the reciprocal presence of oneself and the external objects of the phenomenal world. And for Lucretius it is a far greater poverty not to live in a physical world. So the poem needs to include not only its wide range of mothers and maternal functions but also its vivid evocations of what it means to be a subject with a bounded bodily life, human, mortal, and above all *born*.

Lucretius occasionally registers a muted, implicit attraction to a barely represented life before birth. He has a sense of protected life in the space of the womb, just as he does of hidden places and openings in the maternalized earth. But to be born is far preferable: it is to come from a close, dense, dark space into the Ennian "oras luminis," the shores of light. To dwell in this flood of light is to be living, and there is thus a drive to birth, to be distinct and witness to the fountain of light; this drive is stronger than any for fusion with mother. Being separated also entails, of course, the experience of repeated fragmentation, which can be a kind of phenomenal death or create fantasies of psychic death; this is why, in book 3, Lucretius can tap such deep anxieties about the loss of self-boundedness into a dispersal of atoms. Nonetheless, reversion to a mother earth that would be, for humans, a truly disastrous dispersal, a loss of bounded form. Bounded creatures, we are nonetheless committed to tolerating lives of dispersed paths and exposures to the enormous energies of the world. Lucretius's therapy exhorts us to be strong enough to tolerate voids that guarantee distinctness, and to tolerate nullities or interims that can be a prelude to new condensations and generations. As Winnicott might say, some voids sustain. The anticipated denial or amnesia of separateness, of the achieved quality of bounded distinctness, is a necessary risk in the double aim of facing death and acknowledging a debt to the maternal.

In book 3 these issues constellate in an account of the body that is firmly fixed but also dispersing. In this book of mortalism, Lucretius's project is to evoke in his reader the fear of death; the vital, random atomic flows of matter become "the breath of life" ever at risk of streaming out of the body and dispersing in the air (*eiectis extra vitalibus auris*; 3.577). The speaker of book 3 is haunted by this two-way permeability of the body. The body exists not only as structured matter-with-orifices into which the sensory phenomena of the world stream (a major subject of book 4), but worse, of pores which are even less capable of being guarded and closed than orifices, and of unseen, deeply set, inward recesses, channels, passageways.

> Denique cum corpus nequeat perferre animai
> discidium quin in taetro tabescat odore,
> quid dubitas quin ex imo penitusque coorta
> emanarit uti fumus diffusa animae vis,
> atque ideo tanta mutatum putre ruina
> conciderit corpus, penitus quia mota loco sunt

fundamenta, foras anima emanante usque per artus
perque viarum omnis flexus, in corpore qui sunt,
atque foramina? multimodis ut noscere possis
dispertitam animae naturam exisse per artus
et prius esse sibi distractam corpore in ipso,
quam prolapsa foras enaret in aeris auras.

[Again, since the body cannot endure tearing apart from the spirit without
putrefying with a loathsome stench, why do you doubt that the strength of
the spirit, after gathering together from its depths and inmost recesses, has
oozed out already dispersed abroad like smoke, and that the reason why
the body changing and crumbling in such ruin has collapsed altogether, is
that its foundations to their inmost recesses have been moved from their
place while the spirit was oozing out all through the limbs and through all
the meandering passages and pores that are in the body? So that in many
ways you may learn that the spirit was scattered abroad when it went out
through the limbs, and had been torn all apart within the body itself, before
it glided out and swam into the winds of the air.]

(3.580–91)

It is as if the breath of life or the atoms that comprise it yearn after an
expanded, more fluid existence in light and air, as if they wished to
escape their places in the fixed structures and enlarge into freedom of
motion. The affinities of spirit are with smoke, mist, and cloud
(3.177–230, 425–44); the body is a vessel that breaks all too easily and
disperses its atoms into the air.

But fixed forms remain crucial in this book; the mind desires to live
just as fiercely as atoms wish to stream away into independent life. Book
3 is pervaded by pathos because living bodies are comprised of the
fixed, firm structures that Lucretius has been at such pains to establish—
the tenacious mind, the misty spirit, and the insurgent life of the body,
all pulling against one another:

Et magis est animus vitai claustra coercens
et dominantior ad vitam quam vis animai.
nam sine mente animoque nequit residere per artus
temporis exiguam partem pars ulla animai,
sed comes insequitur facile et discedit in auras
et gelidos artus in leti frigore linquit.

[And the mind is more potent in holding fast the barriers of life, and has
more dominance over life, than the spirit's force. For without the mind and

intelligence no particle of the spirit can abide in the frame for an instant,
but readily follows after it, and departs into the air, and leaves the limbs
cold in the chill of death.]

(3.396–401)

The more an airy freedom beckons, as if Lucretius were articulating
an atomic desire to become Ariel, the more the speaker must resort to
insisting on the tenacity of integral life forms and on grotesque, anxious
examples of the loss of life. The lines cited above are followed by just
this kind of intensification:

quamvis est circum caesis lacer undique membris
truncus, adempta anima circum membrisque remota
vivit et aetherias vitalis suscipit auras.
si non omnimodis, at magna parte animai
privatus, tamen in vita cunctatur et haeret;
ut, lacerato oculo circum si pupula mansit
incolumis, stat cernundi vivata potestas,
dummodo ne totum corrumpas luminis orbem
et circum caedas aciem solamque relinquas.

[He may be a mutilated trunk dismembered all about, the spirit removed
all around and separated from the limbs, yet he lives and breathes the vital
air. Deprived of a great part of the spirit, if not of all, yet he lingers and
clings to life; just as when the eye is lacerated all round, if the pupil
remains unhurt, there abides the lively power of seeing, provided you do
not mangle the whole eyeball and cut round the pupil and leave that isolated.]

(3.403–11)

Imagined violence to the tender eye returns two hundred lines later,
ostensibly a rational example of the argument that neither mind nor
body can function independently, as if the horror of harm to it will not
be quieted: "scilicet avulsus radicibus ut nequit ullam / dispicere ipse
oculus rem sorsum corpore toto, / sic anima atque animus per se nil
posse videtur" [to be sure, just as the eye torn from its roots cannot by
itself distinguish anything apart from the whole body, so it is seen that
mind and spirit can do nothing alone] (3.563–65). The limbless human
trunk also returns in a *tour de force* of the grotesque. The argument that
anything that can be "cleft and divided" cannot be eternal finds its
example in the image of a body sundered in two (3.636–39), then glides
into a gruesome reverie on battlefield dismemberments, which itself

ends with the uncanny shadow of life in the movement of lopped limbs (3.642–51). Even mutilated parts of creatures resist death. To be slowly dismembered in battle is to die, while a severed arm or leg retains a ghastly animation. To live is to be a bounded, integral entity composed of atoms tightly knit in fixed relationships, yet atoms delight in the sensuousness of swimming in air and light—which would be death to the humans they constitute. Humans fear death so much that they come to hate life, devising their own deaths. The whole poem assumes our fear of death. In book 3 we learn that we also have a *rage* for death, perhaps even an instinct for it. Yet it is hard to distinguish this from a craving for amplitude of life and movement in the air.

Lucretius evidently arrives at the intricate paradoxy of Freud's death drive. If death is what fragments, separates, disperses a unitary self, then we find death in the act of running from it, for the fear of death impels us to seek a transcendent stasis beyond mutability. Yet this immobility would count as death too; Lucretius's *ataraxia* is a complex and potentially contradictory ideal.[32] Or again, if the death drive is an attempt to revert to an imaginary wholeness in symbiosis with the mother, then Lucretius recognizes that the death drive is also fueled by a desire for greater, more expansive life. This is why Lucretius never jettisons altogether those mythopoeic representations like *alma Venus*, the Magna Mater, Cybele, a maternal earth. Is death a drive toward dispersal or a drive toward wholeness? Is wholeness a livable possibility or a craving for the stasis of death? Is a craving for reunion with the mother an acknowledgment of her power or a capitulation to her abjection?

These binarisms are not likely to be resolved easily. But those Lucretian atoms yearning for free movement in the air suggest a path for thought, and for feeling about death. Whatever the life toward which the atoms' mobility beckons them, such absolute dispersal would be death for a human creature. To identify with them utterly, to pursue only the element of air and only the condition of random movement, would be to give in to death. But with Irigaray, we might consider that the element of air makes possible the fluent movements of growing into an endless expanse, in an Irigarayan process of becoming. This is certainly the longing that they seem to carry for Lucretius, who loves

32. In this paragraph I am indebted to Margaret Whitford, "Irigaray, Utopia, and the Death Drive," in *Engaging with Irigaray: Feminist Philosophy and Modern European Thought*, ed. Carolyn Burke, Naomi Schor, and Whitford (New York: Columbia University Press, 1994), 379–400, esp. 390, 394, and to DeLacy, "Epicurean Dilemma," who discusses Lucretius's confounding of life and death.

movement through the radiance, clarity, and amplitude of air. But following the paths of atoms into regions of light, into what Stevens calls "the lustrous inundations, / Flood on flood, of our returning sun," requires a certain strength, something like Winnicott's hardiness, or Emerson's sturdiness, or Lucretius's conquering of the fear of death.[33] Or Irigaray's willingness to do the mourning work of birth.

For the claiming of air and movement never comes easily, as we have seen in Winnicott; taking in the first draughts of air at birth is one of Winnicott's chief examples of his peculiar sense of aggression. Irigaray too is at pains to insist on the difficult necessity of claiming a birthright of air. Air is first given to us in utero, by the mother: "She gives—first—air, and does so irrecoverably, with the exception of the unfolding, from and within her, of whoever takes air from her. . . . She gives first. She gives the possibility of that beginning from which the whole of man will be constituted. This gift is received with no possibility of a return."[34] And of the transition to the first vigorous intakes of air by the neonate: "This provenance of life, this mediation and medium of life, offers itself without appearing as these. The first time, these are experienced as pain. Free air represents the possibility for life, but it is also the sign of the loss of that which—of she who—at no remove, with no expectations, and with no difficulty, used to provide everything. In air, life is, in the beginning, the boundless immensity of a mourning. In it the whole is lost."[35] The claiming of air challenges the neonate, and processes of parturition never end. The becoming subject cannot be exultant in air, or even hardy in Winnicott's sense, unless it first mourns the increase of separation from the mother that is birth. "Air is, first, the being of the open expanse whose measure would be that of the yet-to-come of (the) mourning: of she who will never come back. In expectation and oblivion, this mourning is not discernible as such, thanks to air, which is more a sign of life than of mourning. Or it is a sign of one as much as the other."[36]

Lucretius's atoms seek movement and air, and an exhilaration can arise from his descriptions; but there is also a certain poignancy, for the

33. Wallace Stevens, "Meditation Celestial & Terrestrial," in *Complete Poems*, 123.

34. Luce Irigaray, *The Forgetting of Air in Martin Heidegger*, trans. Mary Beth Mader (Austin: University of Texas Press, 1999), 28. As the translator notes, the "she" (*elle*) of this passage, and indeed of the whole book, plays on the triple referents *la femme*, *la nature*, and *la mère*.

35. Ibid., 42–43.

36. Ibid., 43.

human reader, in their flight from a home within bounded creatures. The Lucretian atomistic "fixed mother" is she to whom we must cleave in order to choose life and resist the disordered craving for death; yet this cleaving is also an acceptance of mortality, of merely living as and where we live, since to accept life as a bounded creature is to know the prospect of death. For all his fascination with the fecundity of earth, Lucretius is an anti-chthonic poet: for him it is a false nostalgia running through our religions and philosophies which collapses mother, earth, blood, and death in a single phantasmic desire; it is just as false a rage for death as the temptation to disperse into atomic movement. This is why the sequence of his represented mothers—*alma Venus*, Magna Mater, heifer, mother earth—takes us through a series of increasing distances from the mother; the sequence does mourning work and leaves us with both the burdens and the exaltations of relation to the divided mother. Irigaray, in a different context, articulates what Lucretius values in his series of mothers, and it is not just their nurturing capacity, it is their ability to disrupt nostalgia for the maternal: "If after all this [use by man], she is still alive, she continuously undoes his work—distinguishing herself from both the envelope and the thing, ceaselessly creating there some interval, play, something in motion and unlimited which disturbs his perspective, his world, and his/its limits."[37] Lucretius's sequence of varyingly distant mothers *is* the good-enough mother, and recognizing this is a step toward facing the plague of book 6. Lucretius and his interlocutor are challenged to accept real death (the plague), the elaborate, fixed but mobile structures of our atomistic bodily life, and the real pleasures of inventiveness, representation, and movement. Distinctions of birth are thus simultaneously challenges and privileges.

37. Luce Irigaray, "Sexual Difference" (1982), in *An Ethics of Sexual Difference*, trans. Carolyn Burke and Gillian Gill (Ithaca, N.Y.: Cornell University Press, 1993), 5–19, at 10.

8

Absorption into the Chthonic Mother: Spenser's *Faerie Queene*, Book 4

But it is in vain that an old man yearns for the love of woman as he had it first from his mother; the third of the Fates alone, the silent Goddess of Death, will take him into her arms.

—Sigmund Freud

Stifled beneath all those eulogistic or denigratory metaphors, she [the female] is unable to unpick the seams of her disguise and indeed takes a certain pleasure in them, even gilding the lily further at times. Yet, ever more hemmed in, cathected by tropes, how could she articulate any sound from beneath this cheap chivalric finery? How find a voice, make a choice strong enough, subtle enough to cut through those layers of ornamental style, that decorative sepulcher, where even her breath is lost.

—Luce Irigaray

Western discourses on the creation of the world are steadily reliant on the figures of Natura and a maternal earth, yet also reliant on birth as a figure for the male divinity's primal making of creatures. Such discourses are always answerable to the charge that Irigaray puts here.[1] Like Lucretius, Freud, Klein, Winnicott, and Irigaray, Edmund Spenser launches complex meditations on the drive toward death and its mysterious relations to maternity. In this chapter I deal with book 4 of *The Faerie Queene*, where the allure of the mythic, chthonic mother is most evident and where the strongest of several turns away from her is Lucretian. The first section of this chapter sketches the tangled romance yarn of the first three cantos, in which knights fight and mutilate one another in irritable paroxysms of bloodlust. These cantos have long made readers unhappy and perplexed, not least because they do not rise to the famous homage to Chaucer that Spenser embeds in them.[2] In the second section I will be arguing that the text's deployments of Father Chaucer and deathly mothers articulate a death drive among the knights as a fatal nostalgia for union with something maternal and fecund, a maternal that they envy and wish to identify with. Like Lucretius's atoms, Spenser's knights manifest a search for expanded life through death. But in a turn from such nostalgia, Spenser augments Chaucer's tales with new female characters who offer an alternative to the chthonic mother. In the third section, I propose that Spenser represents one form of romance as a death or fixation of narrative itself, and that he represents Lucretian poetry as a revival of narrative possibilities, first in the Temple of Venus episode and then in the marriage of rivers concluding the book. Lucretian freshenings of romance narrative constitute a second, more radical turn from nostalgia for absorption into the maternal.

1. Luce Irigaray, "Any Theory of the 'Subject' Has Always Been Appropriated by the 'Masculine' " (1974), in *Speculum of the Other Woman*, trans. Gillian Gill (Ithaca, N.Y.: Cornell University Press, 1985), 142–43. Freud's words on the goddess of death come from "The Theme of the Three Caskets" (1913), in *Standard Edition of the Complete Psychological Works of Sigmund Freud*, ed. James Strachey et al., 24 vols. (London: Hogarth Press and Institute of Psycho-Analysis, 1953–73), 17:291–301, at 301.

2. In 1917 Herbert Ellsworth Cory said of these cantos, in which Spenser aims to finish the Squire's Tale, "Spenser evidently felt his own audacity and responsibility keenly and it led him into an extravagance so crude and turgid that it seems almost boyish. . . . Book Four, so chaotic in structure, is like a sky confused with cloud masses through which ever and anon come clean shafts and pillars of the sunshine of a young and wilful spring." *Edmund Spenser: A Critical Study* (Berkeley: University of California Press, 1917), 261, 290. Critics have long repeated versions of these complaints.

My subheads "What a Tangle" and "No End to Possibility" are borrowed from chapter titles in John Crowley's Spenserian-Shakespearean romance, *Little, Big* (New York: Doubleday, 1981).

What a Tangle

The Faerie Queene, book 4, cantos 1–3, tell a tale that readers have often found a perplexing knot of nearly identical and schematic bits of plot: indistinguishable knights in bloody combat, enmities and friendships forming and reforming in new and apparently inconsequential combinations, damsels won, lost, exchanged in an uncritical traffic in women. In spite of sophisticated readings, it is all too easy to feel that in these cantos Spenser is not much better than Chaucer's Squire as a storyteller.[3] Even if we find solace in critics' analyses of the structures of substitution and exchange in the narrative, we still need to consider how, if at all, these cantos give pleasure, and how Spenser negotiates what can seem to us a perplexing use of Chaucer, whom he praises as the "well of English vndefyled" (4.2.32), and whom he hopes to revivify by "infusion sweete" (4.2.34).[4] It is not just that Spenser resorts to Chaucer's tales (Knight's as well as Squire's tales, father's and son's tales) for narrative matter; it is that he also uses them to entertain a cultural nostalgia for the maternal implicit in certain lines of romance, and to pair this speculation on the maternal with the hazards of reviving a father's spirit so as to gain access to poetic origins.

The address to Chaucer functions as a pivot between two long episodes of knightly combat: in the first, knights fight randomly against whomever they meet, in order to win one another's ladies; in the second, the brothers Priamond, Diamond, and Triamond fight Cambello in an organized tournament for the hand of his sister Canacee. The martial engagements display the crudest and most naked motivations for the knights' battles: emulative rivalry and vociferous claims on the ladies. But the first battle segment clearly emphasizes envy, and the second a compulsive violence exerted on the

3. See James Nohrnberg, "*The Faerie Queene*, Book 4," in *The Spenser Encyclopedia*, ed. A. C. Hamilton, Donald Cheney, and W. F. Blissett (Toronto: University of Toronto Press, 1990), 273–80; Nohrnberg, *The Analogy of "The Faerie Queene"* (Princeton: Princeton University Press, 1976), 608–19, 621–25; Jonathan Goldberg, *Endlesse Worke: Spenser and the Structures of Discourse* (Baltimore: Johns Hopkins University Press, 1981); Patrick Cheney, "Spenser's Completion of the Squire's Tale: Love, Magic, and Heroic Action in the Legend of Cambell and Triamond," *Journal of Medieval and Renaissance Studies* 15 (1985): 135–55; A. Kent Hieatt, *Chaucer, Spenser, Milton: Mythopoeic Continuities and Transformations* (Montreal: McGill-Queen's University Press, 1975); Lauren Silberman, *Transforming Desire: Erotic Knowledge in Books III and IV of "The Faerie Queene"* (Berkeley: University of California Press, 1995).

4. Citations are to books, cantos, and stanzas in A. C. Hamilton's edition of *The Faerie Queene* (New York: Longman, 1975).

enemy's body. Thus, the first canto of book 4 begins by reopening the story of Amoret and Scudamour from the last two cantos of book 3, here with the new information that Scudamour had won his bride in "perilous fight . . . / A perilous fight when he with force her brought / From twentie Knights" (4.1.2). Amoret is currently in the custody of the knight who had rescued her from Busyrane's house (3.12). Both Amoret and Scudamour presume wrongly that this knight is male (the knight is really Britomart) and thus has daunting claims on various aspects of Amoret's person: to Amoret, the knight who rescued her "Right well deserued as his duefull meed, / Her loue, her seruice, and her vtmost wealth" (4.1.6). Later in the canto, the hypocritical friends Blandamour and Paridell (paired respectively with Ate and Duessa as their consorts) assume that their chivalric task is to conquer other knights and win the "meed" of their accompanying ladies. When they encounter a knight and lady (Britomart and Amoret), Blandamour easily tosses around the men's rights to the women: "Lo there Sir *Paridel*, for your desart, / Good lucke presents you with yond louely mayd" (4.1.33), he says, and when Paridell retreats from the engagement, the "hot-spurre youth" Blandamour claims the fight and hands Ate to Paridell: "Take then to you this Dame of mine" (4.1.35). Blandamour hates Scudamour with a rancorous envy, "Both for his worth, that all men did adore, / And eke because his loue he wonne by right" (4.1.39), and this grief takes so much psychic energy that it depletes his battle strength. In the next canto Paridell and Blandamour are easily divided over their desire to possess the beautiful false Florimell (riding with Sir Ferraugh), spurred on in their contention by the hag Ate (to whom we shall return, as she is the very fusion of maternity and aggression). Blandamour, himself "prickt . . . / With sting of lust" for Florimell, perversely sets Paridell on: "Sir knight why ride ye dumpish thus behind, / Since so good fortune doth to you present / So fayre a spoyle, to make you ioyous meriment?" (4.2.5). Paridell still declining to fight, Blandamour

> Fiercely forth prickt his steed as in disdaine,
>   Against that Knight, ere he him well could torne:
> By meanes whereof he hath him lightly ouerborne.
>
> (4.2.6)

Inevitably in this homosocial bonding of aggression, the two friends turn on each other:

Exceeding wroth thereat was *Blandamour*,
 And gan this bitter answere to him make;
 Too foolish *Paridell*, that fayrest floure
 Wouldst gather faine, and yet no paines wouldst take:
 But not so easie will I her forsake;
 This hand her wonne, this hand shall her defend.
 With that they gan their shiuering speares to shake,
 And deadly points at eithers breast to bend,
Forgetfull each to haue bene euer others frend.

(4.2.14)

All this exemplifies with diagrammatic clarity a homosocial economy of chivalric desire, and a virulent form of the entanglement of eros with aggression; even the good knights, whom I have not mentioned, and the ladies themselves take for granted these features of their courtly lives. It pertains especially to the good knights Cambello and Triamond and good ladies Cambina and Canacee—the latter also Cambello's sister, whom Triamond has won in the battle described in canto 3. This second battle changes the stakes of knightly combat in more respects than one. It is staged in order to find a suitable husband for Canacee, not just to trade her off to other handy knights. More important for my purposes, Spenser creates for Cambello and the three brothers Priamond, Diamond, and Triamond one of the more uncanny battles of the poem. Its combatants, appalled, find themselves fixed in a nightmarishly endless battle. Because each is protected from death by magic, the battle cannot end, but they can and do keep inflicting ghastly wounds on each other. Cambello has a ring that heals all wounds, given him by his sister Canacee. Priamond, Diamond, and Triamond share a form of extended life such that when one dies, his spirit enters the body of the next, and when the second dies, the two combined spirits enter into the third. I will return to this strange augmentation, but first a comment about the violence and pointed injuries of the battle itself. Cambello first fights Priamond, wounding the latter in the thigh:

With that his poynant speare he fierce auentred,
 With doubled force close vnderneath his shield,
 That through the mayles into his thigh it entred,
 And there arresting, readie way did yield,
 For bloud to gush forth on the grassie field.

(4.3.9)

Priamond, in pain and rage, hurls his spear into Cambello's head. The spear

> Pierst through his beuer quite into his brow,
> That with the force it backward forced him to bow.
>
> Therewith a sunder in the midst it brast,
>   And in his hand nought but the troncheon left,
>   The other halfe behind yet sticking fast,
>   Out of his headpeece *Cambell* fiercely reft,
>   And with such furie backe at him it heft,
>   That making way vnto his dearest life,
>   His weasand pipe it through his gorget cleft:
>   Thence streames of purple bloud issuing rife,
> Let forth his wearie ghost and made an end of strife;
>
> (4.3.11–12)

Priamond's spirit transfers "through traduction" (4.3.13) into his brother Diamond, who now leaps onto the field to take his elder brother's place.

> With that they both together fiercely met,
>   As if that each ment other to deuoure;
>   And with their axes both so sorely bet,
>   That neither plate nor mayle, whereas their powre
>   They felt, could once sustaine the hideous stowre,
>   But riued were like rotten wood a sunder,
>   Whilest through their rifts the ruddie bloud did showre
>
> (4.3.15)

When Diamond is beheaded, his and Priamond's spirits enter into the youngest, Triamond. By now both the onlookers and Cambello are shocked by these weird survivals; soon both Triamond and Cambello are exhausted but find themselves trapped, through their magical protections, in a battle without end. The wounds they inflict become ever more desperate as the combatants seek death or surcease:

> And all the while the disentrayled blood
>   Adowne their sides like litle riuers stremed,
>   That with the wasting of his vitall flood,
> Sir *Triamond* at last full faint and feeble stood.
>
> (4.3.28)

Cambello smites Triamond "through the seame, which did his hauberk close, / Into his throate and life it pierced quight" (4.3.30). Triamond "in [Cambello's] head an hideous wound imprest" (4.3.34). The tournament has deteriorated into mutilations, and the drive toward life—preservation of life in battle—is indistinguishable from the desire for death:

> Ne either cared life to saue or spill
>
> . . . .
>
> So wearie both of fighting had their fill,
> That life it selfe seemd loathsome, and long safetie ill.

(4.3.36)

The phrase "had their fill" carries particular force because Spenser has twice described the knights' motivations in epic similes about the fierceness of ravenous hunger: in one, they are like "two Tygers prickt with hungers rage" who turn on each other in competition for the scarce resource of food, itself described in courtly diction as "a feastfull guerdon"; in the other, they resemble the vulture, greedy through "hunger long," who attacks a heron (4.3.16, 19). What can the hunger be that pricks these knights' devouring rages? I think Spenser here links his own predilection for narrative redundancies with the dead ends of the knights' repetition compulsion. As Irigaray wittily says, a "boredom in repeating the same story over and over again" "is called, in part, the death instinct."[5]

The deepest desire of these knights, or of the courtly culture into which they are interpellated, is not the hand of the lady; it is escape from mortality and boundedness into the larger life of absorption into an encompassing or chthonic mother, a mother identified in fantasy with earth and with deities of the underworld. Their bloodthirst is more accurately an obsessive spilling of blood—an enemy's or their own—from open wounds into the thirsty earth. The desperation with which the knights of book 4 of *The Faerie Queene* fight one another, and the paltriness of their overt objects in contrast to the large and exalted aims of knights elsewhere in the poem, needs accounting for by some such desire, subterranean and unacknowledged.

The cantos' mythological contexts encourage the conception of a

---

5. Luce Irigaray, "The 'Mechanics' of Fluids" (1977), in *This Sex Which Is Not One*, trans. Catherine Porter with Carolyn Burke (Ithaca, N.Y.: Cornell University Press, 1985), 106–18, at 115.

chthonic maternity with occult powers over life and death. There is Ate, participating in events in the form of a romance damsel but aligned with the Furies and living in "a darksome delue farre vnder ground" full of broken or rent objects testifying to the destructiveness of greed and envy.[6] She is the fatal mother, one who battens on the "debates" and even on the bodies and blood of feuding mortals: "For life it is to her . . . / That she may sucke their life, and drinke their blood, / With which she from her childhood had bene fed" (4.1.26).[7] There are the Fates, chthonic weavers of the threads of mortality, who figure in these cantos when they agree to extend the lives of Priamond, Diamond, and Triamond. They do not ask the boon for themselves; their mother seeks it for them. That mother, Agape, is another link between maternity and the chthonic and to fantasies of enlargement of mortal life.[8] When she visits the Fates she asks:

> Graunt this, that when ye shred with fatall knife
> His line, which is the eldest of the three,
> Which is of them the shortest, as I see,
> Eftsoones his life may passe into the next;
> And when the next shall likewise ended bee,
> That both their liues may likewise be annext
> Vnto the third, that his may so be trebly wext.

> (4.2.52)

Agape herself takes this method of extension as a happy thing, and departs "with full contented mynd" (4.2.53). But Spenser embeds her

6. See Dorothy Stephens's fine discussion of Ate in *The Limits of Eroticism in Post-Petrarchan Narrative: Conditional Pleasure from Spenser to Marvell* (Cambridge: Cambridge University Press, 1998), 69–72.

7. John Upton notes that Ate's dwelling "seems imaged from the temple of Mars in Statius, *Theb.* 7.40, etc. And from the same temple described in Chaucer's Knight's Tale"; Henry Lotspeich contributes parallel phrases among the three works. See *Variorum Works*, ed. Edwin Greenlaw et al., vol. 4, ed. Ray Heffner (Baltimore: Johns Hopkins University Press, 1947), 168. Kenneth Gross's comment on the striking passage in *A View of the Present State of Ireland* in which an old woman sucks blood from the head of her just-executed foster child, the rebel Murregh O'Brien, is germane here: "What the poet describes is at once a literalistic and a madly superstitious attempt to master the cutting off of death by rejoining endings to beginnings, the nurse consuming the blood of the child whom her own milk had nourished, now sucking 'death instead of life,' as if through her his divided body could become whole again." Gross, *Spenserian Poetics: Idolatry, Iconoclasm, and Magic* (Ithaca, N.Y.: Cornell University Press, 1985), 103. See the Spenser passage in *A View of the State of Ireland*, ed. Andrew Hadfield and Willy Maley (Oxford: Blackwell, 1997), 66.

8. Nohrnberg discusses Agape as a Venus who is also a Fate in "*Faerie Queene*, Book 4," 278.

happiness in an ominous context. First, the sons need Agape's intervention only because they so eagerly embrace the violence of the masculine
chivalric world, following their father, who had begotten them by rap-
ing Agape:

> Which she with her long fostred in that wood,
>   Till that to ripenesse of mans state they grew:
>   Then shewing forth signes of their fathers blood,
>   They loued armes, and knighthood did ensew,
>   Seeking aduentures, where they anie knew.
>
> (4.2.46)

Second, the Fates themselves are as underworldly and threatening as
one could wish, dwelling "Farre vnder ground . . . Downe in the bot-
tome of the deepe *Abysse*," wielding "cursed knife" (4.2.47, 48), speaking darkly of necessity and the brevity of life.[9] So grim is this fatality that
it evokes from the narrator one of his moving outbursts of pity: "Most
wretched men, whose dayes depend on thrids so vaine" (4.2.48). Third
and most strikingly, the first stanza of the next canto, just after the close
of Agape's visit to the underworld, begins with a more remarkable out-
burst on the part of the narrator, repeating the emphatic "wretched
men":

> O Why doe wretched men so much desire,
>   To draw their dayes vnto the vtmost date,
>   And doe not rather wish them soone expire,
>   Knowing the miserie of their estate,
>   And thousand perills which them still awate,
>   Tossing them like a boate amid the mayne,
>   That euery houre they knocke at deathes gate?
>   And he that happie seemes and least in payne,
> Yet is as nigh his end, as he that most doth playne.
>
> (4.3.1)

The despair of this stanza is cast as a weariness both in experiencing
and in contemplating the ills of human life, as if the narrator spoke from
great age and its potential wish for easeful death. Coming immediately
upon the depiction of the Fates—and leading into the intolerable battle

---

9. Agape's visit to the Fates parallels Duessa's visit to Night, "most auncient Grandmother of all" (*Faerie Queene* 1.5.20–44), and the themes and motifs of that passage anticipate those of 4.1–3.

between the Chaucerian Cambello (out of the Squire's Tale) and the brothers Priamond, Diamond, and Triamond—this passage hauntingly and virtuosically echoes the moving and terrible passage in Chaucer's Pardoner's Tale where the old man seeks death:[10]

> Ne Deeth, allas, ne wol nat han my lyf.
> Thus walke I, lyk a restelees kaityf,
> And on the ground, which is my moodres gate,
> I knokke with my staf, bothe erly and late,
> And seye "Leeve mooder, leet me in!
> Lo how I vanysshe, flessh, and blood, and skyn!
> Allas, whan shul my bones been at reste?
> Mooder, with yow wolde I chaunge my cheste
> That in my chambre longe tyme hath be,
> Ye, for an heyre clowt to wrappe me!"
>
> (Pardoner's Tale 727–36)

The old man's alienation from a maternal earth that refuses to receive him coincides with his bodily vanishing; for this mother, receiving her child would be reuniting him within her own body, so that his own dissolution would also be a new form of life, a new engrossment and absorption. The idea of a longed-for, subterranean mother as an alternative to the burdens of history and "eld" (or age, time) reverberates in the episode of the Fates as it culminates with Spenser's stanza on the desire for death.

These diverse mythic figures ground the cantos' large-scale subtexts in the matter of Thebes, a bloody history of fratricidal violence, incestuous returns to real and phantasmatic mothers, exclusions of real mothers, and violence against the feminine. Theban history is initiated by Cadmus, whose sowing of dragon's teeth in the earth creates the first Thebans, born from the earth, who immediately turn against one another in war and then, in Ovid's words for their dying, "tepido plangebant pectora matrem" [beat the breast of their mother earth warm with their blood] (Metamorphoses 3.125).[11] In Statius these earth-sown

---

10. The *Variorum* lists other possible sources: Todd suggests Psalm 9 or Job 38; Thomas Warton mentions Thomas Sackville's *Induction to the Mirror for Magistrates* or the English *Romaunt de la Rose*. Ray Heffner, editor of the *Variorum Faerie Queene*, book 4, argues most persuasively for the Pardoner's Tale; see *Variorum*, 4:182–83.

11. Ovid, *Metamorphoses*, 2 vols., trans. Frank Justus Miller, 3d ed., rev. G. P. Goold (Cambridge: Harvard University Press, 1977), 1:132–33.

men are hungry for death, or thirsty for a blood that would augment them; the prophetess Manto says that they "alternum sitis exhaurire cruorem" [thirst to drain each other's blood] (*Thebaid* 4.560).[12] The history includes Oedipus, who returned blindly to the place of his conception in the body of his mother; his sons Eteocles and Polynices, who fight for the crown; his daughter Antigone, buried alive by Creon; and, earlier in the generations, Tantalus, who killed his son and fed him to the gods. Statius's *Thebaid*, which Spenser knew well and used often, is heavy with chthonic goddesses, Fates, and Furies, curses against progeny and parents, a maternalized earth that seems to absorb as much blood as violent humans can pour into her, suffering mothers excluded from significant action, Stygian monsters who drink infants' blood, characters whose rage is never sated by violence. As Lee Patterson has argued in relation to the Theban matter of Chaucer's Knight's Tale and the long rivalry between Palamon and Arcite, "Theban history in its pure form has neither origin nor end but only a single, infinitely repeatable moment of illicit eroticism and fratricidal rivalry—love and war locked together in a perverse fatality."[13] Within this impressive mythic and textual matrix, the hunger of Spenser's knights reads as an atavistic and hopeless wish to achieve life, or achieve birth, by means of death: spilling their blood, in this fantasy, would return them to an authoritative source with the power both to absorb them and to augment them. Their death drive is thus also a drive toward some sense of a fuller life. Irigaray puts this as a fantasy of limitlessness: "Does not that limitlessness come from absorbing the mother-nature which [the man] refuses to amputate? Always consuming another, without repaying her, he lacks outlines. He does not acknowledge his source of life. . . . In that appropriation of what he takes from the other, he doubles his life, but loses measure."[14]

Irigaray also speaks often of one Theban matter in the person of Antigone, and Creon's desperate act of burying her alive, all but depriving her of air, light, movement, nourishment—a Theban way (and for Irigaray a masculine way) of encrypting the feminine-maternal so as to

12. Statius is cited from *Thebaid*, Loeb edition, trans. J. H. Mozley, vol. 1 (Cambridge: Harvard University Press, 1967).

13. Lee Patterson, *Chaucer and the Subject of History* (Madison: University of Wisconsin Press, 1991), 77. On Theban fatality in Statius, Boccaccio, and Chaucer, see also Winthrop Wetherbee, "Romance and Epic in Chaucer's Knight's Tale," *Exemplaria* 2 (1990): 303–28.

14. Luce Irigaray, *Elemental Passions*, trans. Joanna Collie and Judith Still (New York: Routledge, 1992), 53.

have it as the ground upon which culture is built.[15] Antigone represents the social order's sacrifice of the feminine-maternal, a sacrifice locking that order in a fascination with the subterranean maternal that it dares not kill outright: "Without friends, without husband, without tears, she is led along that forgotten path and there is walled up alive in a hole in the rock, shut off forever from the light of the sun. Alone in her crypt, her cave, her den, her womb, she is given just enough food by those who hold power to ensure that the city is not soiled and shamed by her decay."[16] Insofar as she remains this sacrifice, encrypted, Antigone cannot be an ethical ideal for Irigaray; Sophocles' Antigone is too much in love with Death for this. In *An Ethics of Sexual Difference* Irigaray returns to the figure of Antigone, "though I shall not identify with it. Antigone, the antiwoman, is still a production of a culture that has been written by men alone."[17] Yet Antigone is to be praised for her insistence upon the blood tie to the mother—her argument for the right to bury her brother because brother and sister derive from the same womb: "the sister will strangle herself in order to save at least the mother's son. She will cut off her breath, her voice, her air, blood, life . . . so that her brother, *her mother's desire*, may have eternal life."[18] She is moreover worth identifying with insofar as she refuses to remain "unconscious ground that nourishes nature."[19] That "unconscious ground" is precisely what the matter of Thebes represents as her tragic, inevitable fate.

Taken together, Irigaray's and Patterson's arguments focus the drives of Spenser's unreflective, battle-engrossed knights. Their bloody nostalgia for a chthonic mother arises from a cultural complacency with easy

15. See Tina Chanter, *Ethics of Eros: Irigaray's Rewriting of the Philosophers* (London: Routledge, 1995), 80–116, for Irigaray's diverse deployments of Antigone.

16. Luce Irigaray, "The Eternal Irony of the Community" (1974), in *Speculum of the Other Woman*, 214–26, at 218. Antigone embodies many of the paradoxes of the death instinct; when Irigaray takes her condition as symptomatic of cultures' situating of women, it is no wonder that she must worry the issue of Antigone repeatedly. Thus: "she is damned, and by consenting to a punishment she has not merited and yet cannot escape, at the least she accepts on her own account the death knell of her jouissance—*or is mourning itself her jouissance?*—by killing herself. Does she thus anticipate the decree of death formulated by those in power? Does she duplicate it? Has she given in? Or is she still in revolt? She repeats, in any case, upon herself the murderous, but not bloody, deed of her mother [Jocasta]" (218–19).

17. Luce Irigaray, "An Ethics of Sexual Difference" (1984), in *An Ethics of Sexual Difference*, trans. Carolyn Burke and Gillian Gill (Ithaca, N.Y.: Cornell University Press, 1984),116–29, at 118–19.

18. Irigaray, "Eternal Irony," 219.

19. Ibid., 225; see also 219.

representations of the maternal: the unconscious in such a culture is free to hunger for a plenum of fusion with mother, which in turn authorizes the knights' exorbitant claims on the ladies' resources.[20] As I said in chapter 1, it is in not acknowledging parturition that such fantasies of fusion with an archaic mother arise. What poets may offer is not just rehearsals of myths that work out this stubborn mythic imaginary, but a willingness to interpret and figure passages of birth otherwise—as an expansion into the distinctness that always exists between mother and infant. Trapped in the melancholia of refusing to symbolize the space between mother and self, the knights of Spenser's Theban textual tradition consign themselves to the pathos of nostalgia for a maternal first home.

Three features of the battles of *The Faerie Queene* 4.1–3 suggest that Spenser depicts his combatants as trapped in a cultural imaginary that they cannot bring to awareness.[21] First, these cantos contain the largest concentration of stupefied knights. Paridell and Scudamour meet so "furiously" "that what of them became, themselues did scarsly weete" (4.1.41); Paridell, revived from a swoon by onlookers, is "yet so mazed, that he nothing spake" (4.1.43); Paridell and Blandamour, after stunning each other, "At length . . . both vpstarted in amaze, / As men awaked rashly out of dreme" (4.2.17); of these last the narrator remarks, "There they I weene would fight vntill this day," had not the Squire of Dames intervened (4.2.20).[22]

Second, the unconscious quality of the compulsion to repeat battles in endless recombinations of knights appears in the extraordinary amount of piercing, pricking, cutting, slashing, incising, and hacking in these hand-to-hand combats. Earlier in *The Faerie Queene*, beginning with the famous first line of the first canto, "A Gentle Knight was pricking on the plaine," "pricking" activities are Chaucerian echoes for Spenser. Book 1, for instance, draws on the comic recurrences of the verb "prick" in Chaucer's Sir Thopas to shape the Redcrosse Knight's adventures. The lexicon also includes the terms "jolly" or "jollity," "courage," "lust," and

20. David Lee Miller (*The Poem's Two Bodies: The Poetics of the 1590 "Faerie Queene"* [Princeton: Princeton University Press, 1988], 245–54) discusses what he perceives as the poet's disgust with a chthonic maternal. See also Walter Kendrick, "Earth of Flesh, Flesh of Earth: Mother Earth in the *Faerie Queene*," *Renaissance Quarterly* 27 (1974): 533–48.

21. On the possibility of speaking of the unconscious of a genre or mode, romance in particular, see Elizabeth J. Bellamy, *Translations of Power: Narcissism and the Unconscious in Epic History* (Ithaca, N.Y.: Cornell University Press, 1992), 27–31 and passim.

22. The editors of the *Variorum* point out that the presence of a stupefied knight is "a common formula in Spenser": 1.5.12; 2.1.45; 3.7.45; 3.10.49; 4.3.31; 5.5.13; 6.3.11 (*Variorum*, 4:175).

"lustfull," all of these in the service of those qualities fueling the achievements of the knights of Spenser's first book— prowess and desire, vigor, lustiness, spiritedness.[23] The same lexical clusters appear in *The Faerie Queene* 4.1–3, but with a much darker tonal coloring and much less distinct characterization of the knights. These cantos tamp down individual characterization so as to emphasize the cultural system's exchanges and substitutions of persons, and to emphasize and deplore the violence of this culture. Blandamour, whose name may derive from Chaucer's Tale of Sir Thopas, "fiercely prickt" (4.1.35); Sir Ferraugh is "a lustie Knight" riding with the false Florimell (4.2.4), and Blandamour finds that the sight of her "prickt his wanton mind / With sting of lust" (4.2.5), upon which he "fiercely forth prickt" in order to challenge Ferraugh (4.2.6). Ate works up Paridell's resentment by pricking him forth (4.2.12) against Blandamour. When the two friends finally fight, they begin a "deadly points [of spears] at eithers breast to bend, / Forgetfull each to haue bene euer others frend," with the result that those pitiless spears "a griesly passage rend" in each of them (4.2.14, 15). In the tournament for Cambina, Priamond is injured by Cambello's "poynant speare" which travels through shield and mail into his thigh (4.3.9), and in the next stanza by Cambello's shield: "nought mote stay the steele, till in his side / The mortall point most cruelly empight" and remains "fast infixed" (4.3.10). Priamond in turn sends his spear "piercing" into Cambello's head. Triamond is pierced through the throat, and repays Cambello with "an hideous wound imprest" in his head (4.3.30, 34).

Third is blood. It is a startling fact that these cantos, composed in a culture so ingrained with what Gail Paster calls the "overall humoral logic of bodily repletion," in which it was "woman's normative condition to leak," represent the knights and not the ladies as those who bleed in copious issuings (and it is the women, traditionally leaky vessels, who embody and urge corporeal integrity and discrete identity, as we shall see).[24] Priamond's blood "gush[ed] forth on the grassie field"; when his body dies it is due to "streames of purple bloud issuing rife" (4.3.9, 12); Cambello and Triamond fight for a long time, "And all the while the disentrayled blood / Adowne their sides like litle riuers stremed" (4.3.28). Spilling blood into a maternalized earth, in the con-

23. See Judith Anderson, " 'A Gentle Knight was pricking on the plaine': The Chaucerian Connection," *English Literary Renaissance* 15 (1985): 166–74.

24. Gail Kern Paster, *The Body Embarrassed: Drama and the Disciplines of Shame in Early Modern England* (Ithaca, N.Y.: Cornell University Press, 1993), 39, 105.

text of Spenser's Theban subtexts mystifying blood's entry into the earth, is in part a phantasmatic wish to get back inside the maternal home, but it may also bespeak a menstrual envy, a way of enlarging one's mortal, bounded identity by opening the body so as to become something like a mother.[25] This Spenserian inversion of cultural truisms about gendered bodies poses an ethical critique of chivalric romance's emulous and combative aspects. All three elements—stupefaction, pricking, bleeding—mark as an urgent imperative the rectifying of an unconscious impulse toward unicity of selfhood in its struggle against other impulses toward brokenness, division, fragmentation.[26]

But if "pricking" and its verbal cohorts adumbrate a critique of romance, Spenser gathers other romance motifs to articulate one alternative to the knights' cultural imaginary. Their irresistible impulses to open wounds and pour blood out of the finite body and into a receptive earth are countered by the cantos' equal insistence on round, spherical, containing, or linked objects. Their crucial feature is that they are blessedly unbroken, as if being whole, with one's lifeblood or sap still sealed within bodily boundaries, were a gift or an achievement that the chivalric social world makes difficult of attainment. They are often magical, as if humans could not be entrusted with maintaining the unicity and integrity of their own bodies. This emphasis on wholeness or its failure appears in connection with every such unbroken object in the cantos, in passages as short as a phrase or as long as a stanza, as figures or as tangible objects within the narrative.[27] The small group of Paridell, Blandamour, Duessa, Ate, and the false Florimell are implicitly rebuked by the narrator's reminder that "vertue is the band, that bindeth harts most sure" (4.2.29); this small group overtakes the true friends Cambell,

25. See Mary Jane Lupton, *Menstruation and Psychoanalysis* (Urbana: University of Illinois Press, 1993), esp. chap. 9, "The Bleeding Body and Male Desire."

26. The poem's quest for bodily wholeness is the subject of Miller's *Poem's Two Bodies*. He writes, for example, "I take the allegory of *The Faerie Queene* to be organized with reference to the anticipated-but-deferred wholeness of an ideal body. . . . This 'body' is an ideological formation derived from the religious myth of the *corpus mysticum* and its imperial counterpart, the notion of the monarch as incarnating an ideal and unchanging political body" (4). This ideological derivation allows Miller to bring Queen Elizabeth into play in his reading of the poem; my concern is more with Spenser's extraordinarily complex and fluent relationship to his genre.

27. On the archaic magical power of such engirdling objects in folklore, see Richard Onians, *The Origins of European Thought: About the Body, the Mind, the Soul, the World, Time, and Fate* (Cambridge: Cambridge University Press, 1954), 315–17, 352–77, 444–60; Albert Friedman and Richard Osberg, "Gawain's Girdle as a Traditional Symbol," *Journal of American Folklore* 90 (1977): 301–15.

Triamond, Canacee, and Cambina, "lincked . . . in louely wise" (4.2.30).
Florimell's girdle, Canacee's magic ring that binds up all wounds, the
entwined serpents of Cambina's caduceus and the olive garland that
crowns them, the snake encased in a new skin to which Cambello is
compared (4.2.23), the cup of nepenthe "to the brim vpfild" with which
Cambina heals the knights' bloodlust (4.3.42), Cambello's wounded
body each time it closes up, even Chaucer himself as "well of English
vndefyled" (4.2.32)—all are instances of the encircling, entwining, or
containing and cherishing objects that protect the violent, mortal
humans. Hence the sinuous Spenserian glide from objects that bind or
weave together with objects that contain: they all become vessels, holding in the "vitall sap" of blood made precious because so easily lost.
Within the narrative, it seems that mostly (but not solely) female characters offer such unicity. The real, bounded, mortal life of the integral
body with its vital sap that they offer seems to be an alternative to
merger with the subterranean mother of fantasy and the opened, bleeding body.

The integral body's association with these female characters constitute the first layer of the cantos' turn away from a chthonic mother and
the melancholic nostalgia she awakens insofar as she blocks adequate
symbolization of birth. When Cambina gives a draught of nepenthe to
the fighting knights, Spenser emphasizes its ability to "asswage /
Harts grief, and bitter gall away to chace, / Which stirs vp anguish
and contentious rage" (4.3.43). In the Theban context of these cantos,
Spenser's nepenthe releases the knights from endless grief for a putatively lost maternal object. After so many hand-to-hand combats,
exchanges, and substitutions among the knights and ladies of these
cantos, it comes as a relief that Cambina—a character whose description owes much to Lucretius's Magna Mater passage—has the power
to awaken a simply natural thirst in them, bringing them back from
bloodshed to the boundedness of their bodily lives: "Thus whilest
their minds were doubtfully distraught, / . . . / Her golden cup to
them for drinke she raught, / Whereof full glad for thirst, ech drunk
an harty draught" (4.3.48).[28] The characteristically ambiguous syntax
of the last line suggests that they are as glad for thirst as for a draught.
And in the atemporal happy end of this tale, they make "ioyous feast"
(4.3.52).

28. See Anthony Esolen, "Spenserian Chaos: Lucretius in *The Faerie Queene*," *Spenser
Studies* 11 (1990), 32–34, for a discussion of Cambina and Cybele.

Mothers to Think Back Through

Irigaray says, "There is a pathos of remembering and forgetting. Moving backward in search of something that has been erased, or inscribing it so that it shall not be erased. Fretting over repetitions, reproductions, over what has been erased and comes back."[29]

Spenser has extremely precise and curious ways of remembering and reproducing the Squire's Tale, and these forge an account of his praise of Chaucer which carries much of the "pathos of remembering and forgetting" of which Irigaray speaks. Chaucer's character Canace in the Squire's Tale is given a magic ring allowing her to understand the languages of birds and the medicinal properties of herbs. This magic has little point in the unfinished tale except to enable Canace's hearing and understanding of the tercel's love complaint. But Spenser's Canacee is a woman whose understanding of the languages of the creatures derives from her erudition, which is made possible by her turn away from courtly culture and its available forms of erotic love (viz., being fought over by aggressive knights):

> *Cambelloes* sister was fayre *Canacee*,
> That was the learnedst Ladie in her dayes,
> Well seene in euerie science that mote bee,
> And euery secret worke of natures wayes,
> In wittie riddles, and in wise soothsayes,
> In power of herbes, and tunes of beasts and burds.
>
> (4.2.35)

This displacement of a Chaucerian magic from the realm of the marvelous to a realm of learning, attributed to a woman who resists participation in the courtly world's traffic in women, is one of Spenser's responses to Chaucer's tale. Moreover Spenser creates a remarkable doubling of Canacee's qualities with a second, non-Chaucerian, character, the fay Agape, also deeply versed in the mysteries of nature and turned away from a social world dominated by violent males:

> Their mother was a Fay, and had the skill
>   Of secret things, and all the powres of nature,
>   Which she by art could vse vnto her will,
>   And to her seruice bind each liuing creature,

---

29. Luce Irigaray, "Love of the Other," in *Ethics*, 141.

Through secret vnderstanding of their feature.
Thereto she was right faire, when so her face
She list discouer, and of goodly stature;
But she as Fayes are wont, in priuie place
Did spend her dayes, and lov'd in forests wyld to space.

(4.2.44)

Furthermore, Agape has a daughter, Cambina, to whom she has passed on this lore, while her brothers, Priamond, Diamond, and Triamond, lack it. When Canacee and Agape turn away from chivalric culture and its pressures on them, and toward learning the riddles and soothsays of nature, they emblematize Spenser's wish, particularly strong in these cantos, for a release from the pressures of poetic textuality, with its precarious history and its patrilineal descents, into an oral and aural verbal culture associated with women and the natural world. This wish is one aspect of his ambition to revivify Chaucer. Through it he broods on the relationships between oral poetry and written poetry, hence on textuality, on the ways that poetic activity has come to be gendered in his culture, on precursor texts and the burdens of old texts: "Of louers sad calamities of old, / Full many piteous stories doe remaine, / . . . / That I . . . / . . . oftentimes doe wish it neuer had bene writ," says the narrator at the start (4.1.1).

Spenser's development of Canacee's and Agape's skills complicate what a father-precursor poet might mean at a moment when he feels textuality itself as a burden. The first burden is the responsibility to re-create, in one's own time and one's own tongue and in one's own hand, both the meaning and the monumentality of the predecessor poet. A second is the responsibility of a son to do right by the father's poetic prowess—something that Spenser seems to register when he completes the Squire's Tale by drawing extensively on the Knight's Tale. Third is the risk of closing out a precious (if idealized) oral tradition: its association with spirit, air, and speech, its evanescent nature, its music—and the fact that it involves living women communicating face to face (Agape and Cambina, Agape and the Fates) rather than a living poet addressing another poet two centuries dead. A fourth burden is the poet's vulnerability to an oppressiveness of the precursor text and the related problem of the text perceived as a falsifying reification. Fifth is the practical problem of the writer's feeling overwhelmed by the density of literary history, and by the multiple texts to be woven into a newly configured tapestry. Last is the painfulness of contemplating the

vast panorama of futility in the history received through texts; this is the
burden of Ate's dwelling:

> And all within the riuen walls were hung
> > With ragged monuments of times forepast,
> > All which the sad effects of discord sung:
>
> . . . .
>
> There was the signe of antique Babylon,
> > Of fatall Thebes, of Rome that raigned long,
> > Of sacred Salem, and sad Ilion,
> > For memorie of which on high there hong
> > The golden Apple, cause of all their wrong.

$$(4.1.21-22)^{30}$$

As if to insist on the violence implicit in his own vocation of poet—a violence to himself, among others—Spenser makes figurative and narrative
links between terms for writing and those insistent terms for fighting.
As Jonathan Goldberg has shown, the lexical field describing the physical act of writing in this period includes many words for cutting, incising, piercing, carving, slitting; writing itself is "pricking."[31] The extensive language of cutting, pricking, and flowing of blood in Spenser's
three Chaucerian cantos constitute an extended figure for the act of writing, linked to his wish to revivify Chaucer, and resonate with a wish for
a kind of death associated with the feminine.

A potential sense of writing as a trauma to both flesh and spirit occurs
throughout *The Faerie Queene*, constantly exerting its pressure against a
sense of writing's generative powers.[32] Spenser materializes this pos-

30. Susanne Wofford's discussion of gender and romance in these cantos credits the
power of allegory more and Spenser's critique of narrative less than I do; thus of Ate's
dwelling she argues that "these defensive displacements [of allegorical figures] have been
so thoroughly subsumed in the poem's allegory that the fictional surface no longer seems
a significant ground for interpretation. The processes of demonization described here
nonetheless come to constitute a major unacknowledged aspect of the poem's treatment of
the feminine, in which the chivalric fiction provides at least a glimpse of the allegory's
efforts to evade or even erase its own misogynistic reliance on female scapegoats." *The
Choice of Achilles: The Ideology of Figure in Epic* (Stanford: Stanford University Press, 1992),
289. But I think that Spenser both critiques romance and exploits romance's own inclination to critique itself.

31. Jonathan Goldberg, *Writing Matter: From the Hands of the English Renaissance* (Stanford: Stanford University Press, 1990), 57–107.

32. Gross (*Spenserian Poetics*) discusses Spenser's sense of violence in representations of
divinity and in iconoclasm alike; Miller (*Poem's Two Bodies*) traces biblical tropes of writing
upon the heart and the letter that kills.

sible violence in terms of the incising upon some smooth surface or interior organ of a human body. Thus Love yearns to engrave his "tri-
umphs" and "battels" upon the enticingly expansive, virgin surface of
Belphoebe's "iuorie forhead . . . / Like a broad table it selfe dispred"
(2.3.24); the locus classicus is Busyrane's torture of Amoret, which
includes excising her heart, writing with sharp implements in an ink
made of her blood, performing magic from the "bloudy lines" of his
"wicked books," and trying to kill Amoret with a "murdrous knife"
(3.12.31, 36, 32).[33] This episode is part of a bridge between the 1590 and
the 1596 editions of *The Faerie Queene*. In the 1596 edition, Spenser recurs
to and expands the violence of writing, alluding to the mechanics of
writing with sharp implements and an ink of blood. In this edition, only
eleven stanzas (excluding the proem of book 4) separate Amoret's
becoming "perfect hole" from Spenser's reminder of Busyrane's "cruell
knife that her deare heart did kerue" (4.1.4). This knife modulates into
more martial weapons, while Amoret's "perfect hole" modulates into
other circlets of healing and wholeness. So all the piercing, cutting,
pricking, and bloodletting of chivalric combat that we have seen constitute a meditation simultaneously on the homosocial world of chivalric
emulation and on the homosocial world of poetic emulation, within
which Spenser hopes to revivify Chaucer. But as his narrative shows,
neither of these masculine enterprises can achieve its ends without the
powers of the feminine, figured as a small feminine culture that arouses
hope of peace among knights as well as hope of a transformed literary
history for poets.

That Canacee and other female characters represent an intertextual
swerve from the burdens of intertextuality is a point supported by sheer
propinquity. Spenser lodges the Canacee stanza immediately after the
well-known stanzas to "Dan *Chaucer*, well of English vndefyled"
(4.2.32):

But wicked Time that all good thoughts doth waste,
    And workes of noblest wits to nought out weare,
    That famous moniment hath quite defaste,
    And robd the world of threasure endlesse deare,
    The which mote haue enriched all vs heare.
    O cursed Eld the cankerworme of writs,

33. There is a flourishing commentary on Busyrane; I am indebted to Miller, *Poem's Two
Bodies*; Gross, *Spenserian Poetics*, 160–70; Stephens, *Limits of Eroticism*, 27–36 and passim.

How may these rimes, so rude as doth appeare,
    Hope to endure, sith workes of heauenly wits
Are quite deuourd, and brought to nought by little bits?

Then pardon, O most sacred happie spirit,
    That I thy labours lost may thus reuiue,
    And steale from thee the meede of thy due merit,
    That none durst euer whilest thou wast aliue,
    And being dead in vaine yet many striue:
    Ne dare I like, but through infusion sweete
    Of thine owne spirit, which doth in me surviue,
    I follow here the footing of thy feete,
That with thy meaning so I may the rather meete.

Cambelloes sister was fayre *Canacee*,
    That was the learnedst Ladie in her dayes,
    Well seene in euerie science that mote bee.

(4.2.33–35)

With this abrupt turn to Canacee, Spenser's aim is not simply to complete the Squire's Tale but to manifest the complexities of the ways that sons follow fathers in the creation of poetry; for the stanza that ends with an exalted praise of Chaucer, stanza 32, moves immediately to lament, adapted from passages not in the Squire's Tale at all—a tale in itself sunnily carefree about the possibilities of narrative poetry—but in *The House of Fame* and *Anelida and Arcite*, poems more complex and brooding about the relationships among writing, love, and time.[34] Spenser's stanzas sustain an unstable suspension of despair and hope, a sense of distance from Chaucer as well as one of intimacy with him, in an art of poetic commemoration; these two affects jointly underscore the courage required for the task of poetic remembrance, in the face of "cursed Eld." This is one reason for the crucial shift from images of poetic creation as monumentality in stanza 33—"That famous moniment," "threasure endlesse deare"—to images of poetic creation as movement, as gesture of spirit, as encounter, in stanza 34: "infusion

---

34. The lines from *Anelida and Arcite*, for instance, somberly contemplate the devouring and fragmenting power of "elde": "For hit ful depe is sonken in my mynde, / With pitous hert in Englyssh to endyte / This olde storie . . . / That elde, which that al can frete and bite, / As hit hath freten many a noble storie, / Hath nygh devoured out of oure memorie" (ll. 8–14). See Vincent DiMarco's notes to these lines in the *Riverside Chaucer*, 3d ed., ed. Larry Benson et al. (Boston: Houghton Mifflin, 1987), 991, for these lines' derivation from Boccaccio.

sweete," "I follow here the footing of thy feete," "That . . . so I may the rather meete." These latter phrases suggest a poetry less tangible and artifactual, less textual, and closer to the realm of oral poetry, than the kind of poetry that can be food for worms.

The first cantos of *The Faerie Queene*, book 4 inhabit and make much of just this ambiguous, potentially anxious transitional space between the oral and the textual. Canacee may have learned much of her knowledge from books, but they are conspicuously absent from Spenser's description of her work. Canacee's culture is apparently free of artifactual texts, but it is vocalic and full of signifiers (those riddles, soothsays, and tunes). It is as if the introduction of Canacee, just after the dense, affectionate, but also anxious stanzas about Chaucer and the burdens of textuality within history, offers Spenser a momentary breathing space, a release into an oral culture, in the turn away from the necessarily vigilant and constantly revivifying activity of the poetic son who would follow his father's footsteps. This is the significance of Spenser's undoing of Chaucer's link, in the Squire's Tale, between an arbitrary magic and linguistic wisdom; in Spenser, Canacee's gifts are born of learning but ally her with nature rather than alienate her within a textual world.

This pattern of women's oral lore recurs throughout the cantos. Canto 2, for instance, opens with a paean to the oral poet-musicians of ancient classical and biblical cultures, Orpheus and David, and defines their art by two features: it is "wise words with time concented" (4.2.2), and it works powerful effects in the world:

> Such as was *Orpheus*, that when strife was growen
> Amongst those famous ympes of Greece, did take
> His siluer Harpe in hand, and shortly friends them make.

> Or such as that celestiall Psalmist was,
> That when the wicked feend his Lord tormented,
> With heauenly notes, that did all other pas,
> The outrage of his furious fit relented.
> Such Musicke is wise words with time concented,
> To moderate stiffe minds, disposd to striue.

(4.2.1–2)

It comes as something of a shock, after this sublime, canonical, and masculine lineage, to learn that Spenser considers Britomart's nurse Glauce as a full member of so distinguished a company, and scolds the glib Paridell for dismissing women's oral and poetic culture:

Such vs'd wise *Glauce* to that wrathfull knight,
    To calme the tempest of his troubled thought:
    Yet *Blandamour* with termes of foule despight,
    And *Paridell* her scornd, and set at nought,
    As old and crooked and not good for ought,
    Both they vnwise, and warelesse of the euill,
    That by themselues vnto themselues is wrought.

(4.2.3)

The assimilation of Glauce—comic, old, superstitious, garrulous, a figure of fun in book 3—to the line of Orpheus and David is a fine stroke on
Spenser's part: he seems to rebuke not only Paridell but also himself, as
creator of Glauce in book 3, and perhaps also the reader for too easily
dismissing the mother-wit, the tradition of learning, and the effective-
ness of poetry freed from the bondage of textuality that she now represents. Glauce is rehabilitated, in book 4, by assimilation to a newly dig-
nified oral culture (contrast the tone of amusement at her superstitious
magic in book 3) in which Canacee, Agape, and Cambina also dwell.[35]
They negotiate some autonomy and agency in the masculine chivalric
world of bonding among men via exchange of women. The women
characters need the power of their oral culture, and it can even be said
that they are the truest agents of the cantos' significant events, while the
men just fight, all the time, in paroxysms of irritability and in pools of
blood. (The Squire of Dames, serving in this book as a peacemaker, is an
important exception.) Glauce creates a temporary peace in Scudamour.
Canacee, besieged by suitors, insists on a temporary freedom from the
code which gives ladies to conquering knights, and when she can no
longer forestall the inevitable, she agrees to the plan of her brother
Cambello that she should wed the victor of a tournament, the combat-

35. Upton suggests, " 'Tis very agreeable to poetical decorum, as well as a just punishment for Scudamore's jealous disposition, that Glauce leaves him thus in ignorance and
doubt"; Warton notes, "The aged dame Glauce might have easily pacified Sir Scudamore,
in this place, by telling him, that Britomartis was a woman; and as she was so much terri-
fied, it was highly natural, that she should assure him of it. But such a declaration would
have prevented an entertaining surprise, which the poet reserved for a future canto
(IV.vi.28)." *Variorum* 4:173–74.
    See Stephens, *Limits of Eroticism*, 64–72, for a fine discussion of Glauce in the company of
women and Spenser's flirtation with a feminized imagination. Stephens also pairs Glauce
with her opposite number, Ate: "Spenser enables Glauce to become an Orphic figure by
giving her some of Ate's demonic power. Indeed, the poem's rewriting of Ate hints that if
Glauce were not an old and inept worker of charms, she might instead be a furious one" (69).

ants of which would agree to fight Cambello as her champion. The odds of her remaining free seem to be in her favor, since she gives to Cambello her curative magic (4.2.39). And it is Cambina, daughter and pupil of Agape, who can finally put an end to the bloody competitions for women.

The natural magic and oral culture of these women thus offer both the writer and the fighters an alternative to the mesmerizing representations of chthonic mothers, an imagined bliss of being able to let go of the effort to create texts and honor fathers, while remaining within a verbal culture, aligned with nature, culturally transmitted through women. That is, in the creation of Canacee, Agape, and Cambina, and the refurbishing of Glauce, Spenser recognizes the need for mothers to think back through—the need to acknowledge the debt to the mother. In the context of the homosocial poetic history in which Spenser joins, it is the mother who functions as the third element to break the hypnotic union of fathers and sons. One risk that Spenser perceives is that the "infusion sweete" of one male poet by another, without the aid of the feminine, could be too difficult or too unnatural a task, allowing both father and son to "vanysshe, flessh, and blood, and skyn." By these lights, his creation of poetic mothers would be less a brief for a heterosexual regime than an acknowledgment of the debt to maternity. Indeed if Spenser is thinking of the Pardoner's Tale in the midst of his own episode of sons who find death difficult to achieve, then he is also thinking of the necessity of bringing parturition into the symbolic: without this work, his characters and his narrator alike face the intolerable desire of the Pardoner's old man to disappear into a maternalized earth.

No End to Possibility

Spenser effects a further turn away from the phantasmatic chthonic maternal, rescuing his romance narratives from the binarisms governing the diagrammatic patterns of battle and exchange among characters in the early cantos. His first turn away from such nostalgia just creates another binarism and another level of nostalgia. On the one hand, fathers, dead poets, and a textual tradition of bleeding warriors and chthonic maternal forces; on the other hand, benign female peacemakers, oral lore, mother tongue, natural magic, freedom from books, and women in living relationship to one another. The second set of terms, though it begins to symbolize mother-daughter relations, to articulate parturition, and to free maternity from the crypt, still participates in a

duality that leaves the maternal (and the knights and poet, for that matter) locked in a structure of nostalgia. For how can the writer of these
narratives find a place for himself in what he imagines to be the freer
movements among the female characters, their freer relations to their
lore and knowledge? His textually transmitted tales still leave him outside a home that some women seem to enjoy by birthright. The characters will still stage a tournament and a beauty pageant involving the
true and false Florimell and Florimell's magic girdle. To celebrate the
alignment of women, nature, and oral traditions is a step, but it still
leaves us inert in the lap of the goddess, comfortable but not in that
movement which is a crucial ideal of subjectivity for Winnicott and Irigaray. There will have to be another, more radical turn from nostalgia
for the feminine, a transformation of the narrative terms of book 4. This
transformation, working its way slowly through the center cantos of the
book, emerges in strength in the episodes of the Temple of Venus and
the marriage of rivers, narrated in the book's final cantos. In that
sequence and the Lucretian roots of its structure we find the book's second, deeper refusal of nostalgia for the maternal.[36]

The stories flanked by the Temple of Venus and the marriage of rivers
are replete with literal mothers, maternal imagery, uterine environ-
ments, and protective surrogate mothers who aid troubled young
lovers.[37] The two pairs of lovers—Scudamour and Amoret, Florimell and
Marinell—both entrained in the various torments of Petrarchan
amorous relations, need to negotiate their relations to the maternal figures and settings in the book in order for their stories to move ahead.
The mothers initially do a great deal of holding, in Winnicott's sense of
total environmental provision. Among the complex activities of holding,
as we have seen, is an infant's gradual introjection of a sense of self
through responsiveness from adults. Such a formation carries with it a
structure of holding, an experience of the early mother not as object but
as process internalized, as we saw in chapter 3. Thus each subject
learns, as Bollas puts it, "to relate to himself as an object within intra-
subjective space."[38] Of Spenser's four lovers it seems that none knows

36. The most explicit study of Lucretius and Spenser's book is Esolen, "Spenserian
Chaos"; see 49 n. 1 for his survey of debates over Lucretius's influence on Spenser.

37. See Bellamy, *Translations of Power*, 198–200, Jonathan Goldberg, "The Mothers in Book
III of *The Faerie Queene*," *Texas Studies in Literature and Language* 17 (1975): 5–26 and Nohrnberg, *Analogy*, 549–651, for discussion of maternal features in books 3 and 4.

38. Christopher Bollas, *The Shadow of the Object: Psychoanalysis of the Unthought
Known* (New York: Columbia University Press, 1987), 45.

One partner in each couple is given no back story of experience of maternal care, and one how to hold himself or herself, much less others, as an intrapsychic object; each one is much handled by others, not in their own keeping at all. Florimell's vicissitudes provide the best instance, not least because her constant flights from one pair of hands to another produce her uncanny double, the false Florimell, who exists precisely for the purpose of passing from hand to hand. But the other three characters also fail to keep or preserve themselves psychically, relying on others to keep them. It is as if they are all stalled in a kind of psychic infancy, and therefore vulnerable to the predations of the world to which they mistakenly look for parenting. In the love relations that Spenser envisions as ideals for his lovers, they would discover a capacity for what Bollas calls "a more generative way of holding the self as an object of care," and this will make it possible to imagine a cherishing of the beloved without the infantile neediness of narcissism or the violence of Petrarchism.[39] This transformation Spenser achieves by introducing into his chivalric romance two elements from Lucretius: the *alma Venus* passage launching Lucretius's poem and the notions of movement and fluidity as conditions of narrative.

Scudamour, giving his account of the winning of Amoret from her protective female enclave in the Temple of Venus, still gives himself over to the specific chivalric unconscious that we saw at the start of book 4. He is the conquering knight; the occasion requires boldness and martial hardiness, for to him Amoret is "this peerelesse beauties spoile" (4.10.3); the Temple is full of signs that spur Scudamour to heroic-erotic action through dread and doubt. In terms of literary history, his description of the Temple borrows local details from Virgil's *Aeneid*, the *Roman de la Rose*, Chaucer's Knight's Tale and *Troilus and Criseyde*. This bricolage could simply figure forth Scudamour's unrectified knightly assumptions about how to win a woman; his reliance on Venus's approval, which he deduces from her smile, suggests as much:

And euermore vpon the Goddesse face
Mine eye was fixt, for feare of her offence,

---

partner in each couple is given strong ties to mothers. Thus Scudamour has no narrative of maternal care, but book 3 has shown the nymph Chrysogonee's birthing of Amoret and Venus's raising of Amoret in the Garden of Adonis. Florimell is given no earlier account of maternal care, but Marinell has an overprotective mother, the nymph Cymoent (renamed Cymodocee in book 4), who first tries to keep her son from erotic maturity but, in book 4, plays a significant role in uniting her son with Florimell.

39. Bollas, 62.

Whom when I saw with amiable grace
To laugh at me, and fauour my pretence,
I was emboldned with more confidence.

(4.10.56)

As in his first appearance in book 3, where a magical wall of fire blocking him from Amoret is a force field created by his own excess of aggression, Scudamour finds in the external world a mirror of his own impulses. The Lucretian set piece of the hymn to Venus, uttered by an anonymous lover in the Temple, cuts across the Scudamourian construction of Venus entirely as received from bits and pieces of the courtly/chivalric culture transcribed in major textual traditions. Suddenly we are back with Lucretius's great Venus genetrix, and Lucretius's much different deployment of the mirroring mother's face—viz., to celebrate natural drives and fecundity within the larger project of coming to face death:

Great *Venus*, Queene of beautie and of grace,
  The ioy of Gods and men, that vnder skie
  Doest fayrest shine, and most adorne thy place,
  That with thy smyling looke doest pacifie
  The raging seas, and makst the stormes to flie;
  Thee goddesse, thee the winds, the clouds doe feare,
  And when thou spredst thy mantle forth on hie,
  The waters play and pleasant lands appeare,
And heauens laugh, and al the world shewes ioyous cheare.

(4.10.44)

What can we make of the dissonance between the great hymn to Venus (stanzas 44–47) and Scudamour's subsequent, triumphal act of taking possession of the shrinking Amoret (stanzas 53–58)? Scudamour cannot pray the hymn; though it perhaps speaks well of him that he can narrate it, he registers no Lucretian sense of its expansiveness. To my mind Spenser flags the dissonance as a way of situating the very problems of courtly/chivalric culture that we have seen throughout book 4, and gestures toward the rectification of Scudamour and Amoret's marriage only in the later event (later for them but earlier in the narrative) of Amoret's nascent friendship with Britomart.[40] Within the incomplete *Faerie*

40. On this friendship, sketched in 4.1, see especially Stephens, *Limits of Eroticism*, 30–41 and passim. Silberman, *Transforming Desire*, argues that in the last line of Spenser's Lucretian hymn, "O graunt that of my loue at last I may not misse," "*Venus genetrix* has been demoted to the status of a dating service" (83). I cannot hear this tone in the line, but her

Queene, Scudamour and Amoret remain dependent on and therefore vulnerable to those they hope will hold them in a parental way.

Nonetheless, the poet and the reader, if not Scudamour, perceive the hymn's gestures toward rectification of desire, which also provide a way out of the narrative exhaustion of chivalric narrative motifs. A cosmological Venus and the lyric possibilities of catalogue and hymn writ large—that is, on the scale of Spenserian narrative intersect with narrative values of a Lucretian fluency and generativity. Certainly Lucretius would spring to Spenser's mind if he were contemplating river poetry, or perhaps how to revise some early river poem of his own.

Lucretius's praise poem, and its rhetorical features of catalogue, hymn, and invocation, open out from the architectural firmness of the Temple of Venus into the marriage of rivers, with its jubilant catalogue of rivers and water spirits. This lyrical catalog intertwines with the narrative of Florimell and Marinell, the second pair of lovers, as a kind of wedding gift to them. What he gives them is this: a capacity to hold both self and other as objects within the mind in a generative rather than a cruel way. We know that these lovers will be united happily. But for the duration of the marriage of rivers and its catalogue, Florimell remains fixed and Marinell hovers around the edges of the feast—gloomy, sulking, without clarity. What is the point of joining Marinell's story to the river marriage while also excluding him from it?

Spenser proffers lyric possibilities of love to counter the narrative Petrarchan imprisonments of both pairs of lovers. This means lyric possibilities emphatically not in the Petrarchan tradition, but in the cosmological tradition with its greater amplitude of eros and the tying of eros to a divine creativity. Thus Marinell cannot "hold" himself, is in the keeping of his mother Cymoent, needs a clout by Britomart and a long immersion in maternal waters before he can hear and respond to Florimell's suffering for him. What happens during this immersion? Or, to get at the same question by querying narrative structure: What is the relation between the marriage of rivers and the events among Marinell, Florimell, Cymoent, and the gods, running literally underneath the river? Why does Spenser, our greatest poet of wedding, not give to Florimell and Marinell's union its own description? In a maneuver made possible by his romance precursors, Spenser holds Marinell

---

reading points to the canto's insistence on dissonant senses of Venus and led me to think about Scudamour's self-interested account of the Lucretian Venus.

in a Winnicottian way during the poetic time of the lyric catalogue of rivers.[41] He also bestows on Marinell's story the possibility of the transformative powers implicit in his catalogue of waters. By "transformative powers" I mean the following. First, I mean the happy erotic union of the Thames and the Medway, which offers the subsequent narratives an ideal eros free of the tainted textual culture of Petrarchan love. Second, I mean the expansive fluidity with which the natures of anthropomorphized deities and natural objects are represented. River nymphs are both rivers and nymphs; their procession is also their flowing. Lucretius, as we saw, intensifies anxiety about integrity of the bounded self in his descriptions of those dissipating atoms. Here, Spenser reassures—or transforms—anxiety about bodily wholeness and bodily boundaries by gliding easily between mingled waters and the human forms of the water spirits. That is why these mythic doublings of identity are free of the pain that they often carry in Graeco-Roman myth, especially in Ovid. For instance, the catalogue purposely risks starting with a familial fatality analogous to that in the early cantos of the book—"*Phorcys*, the father of that fatall brood, / . . . / And tragicke *Inoes* sonne, the which became / A God of seas through his mad mothers blame" (4.11.13)—but subordinates these catastrophes to the sheer abundance and vitalism of the catalogue. Third, I mean the overtly joyful transformational fusions with literary history celebrated in the river catalogue.

It is not that Marinell is meant to perceive these things, as if he were reading the very episode in which he exists, but that these possibilities of the lyric catalogue enter the narrative stream. Mysteriously, while Marinell is thus held by the poet, he becomes gradually capable of responding to Florimell. His past as a dependent of the sea fades, as he comes to hold not the gems that once belonged to others—haunting traces of lives lost—but, internally, his own life: he holds himself as an object, in a generative way. One sign of this is that Marinell awakens to a capacity to think, a point reiterated throughout 3 full stanzas (4.12.12–14): "Then gan [Cupid] make him tread his steps anew, / And

---

41. The narrative technique of many romances that Spenser would have known include two characteristics that Spenser deploys in *The Faerie Queene*. (1) They displace to rhetorical set pieces and objects like landscape emotions and psychology not vouchsafed to their characters. In this they permit the *reader* a gathering of affect and consciousness. (2) They adumbrate a kind of parental holding atmosphere in their mysterious events, unaccountable actions, and sense that experience is available to be used, even when characters cannot understand their experience. I think this is the largest single feature that Spenser absorbed from Malory.

learne to loue, by learning louers paines to rew" (4.12.13). In these same stanzas he begins to perceive Florimell as a subject and an other: the possibility of an ethical relation between them arises. (Winnicott would say that she becomes an object to him at last, and now he can truly use her.) Spenser even maternalizes Marinell when describing his distress at not being able to aid Florimell: he applies the simile of a cow frantic for the welfare of her calf, which seems to owe much to Lucretius's vignette of the heifer whose calf has been sacrificed:[42]

> Like as an Hynde whose calfe is falne vnwares
> Into some pit, where she him heares complaine,
> An hundred times about the pit side fares,
> Right sorrowfully mourning her bereaued cares.
>
> (4.12.17)

If this simile indeed applies to Marinell, its maternal elements are crucial. Marinell's mother, the sea nymph Cymodoce, had appealed on her son's behalf to the gods—first the sea god Tryphon, then significantly the celestial, non-chthonic healer Apollo (4.11.6–7, 4.12.21–33)—roughly as Agape had appealed to the Fates on behalf of her sons. But Marinell learns to take upon himself the tenderness of a mother, or internalizes a structure of maternal care, and thus frees both himself and the maternal from the symbolic demands to provide for him that he made on the maternal sea when he first appeared in book 3, canto 4. It is precisely because he often holds his characters thus, while they are themselves unaware of plots and figures woven around them, that Spenser's fictions so often seem dreamlike to readers. Marinell, though steeped in the sea, apparently has no dreams or dream visions, but Spenser holds him in that curious position vis-à-vis literary events mysteriously essential to his own survival. Their ramifications are *for* him, soliciting and welcoming him, as the dreamer Chaucer is solicited and enrolled by poetic and dream events in the *Parlement of Foules*.

If dream and dream vision provide useful local models for reading the content of the episodes late in book 4, it is Spenser's sense of a Lucretian plenitude and fluency of the natural world that gives them their satisfying narrative difference from the nightmarishly claustropho-

---

42. Hamilton's edition of the poem takes this simile as applying to Florimell. But the context of the whole stanza seems to make it applicable to each of them; certainly Marinell's restless wandering and anguish make him a plausible correlative to the hind of the simile.

bic and chthonic impulses of cantos 1–3. By adapting Lucretius's invocation to *Venus genetrix*, his heifer vignette, and his fascination with free
movement—and by suppressing the atomists' notion of random
swerves of atoms in favor of a more processional kind of movement. The
narrator too finds himself released from the cruelty, sharpness, and
fatigue of memory-through-textuality, from the chthonic obsessiveness,
from the nostalgic idealizations of the feminine-maternal registered in
the early cantos.[43] Here at the end of book 4, in the invocation launching
the epic catalogue of rivers, he happily acquiesces in a fluent interweave
of nature and text:

> All which not if an hundred tongues to tell,
> And hundred mouthes, and voice of brasse I had,
> And endlesse memorie, that mote excell,
> In order as they came, could I recount them well.

> (4.11.9)

In the midst of his catalogue, the narrator recognizes that he may be
overwhelmed by plenitude, but he divests himself of anxiety over the
recording of monuments—the terrible textual burden of the first three
cantos of the book—with the idea that whatever naming and praising he
does accomplish is good enough, because the vitalism of the natural
world sustains and renews his acts:

> How can they all in this so narrow verse
> Contayned be, and in small compasse hild?
> Let them record them, that are better skild,
> And know the moniments of passed times:
> Onely what needeth, shall be here fulfild.

> (4.11.17)

43. As Silberman argues, the marriage of rivers offers "multiple unfoldings of a greater
plenitude [as] an alternative to the castrating economy of absence and presence" that characterizes the behavior of violent knights (*Transforming Desire*, 136). As she points out, there
are implications about Spenser's narrative practice: the fact that "Florimell and Marinell
are brought together through a series of improvisations and spur-of-the-moment shifts in
theoretical commitment" (11) is of a piece with the late cantos' celebration of natural plenitude and flux.
Lucretius is not the only poet of flux and generative waters whom Spenser honors here;
he also draws on the sea-epyllion concluding Virgil's *Georgics*, book 4, about Aristaeus and
his sea-nymph mother Cyrene. In a yet unpublished essay, I argue that Virgil's shaping of
the sea-epyllion as a meditation on natality comprises his response to Lucretius's poem on
death.

It is heartening that the mother of the groom, the River Ouze (Isis), is strikingly free of associations chthonic, sepulchral, fixed; also, the horror of age, so vivid in Ate, is redeemed, and the aged mother is revered—and in motion:

> But much more aged was his wife then he [the Thame],
> The Ouze, whom men doe Isis rightly name;
> Full weake and crooked creature seemed shee,
> And almost blind through eld, that scarce her way could see.
>
> Therefore on either side she was sustained
> Of two smal grooms . . .
>
> (4.11.24–25)

The groom himself honors the Magna Mater, Cybele; and, by wearing a coronet like the goddess's, he permits Spenser to make another bow to Cambina: "Like as the mother of the Gods, they say, / In her great iron charet wonts to ride, /.../ Old *Cybele*, arayd with pompous pride" (4.11.28). Statius, chthonic mothers and deities, blood soaking the ground, the cruelty of memory and textuality to the poet—in book 4 these yield first to nice girls and then, more powerfully, to Lucretius, flowing waters, praise song, ease in the heart of the poet, and mothers on the move.

9

Enough:
The Winter's Tale

Antigone too needs to emerge from the domination, the
empire of one law—in order to move in herself and in the
universe as in a living house. It is important that life, blood,
air, water and fire should be given back to her for her share,
and not simply that she should be there to serve the cult of
something which is already dead: individuals or laws.

—Luce Irigaray

Irigaray, dissatisfied with her early sense of Antigone as the woman
created by masculine culture because that sense leaves her languishing
in the crypt, mounts a kind of rescue mission of the Theban woman,
restoring to her the vital signs of mobility and breath.[1] The relevance
of this restoration to the concluding action of *The Winter's Tale* is manifest, but before turning to Shakespeare's late play and the strange processes by which the restoration occurs, I make a final turn to Winnicott.

As I have maintained throughout this book, we need to change the
common understanding of Winnicott as the man who promulgated the

1. Luce Irigaray, "Love of Same, Love of Other" (1984), in *An Ethics of Sexual Difference*,
trans. Carolyn Burke and Gillian Gill (Ithaca, N.Y.: Cornell University Press, 1993), 97–115,
at 108.

notion that no mother could be good enough yet *must* be so. Rather than positioning him—and the idea of "good enough"—within our usual assumptions about infant insatiability, we should situate him within a tradition of thought that acknowledges universal exposures and vulnerabilities, an ideal of hardy sufficiency for children and mothers, and the interval between mother and child. This is what the idiom "good enough" means, after all. To have enough or do enough is to be content with a limit for both mother and child. But Winnicott's idea of good-enough mothering is sabotaged not only by ideologies of maternity and birth but also by the very history of the concept "enough." As Jill Mann demonstrates in an essay on *Pearl* and Chaucer's Clerk's Tale, the Middle English *ynogh*, like the Latin *satis*, the Italian *assai*, and the French *assez*, "can mean 'rather, moderately'—indicating a kind of halfway house—but can also mean 'fully, completely, abundantly'—indicating the end of the line, the fullest realization of some possibility."[2] Thus the grace of God in *Pearl* "is gret innoghe"; that is, as Mann says, not only is this grace " 'sufficiently' great, reaching to the limit of the demand made on it, but . . . it is 'abundantly' great, limitless, acknowledging no boundaries but those of the [divine] radiating sphere of perfection" (34). So it is part of our linguistic endowment that "enough" might mean "too much": "Enough is enough," we say, or "I've had enough" or "Enough of that now!" These phrases all exemplify problems of psychic, material, and domestic economy.

Winnicott is adamant, as we have seen, that the infant whose hunger needs to be *satisfied* by mother also needs not to be *satiated*. Being given enough up to a limit is what allows the infant to discover its own bounds and therefore its own appetite; this, for Winnicott, is tantamount to feeling real, insofar as it summons the early motility that he calls aggression. The subject needs to traverse that interval in order to know hope. "For if it does not develop appetite," we have heard from Harold Boris, "it only has its grievances as things upon which to nurse and gnaw."[3] Boris's Kleinian/Winnicottian infant needs to want possession of the breast in order to discover that it belongs to someone else, that he wants to take it, and that infancy's way of possessing it is forever precluded from possessing it as mother does. Without this acknowledgment of the verge between mother and infant, an acknowledgment that

2. Jill Mann, "Satisfaction and Payment in Middle English Literature," *Studies in the Age of Chaucer* 5 (1983): 17–48, at 34.

3. Harold Boris, *Envy* (Northvale, N.J.: Jason Aronson, 1994), 36.

gives to the child its own desire, "the frustration of [the baby's] intention to possess the breast and not merely receive from it is all too likely to feel so unendurable that for the infant to take at all (more accurately, to *know* that it is taking) is to feel the loss of possibility as a pain too deep to be borne" (36). Given too much, the infant loses appetite (when properly delineated its name might be eagerness, as Winnicott said). The infant merely complies, and finds an anxiety of excess that it cannot manage, or even experience. Satiation becomes traumatic.

But of course the idea of a *sufficient* maternity is difficult to sustain if we assume that infants are insatiable, and that they have a limitless claim on mothers, born of infinite neediness. If we are to value sufficiency or the good-enough for *mothers*, we must value the hardiness of infancy. This would mean refusing certain kinds of nostalgia about infancy and the infant within grownups. And this in turn would mean acknowledging, mourning, then celebrating the open enclave of air wrought by birth.

To ground the economic problem of "enough" and to link it to Winnicott and Irigaray on movement, I now turn to *The Winter's Tale*, which thematizes the problem of nostalgia for the lost mother so insistently, reiterates tropes of generation so pervasively, and presents such memorable and articulate literal mothers that it easily evokes our own nostalgia and our critical anxieties about excessive nostalgia for the mother. Since it is also the work that first posed the questions spurring this book when I first saw it at age sixteen, it is fitting that I close with it.[4]

The play opens with a marked nervousness about excess and insufficiency among the courtiers at a moment of delicate decorum, the parting of the two kings. Excess and insufficiency have a way of getting mixed up in the courtly gift economy. Anticipating Leontes' visit to Bohemia during the coming summer, when Polixenes' court can repay Sicilia's hospitality, Archidamus of Bohemia frets that words fail to express a sufficiency of gratitude: "our entertainment shall shame us . . .

---

4. It was the 1969 Royal Shakespeare production in London. I was away—far away—from home for the first time, without my family. It was my first introduction to Shakespeare, and I'd never heard of this play. Judi Dench played both Hermione and Perdita. In spite of the fact that I know I was there, and have the program and ticket stub to verify it, I've never been able to remember anything of going to the theater, much less of that production. Nonetheless, since then I've carried a crush on Judi Dench and an obsessive need to write on *The Winter's Tale*—many, many unpublished pages as well as my first published essay. The repression, as it must be, of my memory of it always haunts me, but even my ten years' work on this book, and the working out of this chapter, haven't solved my personal riddle about my relationship to the play.

we cannot with such magnificence—in so rare—I know not what to say"
(1.1.8–13). And the friendly haggling with which Leontes and Polixenes
enter in the following scene—how long will Polixenes stay beyond his
planned time? how will they negotiate the guest/host ritual of depar-
ture?—confounds *enough* and *too much* in the same way, especially in
Polixenes' loading of their conversation with a lexicon of multiple,
crowding things:

> *Pol.* Nine changes of the wat'ry star hath been
> The shepherd's note since we have left our throne
> 　. . . Time as long again
> Would be fill'd up, my brother, with our thanks,
>
> ·　·　·　·　·　·　·　·　·　·　·　·　·　·　·
> 　　　　　. . . I multiply
> With one "We thank you" many thousands moe
> That go before it.
> ·　·　·　·　·　·
> 　*Leon.* One sev'nnight longer.
> 　*Pol.*　　　Very sooth, to-morrow.
> 　*Leon.* We'll part the time between 's then; and in that
> I'll no gainsaying.

(1.2.1–18)[5]

As readers have long noted, Polixenes' language throughout this
scene evokes fullness, pregnancy, and childhood (he misses his own
son, he nostalgically recalls his boyhood with Leontes in a golden glow).
Perhaps encouraged by his spheres of diction, psychoanalytic studies of
the play understand Leontes' jealousy in the same scene as derivative
from *his* nostalgia for an archaic mother. Thus Murray Schwartz, in two
influential pieces written in the mid-1970s, argues that Leontes' attachment to Polixenes masks a desire for infantile union with the mother. C.
L. Barber and Richard Wheeler argue that Hermione's enhancement and
sanctification in the statue scene "has been earned by freeing Leontes'
perception of the maternal in her from the perverse dependence
expressed in his jealousy." Coppélia Kahn argues that Leontes is "stuck
at the developmental stage preceding the formation of identity, the stage
of undifferentiated oneness with the mother, on which his oneness with
Polixenes was modeled." Ruth Nevo speaks of Leontes' "exclusion from
a once experienced plenitude," "undifferentiated oneness with another

5. Citations come from the *Riverside Shakespeare*, ed. G. Blakemore Evans et al. (Boston:
Houghton Mifflin, 1974).

being," and his being "separated or isolated by Hermione's new intimacy with her unborn child."[6]

An assumption of nostalgia for the mother driving Leontes underwrites all these arguments, and has by now gained the force of common sense (although new kinds of psychoanalytic readings are just beginning to gain ground). I am skeptical about the pervasiveness of this underlying fantasy, though. Why should it be Leontes' presumed and Polixenes' real nostalgia that sets our readings of desire and maternity in the play? Here I turn toward Hermione instead, for I think it is *her* forms of mobile desire that ought to launch our reading. Her form of desire is certainly what makes possible a hopeful reading of the play, an Irigarayan vision of what a life of desire could be.

Hermione's relationship to desire, to her own appetite, I want to characterize as *range of motion*, following Irigaray, who speaks so often of subjects in motion, through her figures of passage, flight, crossing, traversal of an interval or of surfaces, figures of emergence from water or stone, and the discovery of free movement in the expanse and amplitude of air. With only one exception, all Hermione's gestures of relationship in act 1 are motions of verging toward or delicately moving apart from those she loves. She expresses desires for proximity and distance openly, in a continually improvised choreography in which her literal, embodied movements figure forth her desire. Her pleasure lies in constantly traversing and changing the shapes of this space between. Thus she would enjoy granting Leontes an extra month when he visits Bohemia, and she enjoys a poignant interplay of distance from and nearness to her son Mamillius. It is as if Hermione presents us with an ideal vision of appetite like that of Irigaray on movement: "To construct and inhabit our airy space is essential. It is the space of bodily autonomy, of free breath, free speech and song, of performing on the stage of life."[7] Hermione's appetite for movement and space as well as love and praise is an appetite for animation and voice, so it is no wonder that her power of voice and assurance in her words' efficacy are central to her easy inti-

6. Murray Schwartz, "Leontes' Jealousy in *The Winter's Tale*," *American Imago* 30 (1973): 250–73, and "*The Winter's Tale*: Loss and Transformation," *American Imago* 32 (1975): 145–99; C. L. Barber and Richard Wheeler, *The Whole Journey: Shakespeare's Power of Development* (Berkeley: University of California Press, 1986), 333; Coppélia Kahn, *Man's Estate: Masculine Identity in Shakespeare* (Berkeley: University of California Press, 1980), 188; Ruth Nevo, *Shakespeare's Other Language* (London: Methuen, 1987), 103, 104, 105.

7. Luce Irigaray, "Divine Women" (1984), in *Sexes and Genealogies*, trans. Gillian Gill (New York: Columbia University Press, 1987), 66.

macy with her own desire: she manifests Winnicott's and Irigaray's pneumatic figures of breath, words, air, movement, and passage as markers of her feeling real to herself.[8]

In just one exchange, Hermione articulates a different model of desire; it happens to occur in her little jest about her appetites as a pregnant woman. Leontes has just remarked on her persuasiveness in getting Polixenes to stay longer; she says, laughingly,

> What? have I twice said well? When was't before?
> I prithee tell me; cram 's with praise, and make 's
> As fat as tame things. One good deed dying tongueless
> Slaughters a thousand waiting upon that.
> . . . .
> My last good deed was to entreat [Polixenes'] stay;
> What was my first? It has an elder sister,
> Or I mistake you: O, would her name were Grace!
> But once before I spoke to th' purpose? when?
> Nay, let me have't; I long.

> (1.2.90–101)

Hermione revels in being filled up: "cram 's with praise, and make 's / As fat as tame things"; this is so frank in its happy greed to take in words of praise as well as to utter them that I think it could make us a little uncomfortable.[9] Or rather, I think her precise utterance makes Leontes uncomfortable insofar as its model for appetite is that of filling up a container—a Kleinian model—and this model coalesces with the salience of her pregnant body, filled up with the infant who owes her existence to Leontes' having "filled" Hermione nine months earlier.

8. Lynn Enterline beautifully traces the motifs of *pneuma*, voice, and animation in the play as derived from Ovid's *Metamorphoses*, with its "pneumatic movement . . . that both fills up speaking subjects and empties them out" (*The Rhetoric of the Body from Ovid to Shakespeare* [Cambridge: Cambridge University Press, 2000], 50). Although Enterline's project involves neither Klein nor Irigaray, her argument suggests to me that part of the pathos of desire in Ovid is a conflict or impasse between a Klein-like sense of the body as container and a Winnicott- or Irigaray-like sense of desire as movement between surfaces. See also my chapter on Virgil and Ovid in *Gazing on Secret Sights: Spenser, Classical Imitation, and the Decorums of Vision* (Ithaca, N.Y.: Cornell University Press, 1990).

9. I had just finished a satisfying draft of this chapter when I happily found that Katherine Eggert argues similarly about nostalgic form in the play: "[Hermione] speaks a language of desire and bodily presence, a language of eagerness and excess that Leontes can interpret only as *sexually* eager and excessive." Eggert, *Showing like a Queen: Female Authority and Literary Experiment in Spenser, Shakespeare, and Milton* (Philadelphia: University of Pennsylvania Press, 2000), 162.

("No barricado for a belly," he broods at 1.2.204.) Leontes seems to take the Kleinian model in its strongest form, as if we were all both pillaging thieves (especially other men) and containers (especially women) vulnerable to pillage by others. I think it's this speech that sets Leontes off, but it is only one of many expressions of mobile appetite by the others around him, making him feel as if their free, fluent, and mobile desires somehow paralyze or crowd in upon his own range of motion. I recall Winnicott's habit of observing infants reach (or not) toward a shining object, and his notion that the interval in which the baby hesitates allows it an id impulse which allows it to know desire, to initiate motion, and thus to feel real. I recall Winnicott's insistence that while satisfaction of an infant's needs might be a good thing, *satiation* is a terrible thing: an impingement that enforces compliance and brings about a loss of hope. An anxiety of excess, precisely like that expressed often in *The Winter's Tale*, arises in the absence of an open space between oneself and the desirable object.

In light of Hermione's model of appetite, I suggest that Leontes is anxious about having too much, too close by. We have heard Emerson speak of "the fearful extent and multitude of objects"; *The Winter's Tale* shows how this multitude could be traumatic, as it proves to be for all the principal characters. Perhaps Leontes feels so crowded in upon that he cannot find his own appetite, and *this* is his early loss. He is used to loving Polixenes by extending over a large distance, as Camillo says: "they have seem'd to be together, though absent; shook hands, as over a vast; and embrac'd as it were from the ends of oppos'd winds" (1.1.29–31). He and Polixenes have just negotiated a renewed distance between them with exquisite care. True, there is the famous pastoral, nostalgic vision of the young friends' having been "twinned lambs" in childhood, but this is Polixenes' fantasy, not Leontes'. Leontes responds to his friend, his wife, and his son rather as someone who cannot find his own distinctness of birth anymore. He may well require a greater space as "enough" to move in between himself and his loved ones.

In her meditation on *The Winter's Tale*, Lynn Enterline also intertwines the issue of Hermione's pregnancy with the issue of her speech: "If, as most critics agree, the spectacle of Hermione's pregnancy troubles the play's language from the start . . . this spectacle works together with her potent tongue to spark her husband's suspicions."[10] And she adapts Shoshana Felman on "the scandal of the speaking body" to discuss the

10. Enterline, *Rhetoric of the Body*, 206.

scandal of the speaking *maternal* body, doubly powerful in appetite.[11] If Leontes condenses Hermione's assured voice and her pregnancy as signs of her unabashed appetite, filling herself up, then perhaps he feels crowded out, or more accurately feels his own appetite crowded out, by the fluent exchanges going on around him. Thus the extreme pitch of his own voice in the tyrannical rants, and his resistance to the very idea of similitude voiced by others. Where is *his* appetite in all the likening, similitude, and reaching across intervals that occur in 1.2? Polixenes interprets his unhappy countenance "As he had lost some province and a region / Lov'd as he loves himself" (1.2.369–70): I think he has lost the space by which he knows himself to have appetite in relation to others, hence to be real, like the Winnicottian infant who suffers impingements that suppress scope of action in knowing and expressing desire. If this is so, then Leontes' musing that Mamillius and he (as people say) are "like as eggs" (1.2.130) manifests not desire for a lost wholeness or unicity but recoil from excess of likeness, from the pressure of others' desires. This would also mean that he cannot acknowledge others' desire. Certainly all his banishments of kith and kin are best heard not as the generalized raving of a tyrant but more specifically as frantic efforts to make a space around himself. It seems to others that his will is excessive but to himself that his real appetite has gone missing altogether. When he has not slept for some time, he orders that "None should come at him" (2.3.32); his illness includes "needless heavings," perhaps a somatic form of trying to distance the objects inside him, crowding him (2.3.35); Leontes rebukes Antigonus upon Paulina's entrance into his chamber, "I charg'd thee that she should not come about me" (2.3.43), and then "Force her hence," "Hence with her . . . out o' door" (2.3.62, 68). Paulina's insistence on bringing the baby to Leontes and making him acknowledge its *likeness* to him would then be exactly the wrong therapy, leading with tragic irony to the royal command for the baby's exposure. Even here, Leontes' unexplained shift from wanting the infant burned to wanting her exposed emphasizes the precision of his wish not to annihilate her but to put topographical distance between himself and her. To him, each such act gestures toward what he vainly, overliterally, hopes will be a breathing space.

Leontes comes to his senses precisely when assured of Mamillius's death: the region most like himself is gone. Just afterward, Hermione is

11. Ibid., 216. Felman's phrase comes from *The Literary Speech Act: Don Juan with J. L. Austin, or Seduction in Two Languages* (Ithaca, N.Y.: Cornell University Press, 1983), 94.

removed and declared dead. There is plenty of space, but not *enough* space. Why, with *her* appetite or eagerness gone, does Leontes not find the interval that he can traverse, in which he can move and so feel real to himself again? Alienation from his own appetite persists throughout the long interim of sixteen years of mourning. Why would this be?

Maria Torok reminds us that bereavement takes on the affective tone of the role that the object played at the time of the loss. If the survivor hasn't acknowledged all the drives that linked him to the dead, then

> Because the unassimilated portion of the drives has congealed into an imago, forever reprojected onto some external object, the incomplete and dependent ego finds itself caught in a self-contradictory obligation. The ego needs to keep alive at all costs that which causes its greatest suffering. . . . We sense the disarray into which the object's disappearance throws the ego. Its destiny having been fixation, the ego is henceforth condemned to suffer the illness of mourning.[12]

Since Leontes has already banished his appetite toward her and hers toward him, these drives aren't available to him for any work of mourning; instead he is locked into an apparently interminable idealization of Hermione. He and Paulina embark on a sixteen-year task of idealizing a dead Hermione onto whom they project all the movement and vitality that Leontes had split off from himself. Since vital signs now belong only to a dead wife, they become inaccessible to him, and he becomes a frozen thing. More complicatedly, although this imago of Hermione has vitality, Leontes can still deny her *appetite* in his idealization of her; as Johanna Drucker says, his bereavement is less a process of mourning than a process of control.[13] It would be hard to give up a pain like that.

Nonetheless, his interminable repentance has bought him a space, of sorts, in which he can own some kind of desire. At the time of Hermione's putative death, Paulina has cursed Leontes:

> A thousand knees,
> Ten thousand years together, naked, fasting,
> Upon a barren mountain, and still winter
> In storm perpetual, could not move the gods
> To look that way thou wert.

(3.2.210–14)

---

12. Maria Torok, "The Illness of Mourning," in Nicolas Abraham and Torok, *The Shell and the Kernel*, vol. 1, trans. Nicholas T. Rand (Chicago: University of Chicago Press, 1994), 116.

13. In a conversation about this play, mothers, and mourning.

This fierce image is strangely consoling, because although it still participates in a figurative economy of excess, it does represent Leontes' wanting something—regard from the gods—and reaching across an icy interval. At this moment Leontes welcomes it: "Go on, go on; / Thou canst not speak too much" (3.2.214–15). The lexicon of too much, related figures of hyperbole, and debates about what would be payment enough also fill up the wide temporal expanse of Leontes' penitence. To kind-hearted observers the excess is patent. Cleomenes objects after sixteen years, "Sir, you have done enough," "indeed, paid down / More penitence than done trespass" (5.1.1–4); the same gentleman remonstrates with Paulina, "You tempt him over-much" (5.1.73).

Persistence in the folly of excess seems to carry both Leontes and Paulina toward new imaginings of desire, figured in their peculiar, shared fantasies—somehow lugubrious and exhilarating at once—of uncanny returns and doubles, excesses, of Hermione. If he violated the imago of the idealized dead Hermione by marrying someone else, says Leontes, this "would make her sainted spirit / Again possess her corpse, and on this stage / . . . appear soul-vex'd" (5.1.57–59); Paulina replies with another fantasy in which she identifies with that specter contemplating a new wife: "Were I the ghost that walk'd, I'ld bid you mark / Her eye, and tell me for what dull part in 't / You chose her" (5.1.63–65). As in a gothic tale for winter, this newly animate corpse would urge murder on the new wife: all around there are too many wives, too many forms of Hermione, and too much of her powerful speech. This is a paradoxical consequence of consolidating vital signs *only* in Hermione, as if withdrawing life from all other real women. *Her* eyes were "Stars, stars, / And all eyes else dead coals!" (5.1.67–68). Leontes remains dependent upon this exquisite corpse because, as Torok says, it "continues to recall the fact that something else was lost" in the illness of mourning: the desires he seems to have lost at the start of the play.[14] This is in part a displacement of Leontes' own vitality and mobility onto a fantasy, when he cannot or will not yet own his appetite and let himself feel real. (Not owning his appetite would also be a continued grief for the fatherhood of which Hermione has bereaved *him* at

---

14. Torok, "Illness," 114. Torok discusses these fixations as forms of encrypting, now a familiar and useful term for certain unconscious dynamics of bereavement. Torok means encrypting as an entirely unconscious process, and to that degree it is unsuitable to describe Leontes' and Paulina's combined elaboration of fantasy about Hermione. But one could say that these fantasies in the play figure our real-world experiences of encrypting lost objects.

the end of her trial, as Marshall Grossman reminded me when he heard a paper based on this material.)

By what sad steps, then, does Leontes move back toward the motility of desire?

The ghosts and possessed corpses of 5.1.56–69, if signs of a failure of mourning, also work as vehicles of returning appetite, insofar as they have value as incipient *narrative*. Welcoming these ghost stories is an odd but vital step that Leontes takes into his future, an unexpected consequence of holding the "congealed imago" of Hermione for so many years. To take to stories in this play is to entrust oneself to what Emerson called the fearful extent and multitude of objects in the world.[15] It is as if he were to say of the ghost-Hermione, "Yes, she would wish that of my new wife and me, she would have a right to wish that, and I can bear her tormenting me that way." At this crucial moment Paulina suggests that Leontes never marry "Unless another, / As like Hermione as is her picture, / Affront his eye" (5.1.73–75). Oddly seeming to capitulate to Leontes' phantasmatic logic of uncanny doublings of the queen, she begins to elicit *Leontes'* appetite; although he is obediently content to abide by her wishes, still he is willing: has he found his own capacity for desire again, through the relay of Hermione's and Paulina's combined aggression?

Stories carry the possibility of engaging with the multitudinous objects of the world when diseased fantasy cannot move flexibly among objects, when fantasy has filled up a cryptlike container with dead idealizations. (So Leontes' mind needs freeing from the law of the dead as much as Hermione does, as much as Irigaray's Antigone does.) This is clearly their function in the pastoral episodes of act 4, and again in the gentlemen's accounts of the reunions (5.2.1–112). In the pastoral, Autolycus purveys stories in the form of ballads; everyone is eager to buy and sell them, to sing them in consort, to listen to them, to use them to court—as Mopsa, Dorcas, and the shepherd's son do. They are frankly objects that convey, awaken, and satisfy appetite (Autolycus "utters them as he had eaten ballads, and all men's ears grew to his tunes," 4.4.184–86). The ballads are the most valued of Autolycus's

15. On narrative at the end of the play, I am indebted to Carolyn Bitzenhofer's unpublished seminar paper "The Transformative Artifact and the Resuscitated Mother in William Shakespeare's *Pericles* and *The Winter's Tale*" (1995) and to Lowell Gallagher, " 'This Scal'd-up Oracle': Ambivalent Nostalgia in *The Winter's Tale*," *Exemplaria* 7 (1995): 465–98: "By inviting Perdita to address the statue . . . Paulina enjoins her audience to read the statue not as the iconic rendering of an established master narrative but as the image of narrativity" (488).

many shining objects—pins, multicolored ribbons, amber necklaces, baubles and gauds of all kinds. And the ballads *contain* amazing objects, monstrous objects; these objects are themselves involved in complicated, comic relationships of filling and being filled. And the dynamics of filling are entirely apt for stories in ballad form, meant to be sung—which means, to move in and out of the body on the breath. Prominent among them is a doleful tune telling "how a usurer's wife was brought to bed of twenty money-bags at a burden, and how she longed to eat adders' heads and toads carbonadoed" (4.4.262–65). This ballad replays in comic-monstrous form the appetite to be crammed in which Hermione had exulted early in the play, and the usurer's wife also gives birth to an excess of shining objects. Moreover, a Mistress Taleporter had been the midwife at this astonishing birth: "Here's the midwife's name to 't, one Mistress Taleporter" (4.4.269–70). Only, in the ambiguous way of Shakespeare's syntax, Mistress Taleporter could just as well be the midwife to the ballad itself. In any case, conveyance and circulation, and free movement among tale, characters, singer, and hearers characterize its actions of appetite, just as much as do containers and things contained.

At the end of the statue scene, when Leontes turns over to Paulina the royal prerogative of leading the company off to hear "Each one . . . his part / Perform'd in this wide gap of time" (5.3.153–54), he entrusts himself to the multitude of objects in the stories that others tell. Leontes represents the play's apprehension that rediscovering lost appetite, giving oneself over to the realm of generation and maternity, and willingness to hear many stories about unbelievable objects and their fates are parallel actions. All these acts constitute some perilous rebirth passage, particularly challenging to the sufferers Leontes, Hermione, Paulina, who are challenged to move across formidable intervals and take up appetite, to animate themselves after terrible events have petrified them. (Shakespeare is not easy on his characters.) Such movements entail rethinking what the characters will henceforth count as excess, and what they'll count as enough.

But we who come to the play with a reading history saturated with nostalgia for the maternal are also challenged to rethink the excess of *that* phenomenon. If Leontes doesn't legitimately carry the affect of nostalgia for the audience, who does? It is distributed among Paulina—who has an oblique relationship to Hermione's maternity, holding it open for her as a space within her marriage—and Hermione and Perdita. Moreover, with our every thought of nostalgia in *The Winter's Tale* we need a thought of aggression. I mean this not just in the sense of aggression as motility or life force that I have emphasized in this book, but aggression as anger and hostility. It is all too easy to use the play's nostalgia for the maternal to screen the aggression of the mothers Hermione and Paulina, and to focus on blaming Leontes as the central critical issue of the play. There is not only victimization in the trial scene but also aggression, in Hermione's choice to let Leontes believe her dead. Her aggression is visible in the ghost of Hermione in Antigonus's dream, and then in the bear who rends and eats Antigonus. Hermione's aggression is carried throughout by her surrogate Paulina; this occurs strikingly in the ghost stories that Paulina and Leontes imagine together.

When Paulina imagines Hermione's ghost, she attributes a strong appetite for aggression to the ghost: "I'ld bid you mark / Her eye [that of Leontes' imagined replacement bride], and tell me for what dull part in't / You chose her; then I'ld shriek, that even your ears / Should rift to hear me, and the words that follow'd / Should be 'Remember mine' " (5.1.64–67). Paulina carries Hermione's aggression in a new way here. Apparently participating in, even guiding, Leontes' morbid fantasy of Hermione's dead/living corpse, she turns it into a story, a little plot, and wins from Leontes an acknowledgment of appetite. If Hermione has suspended her appetite for Leontes in a sixteen-year freeze, then this little plot draws frozen anger through aggression, toward desire for him. It is as if she were to say: "No, my anger toward him makes it intolerable for me to acknowledge any more desire for him. But since I keep myself alive for my daughter's sake, no, I wouldn't want him to take another wife. Therefore using my aggression to hold a space open for my daughter perforce challenges me to acknowledge my frozen desire for my husband. Therefore as a ghost I would haunt him with my mixed desire and rage, inciting him to murder his new wife, demanding from him the acknowledgment of me and my appetite that he failed to give sixteen years ago."

This logic is speculative, of course, since we aren't privy to Hermione's seclusion and the extraordinarily complex psychic life that it implies. What we have, aside from figurative displacements of her presence, is testimony of Hermione's amazing strength to own her appetite—for she has chosen to live this way over sixteen years on the oracle's riddling, subjunctive gesture toward the possibility of her daughter's survival: "and the king shall live without an heir, if that which is lost be not found" (3.2.134–35). Hermione's is the most literal and the most tested parturition of all those I've discussed in this book:

the baby is born during the time of the play; the psychic expanse between them is immediately enlarged beyond bearing by the king's decision to expose it (another reason for the switch from his initial desire to have her killed, in the psychic economy of the play: how large can that space of parturition between mother and child become?); they are separated by a wide geographical and temporal gap; the death of Mamillius must also shadow his mother. The statue scene shows appetite thawing in Hermione only when she blesses her daughter, after a silent, ambivalent embrace or merest touch of Leontes. First the blessing, then a flood of questions in which her characteristically complex periods alternate with the greater pressure of sentence fragments:

> You gods, look down
> And from your sacred vials pour your graces
> Upon my daughter's head! Tell me, mine own,
> Where has thou been preserv'd? where liv'd? how found
> Thy father's court? for thou shalt hear that I,
> Knowing by Paulina that the oracle
> Gave hope thou wast in being, have preserv'd
> Myself to see the issue.

> (5.3.121–28)

These are the "prayers, appeals, graces, cries, dirges, glorias, anger, and questions" of which Irigaray speaks as part of her pneumatology, in a passage that I cited at the beginning of this book; Hermione's capacity for these speech acts needs some attention.[16]

In the Song of Songs, we saw a young adult daughter in love honoring and protecting a figurative space for her mother, and the mother's household which is her literal space. I said then that the very holding open of this space, and the linking of it with desire, counts as aggression in a Winnicottian sense. In *The Winter's Tale* a mother and her representative, Paulina, use aggression in its more usual senses—anger, hostility, outrage, desire to punish—to hold open a space for the daughter. In the process Hermione works out what Winnicott and Irigaray would value as the painful necessity and hope of *movement*. The statue-Hermione could well have said to Leontes what Milton addressed to Shakespeare: "Then thou our fancy of itself bereaving, / Dost make us Marble with too much conceiving"—the excess of Shakespeare crowding in upon

---

16. Luce Irigaray, "Love of the Other" (1984), in *Ethics*, 133–50, at 139.

"us" bereaves us of fancy, vitality, movement, our ability to conceive.[17] So Leontes had felt the excess of appetite in others, especially in Hermione. But Hermione, if we may perceive her through Paulina, gathers her forces of aggression in order to create an enclave of air for her daughter and herself. It is as if upon hearing about the reunions that have already occurred, she accedes to the considerable risks entailed in *breathing* again. As Winnicott, linking his theme of breath with his sense of a creaturely vulnerability before the multitude of objects in the world, reminds us with his gentle understatement, "An important characteristic of breathing is that . . . it lays bare a continuity of inner and outer, that is to say, a failure of defenses."[18] A failure of defense is the chief risk to breathing, mobile creatures, and why it is so distressingly easy to suppress vital signs, range of motion, to become a statue. Irigaray calls on women—Winnicott would call on all mortals—to fight the forces that immobilize and turn to stone "by trying to say, right here and now, how we are moved."[19] In the statue scene Hermione summons all her strength to breathe and move, her capacity for address, her willingness to praise and bless, by saying how she is moved: animated in all the senses that this book hopes to articulate.

17. Milton, "On Shakespeare," in *Complete Poems*, ed. Merritt Hughes (Indianapolis: Bobbs-Merrill, 1957), 63.

18. D. W. Winnicott, *The Family and Individual Development* (London: Tavistock, 1965), 9.

19. Irigaray, "When Our Lips Speak Together" (1977), in *This Sex Which Is Not One*, trans. Catherine Porter with Catherine Burke (Ithaca, N.Y.: Cornell University Press, 1985), 205–18, at 214.

Thanks to my graduate students at the University of Virginia, who were willing to run with me in trying out the argument of this chapter.

Bibliographic Essay:
Debts of Thinking

Many times in this book I've referred to Irigaray's summons to repay the debt to the mother; here I pay my own debt to some of the thinkers who have shaped those traditions and, more immediately, my own arguments. On the cultural force and complexity of the idea of the mother and the experiences of motherhood, attested in a huge outpouring of works in many disciplines, I'm most indebted to Adrienne Rich, *Of Woman Born: Motherhood as Experience and Institution* (New York: Norton, 1976), which continues to stimulate work on the ambivalence within mothers; Alice Adams, *Reproducing the Womb: Images of Childbirth in Science, Feminist Theory, and Literature* (Ithaca, N.Y.: Cornell University Press, 1994); Janine Chasseguet-Smirgel, "Being a Mother and Being a Psychoanalyst: Two Impossible Professions," in *Representations of Motherhood*, ed. Donna Bassin, Margaret Honey, and Meryle Mahrer Kaplan (New Haven: Yale University Press, 1994), 113–28; Rozsika Parker, *Mother Love/Mother Hate: The Power of Maternal Ambivalence* (New York: Basic Books, 1995); Jessica Benjamin, *The Bonds of Love: Psychoanalysis, Feminism, and the Problem of Domination* (New York: Pantheon, 1988); Benjamin, *Like Subjects, Love Objects: Essays on Recognition and Sexual Difference* (New Haven: Yale University Press, 1995); Benjamin, "A Desire of One's Own: Psychoanalytic Feminism and Intersubjective Space," in *Feminist Studies/Critical Studies*, ed. Teresa de Lauretis (Bloomington:

Indiana University Press, 1986): 78–101; Benjamin, *Shadow of the Other: Intersubjectivity and Gender in Psychoanalysis* (New York: Routledge, 1998); Jane Gallop, "Reading the Mother Tongue: Psychoanalytic Feminist Criticism," *Critical Inquiry* 13 (1987): 314–29; Claire Kahane, "Questioning the Maternal Voice," *Genders* 3 (fall 1988): 82–91; Carolyn Burke, "Rethinking the Maternal," in *The Future of Difference*, ed. Hester Eisenstein and Alice Jardine (New Brunswick, N.J.: Rutgers University Press, 1987), 107–14; Sara Ruddick, "Thinking Mothers/Conceiving Birth," in *Representations of Motherhood*, ed. Bassin, Honey, and Kaplan, 29–45; Victoria Hamilton, *Narcissus and Oedipus: The Children of Psycho-Analysis* (London: Routledge and Kegan Paul, 1982). Mothers' published accounts of their relations with their children suggest not desire for fusion but desire for a range of degrees of contact and distance. A very interesting collection, which appeared too late for me to incorporate, links gift, gratitude, and maternity: Linda L. Layne, ed., *Transformative Motherhood: On Giving and Getting in a Consumer Culture* (New York: New York University Press, 1999). Linda Woodbridge offers rich documentation of non-Enlightenment or "magical" thinking on matters of fertility and sexuality in *The Scythe of Saturn: Shakespeare and Magical Thinking* (Urbana: University of Illinois Press, 1994).

Fueling my thinking about nostalgia are Jean Laplanche, *Life and Death in Psychoanalysis* (1970), trans. Jeffrey Mehlman (Baltimore: Johns Hopkins University Press, 1976), chapters 1–2, with its discussion of Freud's concept of deferred action; Karen Horney's essays, for example, "The Dread of Woman: Observations on a Specific Difference in the Dread Felt by Men and by Women Respectively for the Opposite Sex," *International Journal of Psycho-Analysis* 13 (1932): 34–60, reprinted in *Feminine Psychology* (New York: Norton, 1973), 133–46; Dorothy Dinnerstein, *The Mermaid and the Minotaur: Sexual Arrangements and Human Malaise* (New York: Harper and Row, 1976); Nancy Chodorow, *The Reproduction of Mothering: Psychoanalysis and the Sociology of Gender* (Berkeley: University of California Press, 1978); Susan Stewart, *On Longing: Narratives of the Miniature, the Gigantic, the Souvenir, the Collection* (Baltimore: Johns Hopkins University Press, 1984); Marcia Ian, *Remembering the Phallic Mother: Psychoanalysis, Modernism, and the Fetish* (Ithaca, N.Y.: Cornell University Press, 1993); Donna Bassin, "Maternal Subjectivity in the Culture of Nostalgia: Mourning and Memory," in *Representations of Motherhood*, ed. Bassin, Honey, and Kaplan, 162–73; Mary Jacobus, *First Things: The Maternal Imaginary in Literature, Art, and Psychoanalysis* (London: Routledge, 1995); Lynne Huffer, *Maternal Pasts, Feminist Futures:*

Nostalgia, Ethics, and the Question of Difference (Stanford: Stanford University Press, 1998); Katherine Eggert, *Showing like a Queen: Female Authority and Literary Experiment in Spenser, Shakespeare, and Milton* (Philadelphia: University of Pennsylvania Press, 2000), esp. chap. 5, "The Late Queen of Famous Memory: Nostalgic Form in *Antony and Cleopatra*." Writers whose productivity has been stimulated by Winnicott on the specific form of aggression that he elaborates as mobility include Jessica Benjamin; Jane Flax, for example, *Thinking Fragments: Psychoanalysis, Feminism, and Postmodernism in the Contemporary West* (Berkeley: University of California Press, 1990); Adam Phillips, *Winnicott* (Cambridge: Harvard University Press, 1988); Phillips, *On Kissing, Tickling, and Being Bored* (Cambridge: Harvard University Press, 1993); and Phillips, *The Beast in the Nursery: On Curiosity and Other Appetites* (New York: Pantheon, 1998).

While writing this book I have constantly felt an impulse to cross-reference the writings of Julia Kristeva and Jacques Derrida, whose topics continually call to mind those of Irigaray. But their argumentative arcs and engagements with Lacan take directions so different from those of Irigaray that every attempt to situate the two in relation to Irigaray ramified hopelessly. Here I can at least acknowledge Kristeva's influential developments of Lacan in her thinking about the maternal, subjectivity, and language. These are presently more familiar and more intensively worked by literary scholars than Irigaray's work; hence I mention here only Kristeva's *Soleil noir: Dépression et mélancholie* (Paris: Gallimard, 1987) and its English translation, *Black Sun: Depression and Melancholy*, trans. Leon S. Roudiez (New York: Columbia University Press, 1989); the useful earlier work "L'Abjet d'amour," *Tel Quel* 91 (spring 1982): 17–32, now incorporated into *Tales of Love*, trans. Leon Roudiez (New York: Columbia University Press, 1987); *La Révolution du langage poétique: L'Avant garde à la fin du dix-neuvième siècle: Lautréamont, Mallarmé* (Paris; Seuil, 1974) and its English version, *Revolution in Poetic Language*, trans. Margaret Waller (New York: Columbia University Press, 1984); *Pouvoirs de l'horreur* (Paris: Seuil, 1980), translated by Leon Roudiez as *Powers of Horror: An Essay on Abjection* (New York: Columbia University Press, 1982). See also Anna Smith, *Julia Kristeva: Readings of Exile and Estrangement* (New York: St. Martin's, 1996), esp. chap. 4, " 'Into the Cellar of the Native House': Kristeva and Psychoanalysis"; Judith Butler, "The Body Politics of Julia Kristeva," in *Ethics, Politics, and Difference in Julia Kristeva's Writing*, ed. Kelly Oliver (New York: Routledge, 1992), 164–78; Cynthia Chase,

"'Transference' as Trope and Persuasion," in *Discourse in Psychoanalysis and Literature*, ed. Shlomith Rimmon-Kenan (New York: Methuen, 1987), 211–29; Chase, "Desire and Identification in Lacan and Kristeva," in *Feminism and Psychoanalysis*, ed. Richard Feldstein and Judith Roof (Ithaca, N.Y.: Cornell University Press, 1989), 65–83. The work of my colleague Ewa Ziarek on Derrida, Kristeva, and Irigaray is a constant inspiration and provocation; see, among other pieces, "At the Limits of Discourse: Heterogeneity, Alterity, and the Maternal Body in Kristeva's Thought," in *Language and Liberation: Feminism, Philosophy, and Langage*, ed. Christina Hendricks and Kelly Oliver (Albany: State University of New York Press, 1999), 323–46; "Toward a Radical Female Imaginary: Temporality and Embodiment in Irigaray's Ethics," *Diacritics* 28, 1 (1998): 60–75; "Kristeva and Levinas: Mourning, Ethics, and the Feminine," in *Ethics, Politics, and Difference in Julia Kristeva's Writing*, ed. Kelly Oliver (New York: Routledge, 1993), 62–78.

Inquiry into Derrida on the maternal would entail reading *Of Grammatology* and his other long works; one could also look to his briefer "Circumfession," in *Jacques Derrida*, trans. Geoffrey Bennington (Chicago: University of Chicago Press, 1993), and "Otobiographies," in *The Ear of the Other*, trans. Peggy Kamuf and Avital Ronell, ed. Christie McDonald and Claude Lévesque (Lincoln: University of Nebraska Press, 1985). Derrida's work on the gift, on death, on mourning, and on *Beyond the Pleasure Principle* have been in my mind throughout this book, though to engage them would have caused theoretical traffic jams in my chapters; see *The Gift of Death*, trans. David Wills (Chicago: University of Chicago Press, 1995); *The Post Card: From Socrates to Freud and Beyond*, trans. Alan Bass (Chicago: University of Chicago Press, 1987); *Given Time: I. Counterfeit Money*, trans. Peggy Kamuf (Chicago: University of Chicago Press, 1992). I have profited from Kelly Oliver, *Family Values: Subjects between Nature and Culture* (New York: Routledge, 1997); the essays in *Derrida and Feminism: Recasting the Question of Woman*, ed. Ellen K. Feder, Mary C. Rawlinson, and Emily Zakin (New York: Routledge, 1997).

Most of Freud's work is perforce unexamined in this book, and his developments and evasions of issues of maternity are well analyzed elsewhere; here I merely point to the figurative and structural canniness that demonstrates his awareness of the mother as lost object in *Three Essays on Sexuality*, vol. 7 of *The Standard Edition of the Complete Psychological Works of Sigmund Freud*, ed. James Strachey (London: Hogarth, 1974). For Freud's practice of absenting or repressing the mother from crucial theoretical assertions, see Madelon Sprengnether, *The Spectral Mother: Freud,*

Feminism, and Psychoanalysis (Ithaca, N.Y.: Cornell University Press, 1990) and her continuation of this argument in "Mourning Freud," in *Psychoanalysis/Feminisms*, ed. Peter L. Rudnytsky and Andrew M. Gordon (Albany: State University of New York Press, 2000), 11–37; Jim Swan, *"Mater* and Nannie: Freud's Two Mothers and the Discovery of the Oedipus Complex," *American Imago* 31 (1974): 1–64; Coppélia Kahn, "The Hand That Rocks the Cradle: Recent Gender Theories and Their Implications," in *The (M)other Tongue: Essays in Feminist Psychoanalytic Interpretation*, ed. Shirley Nelson Garner, Claire Kahane, and Madelon Sprengnether (Ithaca, N.Y.: Cornell University Press, 1985), 72–88.

Among the most interesting literary studies of longing for the mother and a dual idealization and degrading of her power in early literatures are Philip Slater's groundbreaking *The Glory of Hera: Greek Mythology and the Greek Family* (Boston: Beacon, 1968)—a book that had considerable influence on Nancy Chodorow; Coppélia Kahn, *Man's Estate: Masculine Identity in Shakespeare* (Berkeley: University of California Press, 1980); Page duBois, *Sowing the Body: Psychoanalysis and Ancient Representations of Women* (Chicago: University of Chicago Press, 1988); Janet Adelman, *Suffocating Mothers: Fantasies of Maternal Origin in Shakespeare, "Hamlet" to "The Tempest"* (Berkeley: University of California Press, 1992); Gail Kern Paster, *The Body Embarrassed: Drama and the Disciplines of Shame in Early Modern England* (Ithaca, N.Y.: Cornell University Press, 1993); Nancy Coiner, "The 'Homely' and the *Heimliche*: The Hidden, Doubled Self in Julian of Norwich's *Showings*," *Exemplaria* 5, 2 (1993): 305–23; Gayle Margherita, *The Romance of Origins: Language and Sexual Difference in Middle English Literature* (Philadelphia: University of Pennsylvania Press, 1994); Lynn Enterline, *The Tears of Narcissus: Melancholia and Masculinity in Early Modern Writing* (Stanford: Stanford University Press, 1995); Philippa Berry, *Shakespeare's Feminine Endings: Disfiguring Death in the Tragedies* (London: Routledge, 1999)—a book that links maternity to the period's explorations of materialist vitalism and these with Irigaray, about whom Berry writes elsewhere. Like that of so many critics, my understanding of Renaissance writing generally, and even of medieval writing, is indebted to C. L. Barber—for example, Barber's and Richard P. Wheeler's *The Whole Journey: Shakespeare's Power of Development* (Berkeley: University of California Press, 1986) and Barber's *Creating Elizabethan Tragedy: The Theater of Marlowe and Kyd*, ed. Richard P. Wheeler (Chicago: University of Chicago Press, 1988).

Family history and related historical work on representations of maternity, birth and infancy in nonpoetic genres flourish. On the perils, real and imagined, to mothers and infants, see Donald Redford, "The Literary Motif of the Exposed Child," *Numen: International Review of the History of Religions* 14 (1967): 209–28; Audrey Eccles, *Obstetrics and Gynaecology in Tudor and Stuart England* (Kent, Ohio: Kent State University Press, 1982); Barbara Estrin, *The Raven and the Lark: Lost Children in Literature of the English Renaissance* (Lewisburg, Pa.: Bucknell University Press, 1985); Jacques Brunschwig, "The Cradle Argument in Epicureanism and Stoicism," in *The Norms of Nature: Studies in Hellenistic Ethics*, ed. Malcolm Schofield and Gisela Striker (Cambridge: Cambridge University Press, 1986), 113–44; John Boswell, *The Kindness of Strangers: The Abandonment of Children in Western Europe from Late Antiquity to the Renaissance* (New York: Pantheon, 1988); Nikki Stiller, *Eve's Orphans: Mothers and Daughters in Medieval English Literature* (Westport, Conn.: Greenwood, 1988); Linda Pollock, "Embarking on a Rough Passage: The Experience of Pregnancy in Early-Modern Society," in *Women as Mothers in Pre-Industrial England: Essays in Memory of Dorothy McLaren* (London: Routledge, 1990), 39–67; Clarissa Atkinson, *The Oldest Vocation: Christian Motherhood in the Middle Ages* (Ithaca, N.Y.: Cornell University Press, 1991); William MacLehose, "Nurturing Danger: High Medieval Medicine and the Problem(s) of the Child," in *Medieval Mothering*, ed. Bonnie Wheeler and John Carmi Parsons (New York: Garland, 1996), 3–24; Ronald Finucane, *The Rescue of the Innocents: Endangered Children in Medieval Miracles* (New York: St. Martin's, 1997). Most recently there is the collection *Maternal Measures: Figuring Caregiving in the Early Modern Period*, ed. Naomi J. Miller and Naomi Yavneh (London: Ashgate, 2000).

Work flourishes on late medieval and early modern representations of bodily and spiritual interiority, and the body as container. See, e.g., David Hillman, "The Inside Story," in *Historicism, Psychoanalysis, and Early Modern Culture*, ed. Hillman and Carla Mazzio (New York: Routledge, 2000): 299–324; Michael Schoenfeldt, *Bodies and Selves in Early Modern England* (Cambridge: Cambridge University Press, 1999); Theresa Krier, *Gazing on Secret Sights: Spenser, Classical Imitation, and the Decorums of Vision*; Katharine Maus, *Inwardness and Theater in the English Renaissance*; Peter Stallybrass, "Patriarchal Territories: The Body Enclosed," in *Rewriting the Renaissance: Discourses of Difference in Early Modern Europe*, ed. Margaret Ferguson, Maureen Quilligan, and Nancy Vickers (Chicago: University of Chicago Press, 1986): 123–44; the essays in *The Body in Parts: Fantasies of Corporeality in Early Modern Europe*, ed. David Hillman and Carla Mazzio (New York: Routledge, 1997); all the work on Ben Jonson—notably his play *Bartholomew Fair*—and his relation to his own unwieldy corporeality, for example, Bruce Boehrer, *The Fury of Men's Gullets: Ben Jonson and the Digestive Canal* (Philadelphia: University of Pennsylvania Press, 1997); much work on Hamlet's interiority; much work on late medieval, Reformation, and Counter-Reformation penitential discourses and practices.

On the ways that educational practice and other social institutions shaped constructions of the feminine-maternal and of boys' masculinity, a topic still better elaborated for the Renaissance and the Reformation than for antiquity or any period of the Middle Ages, see Walter Ong's seminal "Latin Language Study as a Renaissance Puberty Rite," *Studies in Philology* 56 (1959): 103–24; Rebecca Bushnell, *A Culture of Teaching: Early Modern Humanism in Theory and Practice* (Ithaca, N.Y.: Cornell University Press, 1996). Related to this topic are William Kerrigan, "The Articulation of the Ego in the English Renaissance," in *The Literary Freud: Mechanisms of Defense and the Poetic Will*, ed. Joseph H. Smith (New Haven: Yale University Press, 1980), 261–308; Boyd M. Berry, "The First English Pediatricians and Tudor Attitudes toward Childhood," *Journal of the History of Ideas* 35 (1974): 561–77; Seymour Byman, "Child Raising and Melancholia in Tudor England," *Journal of Psychohistory* 5 (1978): 67–92; Christine Coch, "'Mother of my Contreye': Elizabeth I and Tudor Constructions of Motherhood," *English Literary Renaissance* 26 (1996): 423–50; Deborah Willis, *Malevolent Nurture: Witch-Hunting and Maternal Power in Early Modern England* (Ithaca, N.Y.: Cornell University Press, 1995). Family history for ancient Rome is a new and active field; I have found help from Judith Hallett, *Fathers and Daughters in Roman Society: Women and the Elite Family* (Princeton: Princeton University Press, 1984); Suzanne Dixon, *The Roman Mother* (Norman: Oklahoma University Press, 1988) and *The Roman Family* (Baltimore: Johns Hopkins University Press, 1992); Beryl Rawson, ed., *The Family in Ancient Rome: New Perspectives* (Cambridge: Cambridge University Press, 1986) and *Marriage, Divorce, and Children in Ancient Rome* (Oxford: Clarendon, 1991); Keith Bradley, *Discovering the Roman Family: Studies in Roman Social History* (Oxford: Oxford University Press, 1991); Richard Saller, *Patriarchy, Property, and Death in the Roman Family* (Cambridge: Cambridge University Press, 1994); Jane Gardner, *Family and Familia in Roman Law and Life* (Oxford: Clarendon, 1998) and, with Thomas Weidemann, *The Roman Household: A Sourcebook* (London: Routledge, 1991).

Every book is indebted to some scholarly works that provide initial scaffolding but then fall away at the end of the process. But this book is also indebted to wonderful writers of other kinds without whom I couldn't have begun to think these thoughts: Emerson, Frost, Thoreau, Angela Carter, John Crowley, Janet Kauffman, Vicki Hearne. In a book so much about gratitude, it seems fitting to end with thanks to them for their good genius.

Index